# Global TESOL for the 21st Century

NEW PERSPECTIVES ON LANGUAGE AND EDUCATION
**Founding Editor:** Viv Edwards, *University of Reading, UK*
**Series Editors:** Phan Le Ha, *University of Hawaii at Manoa, USA* and Joel Windle, *Monash University, Australia.*

Two decades of research and development in language and literacy education have yielded a broad, multidisciplinary focus. Yet education systems face constant economic and technological change, with attendant issues of identity and power, community and culture. This series will feature critical and interpretive, disciplinary and multidisciplinary perspectives on teaching and learning, language and literacy in new times.

All books in this series are externally peer-reviewed.

Full details of all the books in this series and of all our other publications can be found on http://www.multilingual-matters.com, or by writing to Multilingual Matters, St Nicholas House, 31–34 High Street, Bristol BS1 2AW, UK.

NEW PERSPECTIVES ON LANGUAGE AND EDUCATION: 81

# Global TESOL for the 21st Century

## Teaching English in a Changing World

**Heath Rose, Mona Syrbe, Anuchaya Montakantiwong and Natsuno Funada**

**MULTILINGUAL MATTERS**
Bristol • Blue Ridge Summit

DOI https://doi.org/10.21832/ROSE8182
Library of Congress Cataloging in Publication Data
A catalog record for this book is available from the Library of Congress.
Names: Rose, Heath, author. | Syrbe, Mona, 1987 – author. | Montakantiwong, Anuchaya, 1989 – author. | Funada, Natsuno, 1988 – author.
Title: Global TESOL for the 21st Century: Teaching English in a Changing World/Heath Rose, Mona Syrbe, Anuchaya Montakantiwong and Natsuno Funada.
Description: Blue Ridge Summit : Multilingual Matters, 2020. | Series: New Perspectives on Language and Education: 81 | Includes bibliographical references and index. | Summary: "This book explores the impact of the spread of English on language teaching and learning. It provides a framework for change in the way English is taught to better reflect global realities and to embrace current research. The book is essential reading for postgraduate researchers, teachers and teacher trainers in TESOL"— Provided by publisher.
Identifiers: LCCN 2019053931 (print) | LCCN 2019053932 (ebook) | ISBN 9781788928175 (paperback) | ISBN 9781788928182 (hardback) | ISBN 9781788928199 (pdf) | ISBN 9781788928205 (epub) | ISBN 9781788928212 (kindle edition) Subjects: LCSH: English language—Study and teaching.
Classification: LCC PE1066 .R67 2020  (print) | LCC PE1066  (ebook) | DDC 428.0071—dc23 LC record available at https://lccn.loc.gov/2019053931
LC ebook record available at https://lccn.loc.gov/2019053932

British Library Cataloguing in Publication Data
A catalogue entry for this book is available from the British Library.

ISBN-13: 978-1-78892-818-2 (hbk)
ISBN-13: 978-1-78892-817-5 (pbk)

Multilingual Matters
UK: St Nicholas House, 31-34 High Street, Bristol BS1 2AW, UK.
USA: NBN, Blue Ridge Summit, PA, USA.

Website: www.multilingual-matters.com
Twitter: Multi_Ling_Mat
Facebook: https://www.facebook.com/multilingualmatters
Blog: www.channelviewpublications.wordpress.com

The policy of Multilingual Matters/Channel View Publications is to use papers that are natural, renewable and recyclable products, made from wood grown in sustainable forests. In the manufacturing process of our books, and to further support our policy, preference is given to printers that have FSC and PEFC Chain of Custody certification. The FSC and/or PEFC logos will appear on those books where full certification has been granted to the printer concerned.

Typeset by Nova Techset Private Limited, Bengaluru and Chennai, India.

# Contents

# Tables and Figures

## Figures

# About the Authors

**Heath Rose** is an Associate Professor of Applied Linguistics in the Department of Education at The University of Oxford. Heath started his teaching career in Australian and Japanese schools, before eventually moving into teaching in higher education in Australia, Japan, Ireland and now the UK. During this time, he has prioritized applications of teaching research for classroom pedagogy. His research interests are in Global Englishes, English Medium Instruction and Teaching English as an international language He is co-author of numerous books, including *Introducing Global Englishes* (Routledge, 2015), and *Global Englishes for Language Teaching* (Cambridge University Press), and is series co-editor of the upcoming Cambridge Elements Series titled *Language Teaching*.

**Mona Syrbe** has been working as an English teacher since 2010. Currently, she is an Assistant Professor of Bilingual Education at Rikkyo University, Japan. Before this, she was an adjunct lecturer at Trinity College Dublin, where she taught courses in applied linguistics, TESOL and academic English. Her research interests are in teaching English as an international language, specifically with regards to materials design and language assessment. She has published her research in peer-reviewed journals such as *International Journal of Applied Linguistics, Innovation in Language Learning and Teaching.*

**Anuchaya (Anya) Montakantiwong** is an English Language lecturer at Mahidol University, Thailand. She is also a researcher of Global Englishes, focusing on teachers. She is interested in how teacher cognition of Global Englishes affects teacher identity and pedagogical practices.

**Natsuno Funada** is a doctoral graduate of Applied Linguistics in the Department of Education at the University of Oxford. She also researches in the field of Global Englishes. Before coming to Oxford, Natsuno was an adjunct lecturer of English language at Saitama Women's Junior College in Japan.

# Preface

In the 21st century, teaching English has become essentially different than teaching any other language, and it is this book's aim to explore these differences from a teachers' perspective. Never before has the world seen a global language to the extent that English is now used. English is not only the native or second language in over 50 countries, but it is also by far the most widely taught and learned foreign language in the world. Having been spread through British colonialism, English has taken on a life of its own in almost every corner of the world. Expressing local culture and identity, new varieties of English have developed in former colonies in North America, Africa, different parts of Asia, and Australasia. These speakers make up a large part of the global community of English speakers yet find little to no representation in most TESOL contexts. This is also true for the other group of speakers which make English different than any other language – its lingua franca speakers. As the world's main medium of communication between speakers of other languages, English is now spoken by more second language users than first language speakers, and this has significantly shaped the language and the skills required to successfully use it.

## A Professional Rationale for this Book

This globalization of English has clear implications for TESOL, and teachers and teacher educators need to reframe English language teaching in order to match the new sociolinguistic landscape of the 21st century. Yet, the TESOL industry continues to focus on native English norms, and as a result many TESOL practitioners in training continue to receive traditional views of language and language teaching, characterised by an adherence to 'standard' norms. One reason why the industry has been slow to address changes is that pedagogical innovation requires a significant shift in ideology. Moving away from native speakerism requires a change in views of ownership of English and the emancipation of second language speakers from native speaker norms. From this, pedagogical changes can be made, in which new learning targets are identified, language models are changed, culture is repositioned, and the target interlocutor is reconsidered.

Though research and publications have made noticeable headway in the direction of teaching English as an international language (EIL), teaching practices have largely lagged behind. Offering a detailed examination of the incorporation of an EIL perspective into the multiple faces of TESOL, this book is aimed at in-service and pre-service teachers, practitioner-researchers and teacher educators rather than at academic researchers, for which a large number of resources on the topic currently exist. By exploring practical questions in TESOL, this book aims to provide an introduction into the topic and provide practical answers, but also prompt critical discussion and reflection. Beyond that, we further hope to encourage teachers to participate in the still largely untapped research agenda surrounding classroom innovation, which is necessary to make the move from a native speaker model to teaching English as a truly global language.

## A Personal Rationale for this Book

Each of us, as four independent authors, have come together to write this book as a collective team of EIL researchers who are also English language teaching professionals. We each became interested in teaching EIL via our own personal journeys, which have brought with them experiences as teachers and learners. These journeys have helped to construct our own perspectives as practitioner-researchers. Before we venture into our collective perspective on teaching EIL in the remainder of this book, we want to briefly share each of these journeys with the reader. We feel this is important, as it reveals our personal motivations behind writing this book. Sharing our stories as a kind of reflective practice, helps to establish who we are and via what paths our researcher and teacher identities have been constructed.

### Heath's story

For the first few years of my teaching career in high schools in Japan and Australia, I was acutely aware and uncomfortable with my privileged status as a white, male, native English-speaking teacher, but I did very little to challenge this in the curriculum, largely upholding the status quo of established practices. When I returned to Japan several years later to take up a job at a language specialist university in the Tokyo area, I began to make small changes to shift focus away from native and Anglophone norms in my curricula via two content-based courses that I had been given the freedom to create (one was on travel in Asia, and the other on Japanese influence on culture around the world, which aimed to counter balance an existing focus on American and British cultural studies in the program). A colleague of mine (Nicola Galloway) at the time later taught a course called Global Englishes, which was my first exposure to this as a field of academic study. Learning about Global Englishes enabled me to put a label on aspects of the TESOL profession that I'd been uncomfortable with throughout my teaching career. I became interested in the curriculum changes she was introducing, which led to us co-publishing a number of papers on these innovations in subsequent years.

By the time I moved into my next position in a business program at another Japanese university, I was ready to instigate larger changes in the wider curriculum I was put in charge of. In this curriculum, globally-oriented content was taught explicitly to prepare students to use the language as a business lingua franca. Expert ELF-users were hired as teaching assistants instead of native speakers, expert L2 English users were regularly invited to give lectures to provide role models to the students, and business projects centred on using English to plan business ventures in places such as China, rather than in Anglophone countries. When my Global Englishes colleague moved to my university during my fourth year there, we made further changes across the entire curriculum. Seeing the success of these early efforts in raising our students' confidence and awareness of how English is used, I embarked on a research career to communicate to other teachers what a global curriculum could look like.

Now that I have moved into academia, I have lost access to language classrooms of my own to instigate curriculum change, but have been fortunate enough to connect with teacher-researchers around the world, who are equally driven by the notion of teaching EIL. Some of these connections have facilitated this jointly authored book, with each of my co-authors having travelled their own independent journeys to reach this point.

## Mona's story

My teaching career began as an undergraduate and graduate student, aiming to become a secondary school teacher in Germany. During this time, I developed as strong interest in linguistics, which led me to do an exchange at Trinity College Dublin in Ireland. That was when I discovered my curiosity for research and decided to pursue a PhD. In search of a suitable topic, my teacher (and future co-author) Heath Rose, introduced me to the field of Global Englishes, which led me to explore this topic as part of one of my module assignments at Trinity College Dublin and then as part of my postgraduate dissertation back in Germany. This initial research revealed to me the opportunities of working within such a young, dynamic, developing field of study, and I began to realize its practical relevance to not only teachers but learners of English as well.

The more I learned, the more I understood the practical implications of a global approach to English language education. However, I also saw that most of the discussions within this field were rather theoretical, leaving a significant gap between stating what should be done and what is possible to do. While my doctoral research explored lacks in English language teaching materials and tests, my subsequent work has explored avenues to address this gap in practical ways. As an educator and teacher, the value of my work and research lies in the extent to which it helps teachers to bring English as an international language into their classroom. This goal has motivated my work on this book, and continues to be the foundation of my research.

## Anya's story

Back in 2014 when I had crossed the finish line of my TESOL education, I thought I had the entire world of English language teaching figured out. In my master's degree I had been introduced and inspired by the teaching of EIL, which I was eager to put into practice. This degree had granted me access to my first professional journey as a university lecturer in an English undergraduate programme in Thailand where I imagined making my stage debut with some EIL ideas that had captivated the fantasy of my teacher-in-training self. Yet, in reality, such all-consuming aspiration remained well-hidden in the backstage, while I let subconscious native norms have their premiere and 'steal the show.' On reflection, I was gripped by disappointment. Rather than drawing the students' attention to English as fluid and varying across communities of practice, I diverted them to notions of English as a monolithic entity based largely on dominant Inner-circle varieties. Instead of helping them to see 'English' realistically, I covered their eyes and reinforced the misconceptions. Not only did I fail to live up to my pre-defined philosophy, but I also let slip any opportunity for my 'ideal' teacher identity as a 'multilingual instructor' to materialise (see Kramsch & Zhang, 2018).

If there is one lesson I have gleaned from this 'story of failure', it is that I have learned and evolved as a teacher more on account of things going wrong than things going (al)right. Out of crisis has come clarity and commitment to resolution. Where could I have otherwise done better to optimise my students' learning experience as well as my own professional development as a teacher? How do I translate curricular innovations into practice? The answer to these questions, as I realised, lied in the act of self-introspection itself. I went 'backstage' and re-discovered my once-inspiring pedagogical values, which I was able to re-cast in a new light given the newly-acquired freedom as a course coordinator. With heightened awareness of subtle ambivalence within my belief systems, I replaced out-of-context listening activities in my course's commercial textbook with a context-sensitive, EIL-oriented activity. I began to understand small adaptations can lead their way to larger waves of change. I also learned that failure is not necessarily an end point. As I have later come to learn, it is (and should be) a staging post on a journey towards greater success (or something better).

## Natsuno's story

My personal journey begins with my experience as an English language learner. I studied English through Japanese formal education and graduated from a Japanese university with a bachelor's degree in law. In this degree programme, Japanese was used as a medium of instruction and English was not something to which I felt connected in my life at that time. Nevertheless, there were some English language study requirements within the core curriculum, and I accepted the situation.

Later, I became more interested in the ongoing debate on a long-standing issue in Japan and other countries, where many people do not reach a level at which they can successfully communicate in English with people of different cultural and linguistic backgrounds. I originally searched for a solution to the issue through a master's programme in TESOL, however I still could not find anything concrete to address my concerns. Thus, I felt the necessity to investigate the issue beyond TESOL, as I have found the attachment to native English is deeply rooted in society from both narrow and broad perspectives. This results in many people blindly accepting the underlying norms attached to English, such as the legitimacy of the native-speaker.

Eventually, I came across the research area of Global Englishes, which gave me some insights into the sociolinguistic, sociocultural, historical, and political underpinnings of these beliefs. This inspired me to begin my doctoral studies into the attitudes of English language learners in Japan towards the use of English as a global language. As a learner and subsequent teacher of English, my mission is to explore ways of disentangling the complexity of those norms in society, and to encourage learners and teachers in the current globalised world to think critically about what it means to learn English in their respective contexts to investigate this issue, rather than to accept things at face value.

## Book Structure

The book pools collective knowledge from World Englishes, English as a Lingua Franca, Global Englishes, and EIL, and examines the implications of this knowledge on English language education. As such, the book is intended for the use with university students and teachers in applied linguistics and TESOL programs, where research intersects with teacher development. The book is divided into four main content sections – each with a specific focus.

Part 1 focuses on introducing theoretical foundations in the respective fields of World Englishes, English as a Lingua Franca, Global Englishes, EIL, highlighting the implications for English language education. Chapter 1 opens with an introduction to the main conceptual trends in English language education within a global context. This includes an overview of research into paradigms for examining the spread of English, namely World Englishes, English as a Lingua Franca, Global Englishes, and EIL. The implications of all of these paradigms for current TESOL practices are then outlined in Chapter 2. Based on proposals and models introduced by TESOL researchers and researcher-practitioners, there follows a description of how these implications can be operationalised into TESOL practices, especially in terms of classroom innovations.

Part 2 explores how these implications can be translated into language classroom curriculum and language usage in the classroom. One of the challenges in initiating change in TESOL is how to take account of the destabilisation of established norms and standards, such as native-speaker norms, into teaching. Chapter 3 attempts to untangle the complexity of language norms in TESOL by outlining the driving forces behind the growth of English as a global language, and the associated challenges for TESOL that have accompanied this trend. Chapter 4 sheds light on material evaluation and development in EIL. It presents a guided framework with which ELT professionals can analyse and evaluate their teaching materials with regard to the representation of EIL, and how one can utilise alternative materials for EIL-oriented teaching. Chapter 5 introduces the debate around current language assessment, arguing against measures of test-takers' ability to use English against native-speaker norms. It suggests ways in which to radically re-think classroom assessment to focus on evaluating how well students can use the language in global contexts.

Extant research with regard to the global TESOL classroom and curriculum are still mostly theoretical. Nevertheless, a growing number of empirical studies on perspectives of English language learners and teachers concerning EIL and EIL-oriented teaching has been carried out in recent years. These are included in Part 3 of the book. Chapter 6 provides an overview of research into learners' attitudes to English in general and of EIL and EIL activities. Chapter 7 explores teachers' cognition of TESOL practices, outlining their belief systems. It also addresses EIL in teacher education programs and discusses in-service teachers' perspectives about incorporating EIL into their practices. In addition to learners' attitudes and teachers' cognition as addressed in previous chapters, Chapter 8 further explores learners' and teachers' views with regard to EIL in today's world. These are discussed from multiple perspectives on teacher and learner identities.

In the final section, we propose ideas which seek to contribute to a much-needed paradigm shift for 21st century TESOL. Chapter 9 provides a step by step guide for teachers who wish to incorporate EIL change into their own teaching contexts. The concrete examples of introducing and implementing EIL-oriented teaching in teacher education are also showcased in this chapter. The final chapter, Chapter 10, summarises key concepts in the book and makes a call for accumulating evidence for the implementation of EIL innovation in language teaching and language teacher education. It particularly calls for more reporting on practices by practitioner-researchers. In order to encourage the latter to conduct practice-based studies, such as action research, this chapter outlines various research tools that can be used by practitioner-researchers and presents example studies that have used some of these tools.

Throughout these 10 chapters, we hope to illustrate to teachers, teachers-in-training, and practitioner-researchers what a truly global TESOL curriculum can look like in order to meet the needs of English language learners in the 21st century. We hope to inform and inspire teachers to become active agents of change by contributing to an agenda of global classroom innovation to move our profession towards global models of TESOL.

# Part 1

# Theoretical Foundations

# 1 Theorising the Teaching of English in Global Contexts

**Pre-reading Activities**

> ### *Think*
>
> Look at Figure 1.1, which depicts the spread of English as an international language. Think about how the different ways that English has spread may have affected the language used in various global contexts. In what ways does English differ among the contexts with which you are familiar?
>
> ### *Discuss*
>
> In small groups, discuss the following questions:
>
> (1) Why do some fields of study prefer to use the plural 'Global Englishes' as opposed to 'Global English' when referring to English as an international language? Do you think pluralisation is necessary?
> (2) Most statistics suggest that the bulk of English users today are second-language users who have acquired English via Channel 4 spread, and the second most populous English speakers are bi/multilingual speakers from Channel 3 spread. What implications does this have in terms of learners' likely future use of the language?
> (3) What implications does the spread of English have in terms of how the language should be taught in English language classrooms in global contexts?

## Introduction

The rise of English as a global language has been well documented in the linguistic research literature. In just 500 years, the world has seen English grow from a national language spoken by fewer than 3 million people, to a global language with an estimated 2 billion speakers. During the 20th century, the world quickly moved from a situation where first language (L1) speakers constituted the majority of English users to the current reality where second, foreign and additional language (L2) users are in vast majority. The spread of English is a complex, historical phenomenon, that is intertwined with British colonialism and globalisation alongside numerous other political and social forces (see Chapter 3 for an overview of the driving forces). The ways in which English has spread can be viewed include: political, historical and linguistic. Figure 1.1 represents an alternative perspective that captures the sociolinguistic forces of English spread via four main channels.

The first major wave of English dispersion occurred as a result of British colonialism, where the language spread around the world to places as far flung as Australia, Canada, Jamaica, Nigeria, Singapore and India. Subsequent changes to the language greatly depended on how the language was spread, because linguistic change is highly susceptible to exogenous forces (i.e. forces external to the language itself). Exogenous change occurs when speakers of a language come into contact with speakers of different dialects and languages. Change usually occurs in favour of the language that has more social prestige attached to the identities of these speakers. For example, if South-West English, Northern Irish and Scottish speakers came into heavy contact in a new community in the 1700s, the dialects spoken by the Irish and Scottish speakers may have been more likely to change due to the power held by the English during this time. Differences in population size and the context of the language contact gave rise to new Englishes in various parts of the British colonies. In contact situations typified by Channel 1 spread (e.g. in British colonies in New Zealand and Australia), the English language underwent a process

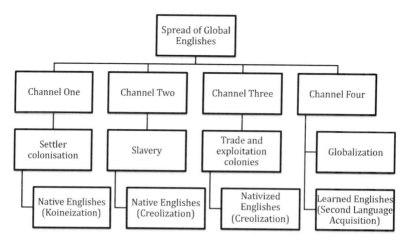

**Figure 1.1** The four channels of English Spread (adapted from Galloway & Rose, 2015: 14)

of *koineisation*, which occurs when speakers of different dialects of English come into contact, and a new dialect emerges as a result. In contact situations typified by Channel 2 spread, the English language was subjected to *creolisation*, which was the result of speakers of languages other than English in sudden intense contact with English. For example, slavery forced different linguistic communities to adopt English as their primary, and often sole, lingua franca in plantation colonies. Both Channel 1 and Channel 2 saw the emergence of new forms of Native Englishes, via different linguistic processes. Channel 3 contact situations also resulted in the *creolisation* of English as a contact language, however this process typically occurred over a long period of time after going through an initial period of pidginisation. This channel of spread was also contextually typified with English being used alongside other more dominant local languages. For example, in Singapore, English was (and still is) used alongside Chinese, Malay and Tamil. In contexts where the role of English was reinforced as a language of education, law or political, it usually gave rise to nativised varieties of English, such is the case in Singapore. In other contexts, the role of English was diminished during post-colonial times, and thus plays a lesser role, such is the case of Malaysia.

The second major wave of English dispersion is seen as Channel 4 spread. As a result of 20th century globalisation, English emerged as a global prestige language due to the economic and political power of the USA during this period. Thus, wrongly or rightly, English was seen by many educational policymakers as a means to facilitate individual and national upward economic and social mobility. Accordingly, globalisation saw the emergence of educational policies worldwide that emphasised the teaching of English as a foreign language in regions which had no previous colonial ties to English-speaking nations. This Channel 4 spread via the educational systems, for example in China, is the cause of the current global boom we are witnessing in the number of L2 English speakers. Thus, the majority of English speakers today can be said to have come into contact with English as a result of Channel 4 dispersion.

Exploring the global phenomenon – the rise of English as a global language – has occupied much applied linguistic and language education research in the previous few decades. The complexity in the ways in which English is used globally now attracts the attention of researchers from multiple perspectives: economic, political, linguistic, sociolinguistic, demographic, national and individualistic, to name just a few. It has also attracted the attention of educational researchers as it is inextricably linked with issues surrounding international education. As Chowdhury and Phan (2014) note, Teaching English to Speakers of Other Languages (TESOL) 'has emerged an important field of choice for international students symbiotically accelerated by the growing dominance of English' (2014: 1). This chapter introduces some of the core fields of research which underpin the concerns of TESOL researchers and practitioners associated with its global growth. The aim of this chapter is to develop a conceptual foundation for teaching English as an International Language in global contexts.

## Key Concepts in Capturing the Spread of English

Research into the spread of English as a global language has resulted in the emergence of a number of interlinked academic fields of research within applied linguistics, which aim to explain the linguistic underpinnings of variation in English. Many of the fields also explore the sociolinguistic implications for the diverse contexts in which the language is now used. Paradigms for examining the spread of English include, but are not limited to:

- World Englishes;
- English as a lingua franca;
- Global Englishes;
- English as an international language.

Even though each of these terms has emerged from research with slightly different areas of focus, they all contain overlapping ideologies. For example, all terms position the English language as globally owned, thereby divulging power from so-called 'native speakers' in terms of informing global English language norms. All paradigms also emphasise the implications of the global spread of English for English language teaching practices – the very focus of this book. In order to understand these terms in more detail, each of them is outlined in turn in this chapter. Building on this foundation, we hope to establish our preferred use of 'English as an International Language' throughout the remaining chapters in this book.

## World Englishes

The theoretical work of Braj J. Kachru and Larry Smith in the 1970s and 1980s is largely credited with kickstarting *World Englishes* as an independent field of study (see Kachru, 1976). Historically, the field was mainly concerned with exploring linguistic variation in English used around the world, with a particular emphasis on phonological and grammatical variation of English in British post-colonial countries. Figure 1.1 shows that the areas of interest to most World Englishes researchers were the Englishes formed via Channel 2 (Slavery) and Channel 3 (Exploitation colony) spread. World Englishes research also had a sociolinguistic aim: by linguistically codifying varieties of English according to their patterned structures and prevalence of use, World Englishes scholars aimed to legitimise other forms of English beyond those considered as 'standard'. In naming this emergent field of study 'World Englishes' scholars adopted a pluralisation strategy in their neologism, which emphasised the diverse and multiple forms that the English language had taken as a result of its global dispersion.

World Englishes research also had a socio-political agenda at its core, which gave rise to the work of critical applied linguists. These scholars aimed to disrupt the status quo, due to observations of an unjustified power hierarchy of Englishes, which placed standards of British and American English at the top, followed by other regional 'native' standards, which were mostly confined to those that had emerged in settler colonies such as Australia and Canada (see Channel 1, Figure 1.1). Other nativised Englishes were seen to be treated as the 'illegitimate offspring' of English (Mufwene, 2001: 107), despite many of them being older, having a greater number of speakers, or being underpinned by more stable linguistic structures than other 'native' Englishes.

This lack of legitimacy ascribed to nativised Englishes has had tremendous implications for language policy and educational curricula in many former British colonies, which in turn has caused harm to the identities of English language users. Through schooling, many students were told that the language they spoke at home was 'broken' or 'inferior'. Adherence to standard norms of English was seen as a social status divide between educated classes and the general masses in many former colonies. World Englishes research has done much to rectify this by justifying new varieties in their own right.

Over the years, there have been a number of attempts to theorise the spread of English around the world. Strevens' (1980) *World Map of English* is an example of an early attempt to categorise varieties of English. This map, however, places American and British English at its top, and is problematic in its regional, rather than linguistic or sociohistorical, focus in organising other global varieties. McArthur's (1987) *Circle of World English* organises varieties of English into a wagon-wheel formation, and places regionally focused varieties between each of its spokes. Its positioning of 'World Standard English' in the hub of the wheel is a positive movement in that power is taken from traditional standards such as American and British standard English, which are placed on par with other regional standards. While an ideology of equality underpins the model, its declaration of a World Standard and regional standard varieties of English is closer to fantasy than representing the actual messy reality of how English is globally used in the world today.

The most influential model of World Englishes is indisputably Kachru's Three Circle model, which has been described as the 'standard framework of World Englishes studies' (Yano, 2001: 121). This model places varieties of English within three overlapping circles:

(1) The Inner Circle, which depicts nation states where English is used as a prominent native language (e.g. England, Ireland, Australia, USA, New Zealand);

(2)  The Outer Circle, which depicts nation states where English is used as a second language alongside other national languages (e.g. Hong Kong, India, Nigeria, Singapore);

(3)  The Expanding Circle, which depicts nation states where English did not have a historic colonial presence, but is learned as a foreign language (e.g. Germany, China, Russia, Brazil).

These three circles are representative of previous divisions between language users, such as Strang's (1970) three categories which led to the eventual labelling of speakers as: English as a native language (ENL) speakers; English as a Second Language (ESL) speakers; and English as a Foreign Language (EFL) speakers.

While Kachru's model of World Englishes has been influential, it is not without its problems. Galloway and Rose (2015) note that 'the model is severely flawed in a number of aspects' (2015: 18). Some of these criticisms include the following:

- it does not account for global mobility, where different types of English speakers live in different circles;
- it takes a reductionist approach to the realities of how language is used in each of these circles;
- the models focus too much on the colonial history in some nations, while overlooking the historical influence of English in others;
- it fails to capture the multi-ethnic and multilingual realities of the world;
- it does not clarify where native Englishes that have been formed via creolisation should be placed;
- it positions the Inner Circle as 'norm-providing' and thus does not disrupt the status quo as much as it proclaims it does;
- it does not capture the way English is used as a lingua franca within and across these circles.

In Bruthiaux's (2003) detailed critique of Kachru's model, he observes that the model 'is a twentieth-century construct that has outlived its usefulness' (2003: 161), and concludes that we need to move more towards a usage-based model. In a similar vein, Pennycook (2010) notes that 'we need to choose carefully between the available models of pluricentric Englishes, avoiding the pitfalls of states-centric pluralities ... in order to deal with globalized linguascapes' (2010: 685). He argues that as a discipline we need to move away from models depicting nation-based circles altogether.

In terms of pedagogical implications (discussed further in Chapter 2) World Englishes research has emphasised the need for students to develop an awareness that speakers of English today adhere to a diverse range of grammatical and phonological norms. Thus, an education that seeks to only teach one standard of English might not prepare students to use the language with the majority of its speakers. World Englishes research has also helped to establish the legitimacy of a number of English varieties, and seeks to empower L2 users of the language as not needing to adhere to so-called 'native' English norms.

## English as a lingua franca

The theoretical work within the field of English as a lingua franca (ELF) first emerged to meet the shortcomings of World Englishes, as outlined above. The focus of initial ELF research sought to explore how English was used in dynamic and fluid global contexts, where speakers of different first languages (L1s) used English for communication purposes. At its core, ELF research sought to break down traditional state-based depictions of English language use. Early work in ELF research emerged within the European context, as English rapidly gained a foothold as the European Union's de facto lingua franca for business, political and social communication. Researchers such as Jenkins (2000), Seidlhofer (2001), and Mauranen (2003), explored the ways in which ELF challenged the established norms of English language use.

The early work in ELF was similar to that of World Englishes, in that much of the research of this time focused on understanding the linguistic features and patterns in ELF communication. Some of the research aimed to explore similarities in these features across diverse contexts. This early work into the features of ELF was underpinned by a number of corpus studies, and was the basis of some now refuted claims that a distinctly European variety of English was emerging. Modiano (2003), for example, claimed that a codifiable variety called 'Euro-English' would emerge due to ongoing ELF interactions across Europe. In hindsight, many ELF researchers today see this earlier work as somewhat problematic, because codifying patterns and features of English use in these diverse contexts was at odds with the field's later stance that ELF was not a codifiable (and therefore teachable) variety. As a result, many critics of ELF are quick to overly focus on this work. They argue ELF upholds an 'anything goes' ideology – a stance which ELF researchers have vehemently refuted.

In an effort to move away from its World Englishes orientation to early research, a second phase of ELF work emphasised a fluidity of norms in each ELF communication, which were later placed at the core of much of its research focus. These norms are variable and changeable with each ELF encounter, and are underpinned by the parameters of the context, the communicative aims of the discourse, as well as the needs of the interlocutors. Because of its focus on dynamism and variability, much ELF research conducted in the late 2000s and early 2010s explored the way in which speakers used English to communicate. During this time, we saw research emerge on topics such as Business English as a Lingua Franca (e.g. Kankaanranta & Planken, 2010) and English as an Academic Lingua Franca (e.g. Mauranen et al., 2010).

More recent work in ELF has emphasised the importance of English in multilingual contexts. As the multilingual turn in applied linguistics (discussed later in this chapter) has made inroads into numerous fields of study, ELF researchers have become more interested in exploring how English is used alongside other languages in lingua franca encounters. Jenkins (2015b) refers to this current phase of research as ELF 3. We would argue this brings ELF research closer in its focus to the field of Global Englishes.

In terms of pedagogical implications (discussed further in Chapter 2) ELF research has emphasised the need for students to develop the communication strategies to successfully use the language with a range of speakers of different linguistic and cultural backgrounds. ELF-aware pedagogy seeks to enable students to adapt their English to various communities of practice, whose norm and expectations might differ according to each context.

## Global Englishes

The term Global Englishes was first adopted by researchers who have been described as *critical applied linguists* (e.g. Suresh Canagarajah & Alastair Pennycook). Rose and Galloway (2019) also link their more recent theorization of Global Englishes with critical applied linguistics. Critical applied linguistic researchers saw the conceptual shortcomings of World Englishes and early ELF research, and sought a new term to unite a shared interest in research that explored the fluidity of language use, globally. Pennycook (2003, 2007) used the term Global Englishes to describe the global spread and use of a diversity of Englishes as part of larger globalisation processes. Other researchers (e.g. Galloway & Rose, 2015) see Global Englishes as an inclusive field of study, where traditional ideologies surrounding language and identity are challenged. Canagarajah (2013) has also used Global Englishes in a similar way to refer to the way in which users reconstitute English for their local purposes. Canagarajah prefers to focus on contact practices rather than static views of 'nativeness' and regionality. Global Englishes research tends to not focus on codifying varieties of English at all, thus moving beyond state-based and community-based constructs of language, by challenging the very boundaries between varieties, languages and communities. It does, however, draw and build on such research, thus incorporating, rather than discarding, previous understandings of English language variation and change.

In terms of pedagogical implications (discussed further in Chapter 2) Global Englishes research has emphasised the need to raise awareness of the current sociolinguistic landscape of English language use. Global Englishes research has also helped to challenge widely held perspectives in TESOL that centre on notions that learners aim to use the language with L1 speakers.

## English as an international language

English as an international language (EIL) as a field of study has largely focused on the implications of the spread of English rather than the language itself. Accordingly, EIL research has been less characterised by a linguistic interest in variation. As such, it stands a little separate in its focus from World Englishes and ELF research, and a little closer to Global Englishes in its universal scope. EIL scholars are particularly interested in the sociolinguistic, political, economic and educational implications for the global spread of English. Under the EIL banner, researchers have explored the implications of global English use for society, and language education, drawing on both World Englishes and ELF scholarship, as well as related fields of study such as native-speakerism (discussed later in this chapter). While EIL as a field has broad similarities to Global Englishes, it has not grown out of movements in critical applied linguistics, and accordingly could be described as embodying a pragmatic perspective, which has made it attractive for the TESOL profession. However, in relation to the practical implications of both fields for English language teaching, it is safe to state that EIL and Global Englishes scholars are on a broadly similar page. EIL scholars of TESOL such as McKay and Brown (2016) and Matsuda (2012, 2017), for example, purport broadly similar messages and ideologies of Global Englishes scholars of TESOL such as Galloway (2017a).

## Teaching English as an International Language

Due to the pragmatic nature of EIL, it is the term that has mostly been adopted into mainstream of TESOL research and TESOL literature, as evident from a string of authored publications (e.g. McKay & Brown, 2016), edited collections (e.g. Alsagoff *et al.*, 2012; Matsuda, 2012, 2017b) and even an entire volume on Teaching EIL in the recent Encyclopaedia of English Language Teaching. Rose and Galloway (2019) state that EIL 'has been used a catch-all term for the use of English in general, as a strategy to eliminate traditional distinctions between English as a Native, Second, Foreign and Additional Language (ENL/ESL/EFL/EAL), as these distinctions are seen as increasingly irrelevant in today's globally integrated world' (2019: 8).

As this book is aimed at TESOL professionals and TESOL researchers, we choose to adopt the terms 'English as an international language' and 'Teaching English as an International Language' to refer to the shared agenda of all of these fields to inform and innovate the English language teaching industry. We see EIL as an easily and widely understood term for this purpose. Nevertheless, throughout this book, we acknowledge that this may not be the preferred term of many of the researchers whose work we draw on, and thus, when directly referring to other authors' scholarship we try as much as possible to retain their preferred terminology. What is important to understand, however, is that

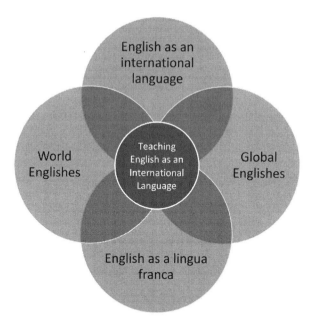

**Figure 1.2** The theoretical positioning of Teaching English as an International Language in this book

the weight of shared endeavours of all of these interrelated fields outweighs any proclaimed differences. Thus, it is this book's stance that, when it comes to pedagogical implications in particular, the four fields are more broadly similar in scope than they are different. We have captured our positioning of Teaching EIL in Figure 1.2. It is important to note that Rose and Galloway (2019) adopt a similar Venn diagram strategy to depict their Global Englishes Language Teaching approach (discussed further in Chapter 2). Thus, different terminology are used to communicate broadly similar ideas.

## Challenges to the 'Native-Speaker'

EIL in this book is positioned as both a sociolinguistic and a political ideology. As such, it aims to disrupt the status quo in TESOL, where the native speaker has long been held a prestige position. It is important to note that the continued prevalence of native speaker hegemony in TESOL has been challenged and problematised for decades (see Cook, 1999; Davies, 2003; Holliday, 2005, 2015; Paikeday, 1985; Rampton, 1990). Galloway and Rose (2015) state that the term of native speaker is incredibly difficult to define, and when one picks at the term, it becomes apparent that neither proficiency, nor timing of acquisition are necessary criteria to be labelled as a native speaker. The most accurate definition of a native speaker is that a native only becomes a native speaker if they are identified as such by other native speakers. The native speaker identity, therefore, is like joining an exclusive club, where there are no membership criteria for joining, but rather other members and gatekeepers decide whether you are 'club material'. Because of the difficulty in defining what a native speaker is, the term has been described as a linguistic 'figment' (Paikeday, 1985); a 'fallacy' (Phillipson, 1992); and a 'myth' (Davies, 2003). Scholars working in this area have called for greater use of alternative terms to the native speaker such as 'multicompetent' users (Cook, 1999, 2016), 'proficient user' (Paikeday, 1985), or 'language expert' (Rampton, 1990). Selvi (2014), however, argues that using different terms in scholarship does not detract from the power of the 'native speaker' label due its continued use in society and in TESOL. Thus, the term 'native speaker', if used critically to describe this social construct, has purpose for the profession and for research.

## The native-speaker teacher

Challenges to the idea of the native speaker are arguably of more relevance to TESOL than other modern foreign languages. For many taught languages, the position of the native speaker as future target interlocutor for learners can be somewhat justified on the basis that native speakers are the majority speakers – but the same cannot be said for EIL. For example, learners of the Japanese language in Australia may indeed see that their future target interlocuter of Japanese will be Japanese people they will encounter in Japan or their home countries. For this reason, it may be natural for such learners to desire to learn a variety of Japanese that adheres to the native linguistic and pragmatic norms of the language. Desires for learners of Japanese in Australia to have a native Japanese speaking teacher (or a non-native speaking teacher who has spent considerable time living within Japan) may thus be somewhat justified, as these teachers are positioned as gateways for learners to interact with the target culture. The situation for TESOL, however, is very different, as English has become a global language with global ownership, where L2 speakers are in the majority.

For most EIL learners, future interlocutors are more likely to be other second-language users of English. Moreover, future contexts of English use may be domestic or international and in non-Anglophone countries (e.g. for the purposes of business, academic study, or even social interaction). For many learners of English, the majority of their English language interactions outside of the classroom might not involve a 'native' speaker of English at all. Thus, preference for native English linguistic and pragmatic norms, and native-English speaking teachers as a gateway to their future target culture, soon unravel and become unjustified. In contrast, teachers who are L2 users themselves, and who have different L1s to their students, may be more authentic role models for students in terms of representing their likely future interlocutors and target English-using cultures. This has led some scholars to call for more emphasis on hiring

'Multilingual English Teachers' (Kirkpatrick, 2011, 2012). Galloway and Rose (2015) concur with Kirkpatrick's call, and state that stakeholders in TESOL need to critically engage with the notion that monolingual English teachers, who have never learned a second language themselves, may not necessarily make the best English teachers. There has been large call in recent years for greater global mobility of NNESTs (non-native English-speaking teachers) via more inclusive hiring practices.

## The NNEST movement

Challenges surrounding the treatment of NNESTs in TESOL have given rise to large amount of scholarship and activism, which has been described as a *NNEST movement* (Braine, 2010). The NNEST movement emerged in TESOL as a means to counter discriminatory practices, and to promote democracy, justice, equity, participation and professionalism (Braine & Selvi, 2018). Selvi (2014) further describes the movement as such:

> Theoretically, it builds a more inclusive intellectual space defined by a shift from the traditional monolingual, monocultural, native-speakerist approach to teaching, learning, and teacher education in TESOL. Practically, it brings together and supports a wide spectrum of threads from the research, teaching, and advocacy realms to promote and institutionalize discourses of multilingualism, multiethnicism, and multiculturalism. (2014: 574–575)

Thus, the NNEST movement is inextricably linked to the scholarship of EIL, World Englishes, ELF and Global Englishes. It, too, lobbies for more equality and representativeness in TESOL, which can be realised via a paradigm shift of the very ideologies which underpin the field.

## Native-speakerism and centre-periphery

Related to the NNEST movement, is the broader research area of native-speakerism, which explores the explicit and implicit creation of inequalities based on a perceived characteristic of nativeness. As Holliday notes:

> Native-speakerism is a pervasive ideology within ELT, characterized by the belief that 'native-speaker' teachers represent a 'Western culture' from which spring the ideals both of the English language and of English language teaching methodology. (Holliday, 2006: 385)

Native-speakerism is underpinned by the concept of 'Othering', because the ideology creates dichotomous categories. Speakers are categorised according to their differences rather than the characteristics they share. Native-speakerism is seen to uphold unequal power dynamics in TESOL, and is especially prevalent in teacher hiring practices, where many advertisements still explicitly place a teachers' nativeness as an essential hiring criterion, and thus a barrier to professional opportunities (Selvi, 2010).

Other scholars in TESOL have explored the othering of NNESTs in terms of centre-periphery theory. In the TESOL industry, various powerful 'centres of English' (i.e. native speakers and native speaking countries) have the lion's share of influence, while others are related to the 'periphery'. There is an imbalance in power between the centre and periphery, which feeds into all related decisions in language teaching policy and practice. Hilgendorf (2018) states:

> Given how widely English is learned and used in so many communities around the globe, a complex set of dynamics and tensions exists between these centers and perceived peripheries. For both native and non-native English-speaking teachers (NESTs and NNESTs), a critical understanding of these dynamics and tensions is imperative, as they have significant ramifications for curricular design and pedagogical practice. (2018: 1)

EIL scholars aim to disrupt the power dynamics between the centre and the periphery by emphasising the important role that the peripheral majority have (and will have) in terms of English language learning and use in the 21st century.

## Multilingualism in TESOL

It is important to note that the field of EIL is further influenced by numerous tangentially related topics within the broader fields of applied linguistics and second language acquisition. These topics include, but are in no way limited to: translanguaging; multilingual turn; and plurilingualism. While each of these fields are not exclusive to TESOL, as they impact all language learning and use, much of the work that has been carried out within these has been within an English language learning context. Each of these are briefly touched upon in this section.

### Translanguaging, translingual practice and plurilingualism

Developments in translanguaging research have been linked to Global Englishes (see Rose & Galloway, 2019), and thus are also of relevance to teaching EIL. Translanguaging challenges monolingual orientations to language learning and language teaching by viewing languages as part of the interwoven linguistic system of a user, rather than as separate entities. Translanguaging is a term that is growing in importance in applied linguistics, touching on all facets of second language acquisition and linguistic research. Nevertheless, its educational connections remain strong, as illustrated by the following observation by García and Li (2018):

> As a critical sociolinguistic theory, translanguaging has had the most application in language education, especially in the education of language-minoritized students and in bilingual education and increasingly in what are considered foreign language programs. It has been seen to have the capacity and potential to transform the way we see, use, and

> teach language, literacy, and other subjects… [T]ranslanguaging has impacted language education, transforming how we teach students for bilingualism as well as how bilingual students learn. (2018: 1)

It is no surprise that translanguaging research has been applied most broadly to education, as the term itself grew out of bilingual education research and practice in Welsh immersion schools (see Baker, 2001; Williams, 1996), before later being repurposed as a broader theory of second language acquisition. From a practical classroom-based perspective translanguaging would involve the encouragement of students to use their other languages in the classroom to support their learning of the second language. These languages can be informally used by learners, or formally integrated into tasks: for example, students could read a text in their L1 to inform them for a project presented in the L2.

Translanguaging has clear similarities to the term code-switching, which has a longer tradition in second language research. Code-switching refers to the act of switching from one language to the other within speech, usually in the context of bilingual communication. Proponents of translanguaging argue that the two constructs are different: codeswitching adopts an external perspective and reinforces power hierarchies between two named languages, but translanguaging views all languages as part of a user's entire linguistic repertoire (see Garcia & Li, 2014 for more detail). In terms of a difference in TESOL practices, therefore, code-switching might imply a learner or teachers switches to another language due to perceived deficiencies in the target language, whereas translanguaging is viewed as a positive act, which embraces a learners' multilingual identity.

Related to translanguaing is the term *translingual practice*, which is Canagarajah's own version of translanguaging. Canagarajah (2016) observes:

> There is now a growing realization that English cannot be separated from other languages. This is true not only of the contemporary global contact zones where languages intermingle, but of all communication, because languages are always in contact. (2016: 16)

Rose and Galloway (2019) note that 'Translingual practice showcases linguistic hybridity, and helps to inform our understanding of how speakers of English as a global lingua franca utilise their multilingual, or translingual, repertoires to communicate' (2019: 9). Thus, the similarities between this term and translanguaging are clear. Both translingual practice and translanguaging similarly challenge the theories that depict languages as separate social, cognitive, psychological or linguistic entities, which underlie many TESOL practices.

The term *plurilingualism* 'refers to the unique aspects of individual repertoires and agency, and multilingual(ism) to refer to broader social language context/contact(s) and the coexistence of several languages in a particular situation' (Marshall & Moore, 2013: 474). In a similar way that translanguaging contrasts with code-switching, advocates use the term plurilingualism to challenge traditional definitions of multilingualism which view language and language proficiencies, as separate. Marshall and Moore (2013) argue, 'the focus on plurilingual competence allows researchers to dismantle perceptions of arbitrary boundaries within individuals' linguistic repertoires, and relates to broader issues such as individual agency, knowledge formation, and engagement' (2013: 474). Plurilingualism research, as it pertains to TESOL, also seeks to create a more multilingual/plurilingual TESOL (Taylor & Snoddon, 2013).

## The multilingual turn

Movements and interest in emerging neologisms such as translanguaging and plurilingualism (alongside numerous others) have been described as being part of a larger trend in second language acquisition and language education research, which has been termed the 'multilingual turn' (see May, 2014b). The multilingual turn has been used as an umbrella term to show the importance now placed on multilingualism, rather than monolingualism, in language research. Rose and Galloway (2019) place Global Englishes (and therefore EIL as part of their conceptualisation of it) within the multilingual turn.

To some TESOL practitioners and researchers, it may be strange to read that the field of second and foreign language education has been historically underpinned by monolingualism. It would seem that the very nature of second and foreign language education implies that stakeholders within this context are, in themselves, multilingual learners and teachers of English. However, if we consider practices which have underpinned TESOL throughout the 20th century, we soon reveal a monolingual bias. For example:

(1) many standard examinations of English are pegged to monolingual native English standards;
(2) in evaluating the proficiency of a learner of English, a native speaker of English is often regarded as the ultimate goal of attainment;
(3) many educational policies encourage teachers to create 'English-only' monolingual environments for their learners;
(4) globally, teacher hiring practices favour native English-speaking teachers, where knowledge of the students' first language may not be a necessary requirement for employment;
(5) many native English teachers are discouraged from using the students' first language, even if they are proficient in it;
(6) communicative language teaching methodologies often depict monolingual English speakers as a learner's target interlocutor;
(7) in task-based language teaching, students in English classrooms are often berated or punished for using their first language during group work, even if the use of this language helps them to complete the task;

(8) research into the English language development of learners (whether it be phonological, grammatical, lexical, or pragmatic linguistic development) often uses a group of monolingual English speakers as a comparison group;

(9) research into the lexical knowledge of younger bilingual users of English (such as EAL learners), often only take account of knowledge in English, ignoring knowledge in other languages.

The monolingual bias further extends to other areas of language learning outside of the classroom, such as the widely prevalent practice of advising immigrant families to speak English at home to better facilitate the English language development of their children (although this advice has lessened in recent decades in many contexts). Even when families adopt a bilingual language policy at home, many families apply a 'one parent one language' practice, thus discouraging the mixing of languages for communication within the family, which can be at the detriment of communication between all members of the family.

In a seminal paper on the multilingual turn, Ortega (2013) predicted that the current observable pivot towards multilingualism will impact the fields of SLA (and by association, TESOL), in a similar manner to that of the social turn in the 1990s. The social turn, over a period of two decades, saw a general movement away from cognitive traditions in SLA towards more social and interactional perspectives of SLA. Social perspectives facilitated the exploration of language learning as a social phenomenon, wrapped up in learner identity and sociocultural theories of education (see Atkinson, 2011 for an overview of these alternative theories). These *turns* have seen the emergence of new theories of language learning such as the 'transdisciplinary framework for SLA in a multilingual world' (Douglas Fir Group, 2016), which has since been used as framework for rethinking language teacher education (Gao, 2019).

Scholars within the multilingual turn have been increasingly vocal with calls for change in TESOL (e.g. Canagarajah, 2014; Leung, 2014; May, 2014a; Norton, 2014), with Meier (2017) referring to it as 'a critical movement in education' (2017: 131). Thus, there are clear links between the work being conducted by multilingual researchers, who are exploring the nexus of language education and multilingualism, and the work being conducted by EIL scholars, who are exploring similar implications for TESOL. The multilingual turn encapsulates a growing trend in TESOL to reject a monolingual bias, and to also be inclusive of the social realities and complexities of how languages are used in our globalised world. Thus, many of the topics we explore in this book, whether it emanates from World Englishes, ELF, Global Englishes, or EIL paradigms of research, may touch on similar work in the multilingual turn.

While the 'E' in EIL clearly stands for 'English', it is important to emphasise that the term itself is not underpinned by a monolingual ideology. EIL is a sociolinguistic and highly politicised paradigm of study, that is highly attuned to the fact that English users in the 21st century are multilingual users. The majority of speakers of English today use the language within their wider linguistic repertoire. This has clear implications for TESOL practice, as subsequent chapters will explore.

## What Does the Research Tell Us?

In each chapter in this book, we explicitly include a section which showcases important empirical research on the topic of the chapter in order to engage the reader directly with relevant research. This is done to emphasise the fact that the ideas presented are empirically founded and not merely 'soap box' ideology. However, as this first chapter is a theoretical one, which is intended to offer a conceptual foundation for subsequent chapters, we mostly draw on important conceptual, rather than empirical, research. In particular we draw attention to what we consider to be key pieces of scholarly work that have helped to inform 21st century TESOL innovation in global contexts. These papers are outlined in Table 1.1.

Ortega (2013) focuses on the broader implications of the multilingual turn for second language acquisition as a whole, but nevertheless, provides an excellent summary for TESOL practitioners of emerging trends in applied linguistics that aim to embrace multilingualism, rather than

**Table 1.1** Theoretical papers related to 21st century TESOL

| Researchers | Topic | Focus |
| --- | --- | --- |
| Meier (2017) | Multilingual Turn | The implications of the multilingual turn for language education, including TESOL. |
| Ortega (2014) | Multilingual Turn | The trends and implications of the past 15 years of research that indicate a major turn in applied linguistics towards multilingualism. |
| Matsuda (2003) | English as an international language | Implications of EIL for the field of TESOL and for English language curricula. |
| Brown (1993) | World Englishes | The incorporation of World Englishes in TESOL programmes. |
| Jenkins (2006) | English as a lingua franca | Perspectives on teaching World Englishes and ELF in English language curricula. |
| Selvi (2014) | NNEST movement | Debunking the myths and misconceptions about non-native English speakers in TESOL. |
| Canagarajah (2007) | Multilingualism and SLA | A theoretical exploration of the implications of lingua franca English and multilingualism for SLA. |
| Lin (2013) or Creese and Blackledge (2010) | Plurilingualism | A current paradigm shift in TESOL methodology towards plurilingualism. |

monolingualism, as a global norm. This has implications for the use of other languages as resources in the classrooms, and challenges some prevailing TESOL ideologies such as the perceived importance of English-only classrooms. Similar perspectives, which are more oriented towards language education and TESOL, can be found in an edited collection on the topic by May (2014a). This book also contains a similar chapter by Ortega (2014).

Meier's (2017) paper offers a more accessible overview of work within the multilingual turn in terms of its direct implications for language education. It reports on an empirical study of key works within the multilingual turn, including May's (2014) edited book, in order to synthesise key areas of interest and to reflect on challenges to innovate change in language education. A similar paper can be found in Sambiante (2017), which also addresses the implications for language education by comparing and synthesising key scholar's work on the topic.

The work of Canagarajah in the 2000s established him as a key scholar of critical applied linguistics. Such scholarship is illustrated in his 2007 paper, which explores the implications of lingua franca English and multilingualism for second language acquisition theory. In this paper, Canagarajah (2007) challenges some of the long-upheld simplifications of the language learning process, and encourages researchers to embrace ideologies that centre around multilingual competence. While very theoretical, many TESOL researchers have found inspiration in Canagarajah's work. For example, Galloway and Rose's (2015) six proposals for change in TESOL, which are presented in Chapter 2, are informed in part by the earlier work by Canagarajah around this time.

Selvi's (2014) article in *TESOL Journal* is a powerful evaluation of nativespeakerism in TESOL. In this paper, he delineates the non-native speaker teacher movement in TESOL, debunking myths and showing a transformation of TESOL in recent years. Later, Selvi (2018) states that he hopes this paper 'will serve as an orientation for TESOLers who might be interested in learning more about the NNEST movement' (2018: 1). It certainly achieves this aim while also highlighting areas of needed attention in the future.

The article by Jenkins (2006) is one of many influential papers which have explored the implications of ELF and World Englishes research for the field of TESOL. Published in *TESOL Quarterly*, the paper explores the differences between EIL, ELF and World Englishes, before then outlining the implications of this research for challenging yardsticks and standards used in TESOL. Unfortunately, the conceptual and theoretical focus of the paper is not articulated in terms of real concrete proposals for change that teachers can readily integrate into the classroom. Nevertheless, the paper has been widely cited and its influence is undeniable.

Matsuda's (2003) paper, also in *TESOL Quarterly*, is more pragmatic in its approach compared to Jenkins' later article. In the paper, Matsuda uses the context of English language education in Japan as an anchor to concretely outline a number of areas in TESOL in need of reconsideration within the EIL paradigm. These areas of change include: a re-assessment of EIL learner needs; direct teaching of issues surrounding language ownership; shifts in assessment towards communicative effectiveness; increased interaction among EIL users; and greater representation of EIL in teaching materials.

Brown's (1993) paper is included here to show that calls for innovation in the TESOL curriculum are not by any means new. In this paper, Brown draws on calls from World Englishes scholars for a paradigm shift in TESOL. Brown's ideas are presented in the form of eight recommendations that promote the incorporation of a World Englishes perspective within TESOL in general, within teacher training courses, and within the broader academic and practitioner community. Twenty-five years since this article, continued calls for innovation are still ongoing (see Galloway, 2017a; Kumaravadivelu, 2012a; Matsuda, 2017a).

Lin's (2013) paper explores plurilingual pedagogies in content classrooms in Hong Kong, which could be seen as evidence of paradigmatic change in TESOL methodologies. Lin draws on case study data from classrooms in Hong Kong to illustrate her points. A similar perspective on translanguaging can be found in Creese and Blackledge (2010). (Although their context is not an English language learning one, the theoretical underpinnings of what they found in the modern language classrooms may be of interest to TESOL practitioners who wish to explore what plurilingualism might look like in bilingual educational contexts.)

## Implications for Teachers in Global Contexts

The theoretical fields of study outlined in this chapter (ELF, Global Englishes, translanguaging, the NNEST movement and the multilingual turn) have all expressed clear implications for language teaching as part of their scholarship. All of these fields of study further emphasise the need for a paradigm shift in TESOL to achieve these aims. As Rose and Galloway (2019) observe: 'Underpinning this paradigm shift is a change in views of ownership of English, the emancipation of non-native speakers from native speaker norms, a repositioning of culture within the English language, a shift in models of language, and a repositioning of the target interlocutor' (2019: 4).

In this book, we group these shared endeavours under the term teaching EIL, which we see as a TESOL-led movement that has actively lobbied for a change in TESOL practices by challenging the prevailing ideologies of current English language pedagogy. We, like Kumaravadivelu (2012a) before us, call for a meaningful break from traditional English language teaching practices. The following chapter (Chapter 2) outlines explicit frameworks for achieving this break.

Nevertheless, the theoretical grounding of this chapter has raised a number of points for teachers to consider before reading further. Teachers in global contexts may want to consider their answers to the following questions:

- Drawing on World Englishes, what varieties of English are most salient to their learners and their teaching context?
- Drawing on translanguaging and translingual practice, how can other languages be used as a resource in their English language classrooms?
- Considering the growing ELF opportunities for students, how can teachers better prepare their students to be successful in lingua franca contexts?
- In light of the NNEST movement, in what ways can schools ensure equality for all teachers?
- Drawing on the wider field of Global Englishes, how can teachers raise student awareness of the global realities of English language use?
- Taking into account movements within the multilingual turn, how much of current teaching practices are informed by a monolingual bias?
- Reflecting on native-speakerism, in what ways do teachers' current teaching contexts show a preference towards the 'native speaker'?
- Taking into account all of the factors surrounding the teaching of EIL, what changes can be made to English language curricula to improve practices?

Overall, teaching EIL requires a shift in perspective of all stakeholders in TESOL, however change cannot occur without the support from teachers. Both Dewey (2012) and Widdowson (2012) note a need for teachers to reconceptualise the notion of language they teach. For the teaching of EIL to become the global norm, we need this to become a grassroots movement, led by teachers for the benefit of their students. The following nine chapters in this book will explore implications of this movement for various facets of TESOL to further explore how teachers can be central to achieving this needed change. It is a hope that this knowledge will better equip teachers (and practitioner-researchers) to meet their students' needs in 21st century global TESOL contexts.

## Post-reading Activities

### Reflect

Think about aspects in a teaching/learning environment you are familiar with, and consider the possibilities for innovation in light of the ideas presented in this chapter.

*Discuss*

(1) This chapter has covered many terms related to the spread of English as a global language (Global Englishes, World Englishes, EIL, ELF) as well as those connected to multilingualism (translanguaging, translingual practice, plurilingualism). Which of the terms resonate most with your own beliefs regarding language norms and language use?

(2) This chapter concludes with a statement that teachers need to reconceptualise the notion of language. If you agree with this, what aspects are most necessary for teachers to reconceptualise?

(3) Both May (2014b) and Ortega (2013) lobby for teachers to reject a monolingual bias. Kirkpatrick argues that multilingual English teachers should be valued over monolingual English teachers. In what way do you agree or disagree that multilingual ideologies are relevant to the profession of English language teaching? In what ways, if any, can multilingualism be valued more in TESOL?

*Apply*

This chapter suggests that the English language teaching industry needs to change. Using the list of questions in the section 'Implications for teachers in global contexts' to guide you, write (or present in a group) a reflection in answer to these questions regarding a teaching context with which you are familiar.

## Resources for Further Reading

May, S. (ed.) (2014) *The Multilingual Turn: Implications for SLA, TESOL, and Bilingual Education*. Routledge.

This book contains nine chapters written by 12 of the leading scholars in the field of multilingualism. Many of the initial chapters lay a strong theoretical foundation for a pivot in second language acquisition towards multilingualism as the norm in informing both theory and practice. Later chapters explore more contextualised realities of how these new perspectives should underpin policy and practice in language education. Please note, this is not a resource for concrete proposals of change in TESOL, but rather an influential resource which covers key movements in SLA theory which underpins TESOL practices.

Galloway, N. and Rose, H. (2015) *Introducing Global Englishes*. Routledge.

Whereas the edited book by May (2013) contains contributions by key SLA theorists in the field, *Introducing Global Englishes* is written by two teacher-researchers and targeted for a more general audience. The book takes a macro perspective of Global Englishes, which they use as an umbrella term to capture the shared ideologies of World Englishes, ELF and EIL. Chapter 1 provides an overview of key topics in much the same way as this book's chapter has done. It then devotes two additional chapters to EIL issues, a chapter on language variation and change, and two ELF-centric chapters on global language use. Chapter 9 is devoted entirely to the topic of implications for TESOL. This chapter contains proposals for change in TESOL, as well as introducing a framework for TESOL innovation to help teachers move towards a Global Englishes-oriented form of practice.

# 2 Models for Teaching English as an International Language

### Think

What might a good EIL course look like? What could teachers do to ensure their students are prepared to use English in global contexts?

### Discuss

Look at the components of the TESOL curriculum in Figure 2.1. For each component, discuss what a curriculum coordinator could modify in an English language course to ensure that it is EIL-oriented. Please note: *Needs* refers to the future needs of learners of the course to be able to use the language; *Goals* refers to the explicitly stated outcomes for a course; *Syllabus* refers to the materials used for teaching and way in which these are sequenced and organised; *Methodology* refers to the teaching approaches used; *Assessment* refers to ways in which students are evaluated as having reached the outcomes of a course; *Evaluation* refers to the way in which the quality of a course is monitored and modified according to feedback.

## Introduction

The previous chapter outlined some of the main conceptual trends in English language education, which have been associated with the spread of English as a global language. All of these paradigms for thinking have highlighted a need to innovate current TESOL practices to better address the global sociolinguistic realities of how English is used in the 21st century. For example, World Englishes research has suggested that this new reality has clear implications for English language learning goals and, as a result, for the whole curriculum (see Kirkpatrick, 2012). The EIL paradigm argues that these new realities challenge some of the long-held fundamental assumptions underpinning TESOL, and that it requires teachers to revisit their teaching practices (see Matsuda & Friedrich, 2012). Even though many scholars argue for a paradigm shift in TESOL, it is now up to teachers and teacher educators to translate these ideas into pedagogical change. Therefore, this chapter begins to explore the implications and translation of EIL knowledge for (and into) EIL practices. It explores proposals and models that have been introduced by TESOL researchers and researcher-practitioners to help operationalise ideas into tangible approaches for curriculum innovation.

## Key Concepts

Three key concepts that are essential to frame good teaching practice in general, and therefore good EIL instruction, are: curriculum development, needs analysis and teaching approaches.

### Curriculum development

A key concept underpinning language teaching is curriculum development. Richards (1982) who is possibly the foremost scholar of curriculum theory in TESOL, explains '[l]anguage curriculum development, like other areas of curriculum activity, is concerned with principles and procedures for the planning, management, and assessment of learning' (1982: 1). In short, a curriculum tells teachers what to teach, how to teach, what to assess, what the lesson goals are, and what the students need (Mickan, 2012). Typically, a curriculum incorporates the following components in its development: Needs; Goals/Objectives; Syllabus; Methodology; Assessment; and Evaluation (see Figure 2.1). Rose and Galloway (2019) have been instrumental in using these components of curriculum development to provide structure to curriculum innovation in Global Englishes (and therefore also EIL).

In order to operationalise EIL change within the TESOL curriculum, Rose and Galloway (2019) argue that further questions can be asked within each component of the curriculum in order to adopt a global perspective. For example, additional questions might include:

(1) Needs: Who are the learners' likely future interlocutors? Will they need to use English as a lingua franca?
(2) Goals and objectives: Do the goals of the curriculum need to prepare students to use English as a global language in global contexts?
(3) Syllabus: Is the syllabus organised to include EIL elements and globally oriented materials?
(4) Methodology: Is the pedagogy appropriate to achieving EIL-related goals, such as facilitating activities to improve students' strategic competence for diverse types of communication?

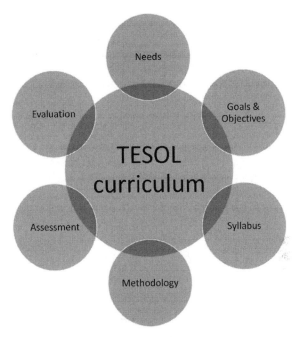

**Figure 2.1** The TESOL curriculum (Richards, 1982)

(5) Assessment: Are the chosen assessments EIL-oriented, focusing on the use of language, rather than knowledge of it?
(6) Evaluation: Is the curriculum being revisited regularly, and evaluated against the dynamic benchmarks of global use? (adapted from Rose & Galloway, 2019: 31)

Although all parts of the curriculum are equally important to inform good pedagogy, we argue that all good EIL curriculum development must be underpinned by good needs analysis, hence we have placed *needs* at the top of Figure 2.1, and discuss it in further detail below.

### Needs analysis

Needs analysis in EIL curriculum development is of particular importance, as it affects all other curriculum components. The needs of learners should inform a curriculum's goals and objectives, which in turn inform the best way to structure lessons within a syllabus, as well as the best methods to achieve these goals. These needs-based goals also dictate what aspects of language use should be assessed, and how assessment should occur to accurately measure achievement against these benchmarks. In the evaluation phase, curriculum developers must always return to student needs in order the evaluate whether the curriculum is targeting the right language skills. If evaluation reveals an incongruence, or if student needs change over time, then appropriate modifications need to be made to *all* curriculum components. If the needs for EIL users cannot be met within a traditional TESOL curriculum, then this is an indication that the curriculum may need a complete overhaul towards EIL-oriented outcomes.

As the world has globalised and English has spread into different social domains and contexts, measuring students' needs has become far more complex. Different students in different contexts (and even students within the same classrooms) might have vastly different requirements to use the language successfully in their futures. Fortunately, the growth in English has been accompanied by a boom in research which examines how English is used – often built on evidence from corpus linguistic methods. This research can help to inform the TESOL profession of the diverse ways in which language is used in a variety of global settings.

If resources permit, some educational institutions are able to conduct their own needs analysis by tracking their students after they graduation from a course. Needs analysis can aim to gather information on how well the course provided them with the *necessities* (knowledge and skills) required to successfully use the language. Needs analysis should also seek to understand where linguistic knowledge is *lacking*, as this can then be fed back into the curriculum via modifications to address these *lacks*. Further to this, Nation and Macalister (2010) state that good needs analysis should not only include *necessities* and *lacks*, but also consider learners' *wants*. This is because not all language learning is instrumentally driven, and students may want to develop linguistic knowledge and skills in areas that might not be immediately applicable. For example, in an English exam preparation course, the learning of low-frequency vocabulary might be a *necessity*, knowledge of reading comprehension strategies might be a *lack* for many students, and student might *want* to engage in regular group work – and all of this informs the needs of the course.

When students are in a course which has *situational* or *specific* needs, such as an EAP course to prepare them for university postgraduate study or an ESP course to prepare nurses to use English in professional contexts, needs analysis is often easier to conduct, as it is targeted to these specific domains.

## Teaching approaches

A further key concept for this chapter is realisation of the fact that throughout history, approaches and ideologies underpinning language teaching have always changed according to the sociolinguistic needs of learners (see Figure 2.2). As Rose (2018) observes, 'Since the early years of mass language education, approaches have adapted according to the needs of the learner' (2018: 6). Taking Europe as an example, Grammar Translation prevailed in the school system well into the 1900s, where language acquisition was seen as part of students' academic development, and

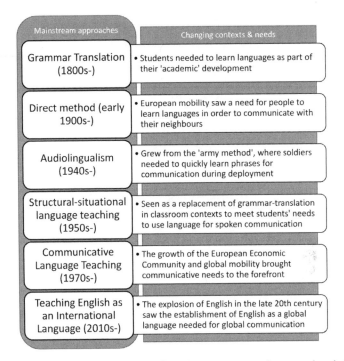

| Mainstream approaches | Changing contexts & needs |
|---|---|
| Grammar Translation (1800s-) | • Students needed to learn languages as part of their 'academic' development |
| Direct method (early 1900s-) | • European mobility saw a need for people to learn languages in order to communicate with their neighbours |
| Audiolingualism (1940s-) | • Grew from the 'army method', where soldiers needed to quickly learn phrases for communication during deployment |
| Structural-situational language teaching (1950s-) | • Seen as a replacement of grammar-translation in classroom contexts to meet students' needs to use language for spoken communication |
| Communicative Language Teaching (1970s-) | • The growth of the European Economic Community and global mobility brought communicative needs to the forefront |
| Teaching English as an International Language (2010s-) | • The explosion of English in the late 20th century saw the establishment of English as a global language needed for global communication |

**Figure 2.2** The relationship between changing contexts and approaches (adapted from Rose, 2018; Rose & Galloway, 2019)

any communicative purpose would mostly be in the form of reading literature and writing papers or letters. As European mobility increased in the 1900s, some learners who needed language for use in politics, commerce, or travel turned to language schools that offered a more Direct Method such as the Berlitz Method, where language was learned via intense spoken communication with orally fluent (often native) speaking teachers. Then, wartime needs in Europe saw the rise in use of the Audiolingual Method by US military stationed in Europe, which aimed to teach phrases for communication to large groups of learners, so they could linguistically operate during their deployment. After the war, such methods were developed into teachable classroom methods such as *structural-situational language teaching* in the UK, which was seen as the first feasible replacement to grammar-translation in schools (as the Direct Method was too resource intensive, requiring small classes, native speakers, and motivated learners).

In the 1970s, the growth of the European Economic Community and an increase in European mobility brought communicative needs of learners to the forefront, giving rise to communicative language teaching, which is still the current prevailing method in most European contexts. As communicative language teaching is an approach, and not a method, it exists in multiple forms. These include 'weaker' forms that follow a similar approach to structural-situational language teaching (such as utilisations of the present-practice-produce technique), and 'stronger' forms (such as task-based language teaching). Now, however, the explosion of English in the late 20th century has seen the establishment of English as a global language, which students need for global communication. This new reality, and the new needs that have accompanied it, are ushering in new ways to explore what teaching English as a global language should look like.

## Proposals for Change

Suggestions for a change in TESOL in order to keep pace with the dramatic sociolinguistic changes in global English language use stretch back decades, and can be found sprinkled throughout linguistic and educational literature. In order to organise these calls into key areas that required the attention from TESOL practitioners, Galloway and Rose (2015) grouped them into six broad proposals for curriculum change. These proposals claim for a need to:

(1) increase World Englishes and ELF exposure in TESOL curricula;
(2) emphasise respect for multilingualism in TESOL;
(3) raise awareness of Global Englishes in TESOL;
(4) raise awareness of ELF strategies in TESOL curricula;
(5) emphasise respect for diverse culture and identity in TESOL;
(6) change English language teacher hiring practices in the TESOL industry.

Together, these proposals seek to achieve innovation with a TESOL curriculum, and within language learning institutions.

The first proposal seeks to rectify an imbalance in current language norms in TESOL (especially the spoken language norms), which are presented to learners of English. It increases awareness that the dominant educational norms of 'British' (i.e. received pronunciation) and 'American' (i.e. General American) are only spoken by a fraction of the global English-using population. In the 21st century, students need to understand a diverse range of speakers (McKay, 2012). The second proposal ties in with movements in the multilingual turn, and embraces an increased awareness that other languages can add efficacy and authenticity in the language classroom. The third proposal promotes the notion that students need to be educated in the language itself, and also with regards to how it is used, so that they can better prepare themselves as global English users. The fourth proposal sees the need to focus on the communication strategies that might help learners to successfully converse with interlocutors of varying Englishes and proficiencies. These include, but are not limited to, negotiation and accommodation strategies. The fifth proposal emphasises a global ownership of English, and seeks to situate English use in diverse contexts and cultures, rather than Inner Circle-situated ones. The sixth proposal lobbies for change in hiring practices, drawing on the work in NNEST movement (discussed in Chapter 1).

However, despite the push for pedagogical change in EIL, there have been relatively few models proposed that detail what such change should look like. This has led some scholars to observe that 'the volume of such academic attention does not seem to have had a tangible impact on actual classroom reality' (Saraceni, 2009: 177). Galloway and Rose (2015), alongside others, have described this mismatch as a theory–practice divide, which they define as both an 'incongruence between what experts claim is the case (or prescribe should be the case) and actual practices' and an ' incongruence between [substantial] theoretical-level discussions and a lack of practical, empirical research at the classroom level in relation to ELT' (2015: 259).

## Models to Innovate the Curriculum

In order to close the theory–practice divide, some researchers have specifically explored ways to operationalise theory into tangible practices, which can be implemented into classrooms. In this section, we explore three movements that have grown out of the three areas of EIL scholarship outlined in the previous chapter (World Englishes, English as a lingua franca and Global Englishes). Each of these fields has produced models, frameworks or blueprints for change, which can broadly be described as: World Englishes-informed ELT, ELF-oriented pedagogy and Global Englishes Language Teaching.

## The EIL curriculum blueprint and World Englishes-informed ELT

Over the past two decades, Aya Matsuda has actively explored the implications for World Englishes research for TESOL in quite concrete ways. Together, this work could be seen to inform a pedagogical model for EIL. In 2011, Matsuda and Friedrich observed that much of the discussion surrounding the pedagogical implications of World Englishes had 'remained at an abstract level and [had] not provided pedagogical ideas that [were] theoretically sound, informed by research, and at the same time specific enough to be useful in the classroom' (2011: 332). In answer to this gap, Matsuda and Friedrich (2011) introduced their EIL 'curriculum blueprint', which was underpinned by World Englishes scholarship. The blueprint is presented according to its crucial components, which include:

(1) the selection of the instructional model(s);
(2) ensuring exposure to Englishes and their users;
(3) facilitating strategic competence;
(4) providing appropriate cultural materials;
(5) increasing awareness of the politics of Englishes.

The authors also note that these steps are just a starting point for further curriculum innovations and development.

In terms of selecting an instructional model, the authors state that teachers can decide from three options, and that 'such a decision needs to be based on various factors such as students' goals and needs, teachers' expertise, and availability of materials and resources' (Matsuda & Friedrich, 2011: 334). These include choices between the selection of: An international variety of English; The learners' own variety; An established variety; and A dominant instructional model, which is salient to the learners. These are discussed further in Chapter 3. Whatever model is selected, the authors emphasise the second component of the blueprint should ensure that learners also receive exposure to other Englishes to better prepare them for future communicative success with a wide range of English speakers.

The third item in the blueprint emphasises the importance of teaching communication strategies to facilitate students' communicative competence. The authors note that 'it is crucial that students are equipped with – and be aware of – both the linguistic and strategic repertoire that they can draw from in situations where they use English to communicate with those who do not share their first language and culture' (Matsuda & Friedrich, 2011: 340). Further to this, the fourth component in the EIL blueprint highlights the importance of appropriate depictions of culture in the curriculum and in materials. These cultures need to move beyond a traditional focus on Inner Circle cultures, and also beyond stereotypical depictions of culture. The final component emphasises the need to explicitly discuss the politics of English with learners so that they are critically informed on issues that affect the way it is globally used. That is, successful EIL instruction should entail not only the teaching of language, but teaching about language, so that students are able to read, watch, discuss and write about global issues surrounding the English language (Matsuda & Friedrich, 2011).

In Matsuda and Matsuda (2018), the authors introduce a World Englishes-informed paradigm for English language teaching, exploring how the field of World Englishes has enriched, challenged and complicated multiple facets of the TESOL profession from theory to practice. Much of this model expands on Aya Matsuda's earlier work on the EIL blueprint.

## ELF-oriented pedagogy

Scholars in the field of ELF have also been relatively active in their promotion of an ELF-informed, ELF-aware or ELF-oriented pedagogy. In his conceptual paper on the topic, Dewey (2012) asserts that raising teacher awareness of ELF is an important first step to making adaptations to existing pedagogy so that it is more ELF-oriented. He argues that teachers are able to apply this heightened awareness to aspects of their existing professional knowledge. More specifically, he suggests the following types of innovations:

- Investigate and highlight the particular environment and sociocultural context in which English(es) will be used.
- Increase exposure to the diverse ways in which English is used globally presenting alternative variants as appropriate whenever highlighting linguistic forms.
- Engage in critical classroom discussion about the globalisation and growing diversity of English.
- Spend proportionately less time on ENL forms, especially if these are not widely used in other varieties; and thus, choose not to penalise non-native-led innovative forms that are intelligible.
- Focus (more) on communicative strategies. (Dewey, 2012: 163)

He further asserts that the adoption of an ELF perspective does not need to entail a radically different approach to teaching, but rather take the form of smaller modifications to TESOL materials and syllabi in response to ELF.

The closest model of an ELF-oriented pedagogical approach is Dewey's 'post-normative approach', in which he depicts as six questions that teachers must ask themselves in a systematic way in order to inform their practices. The model is depicted in Figure 2.3.

Unfortunately, ELF-oriented pedagogy is currently lacking in substantial research which reports on its proposed innovations in action. Upon inspection of the bulk of research emerging under this banner, one soon discovers that much of the extant research has focused on teacher education, as opposed to investigating pedagogical innovation itself. The closest thing to a framework might be Sifakis's (2017) ELF Awareness continuum, but once again the focus remains on teachers as the source of change

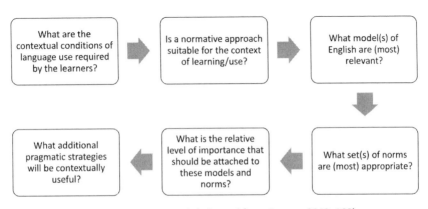

**Figure 2.3** Post-normative approach (adapted from Dewey, 2012: 168)

rather than a framework to help inform the curriculum or to raise aware-ness of the students themselves. Indeed, Dewey (2012) notes that '[u]nder-standing what teachers might do in order to incorporate ELF research in practice is not immediately obvious' (2012: 162), and that 'there has been relatively little in-depth exploration of what teachers might reasonably do to incorporate an ELF perspective in practice' (2012: 167). In more recent years, however, we have seen a few classroom-based studies emerge that could be described as adopting an informed ELF perspective – three of these are discussed later in this chapter: Baker (2012), Vettorel (2013) and Sung (2015). The field of ELF is still missing a concrete framework within which to frame innovation in ELT.

## Global Englishes Language Teaching

Galloway and Rose's (2015) *Global Englishes Language Teaching* framework, hereafter the GELT framework, is arguably the field's most comprehensive endeavour to synthesise calls for TESOL innovation. The attraction of the GELT model is that it builds on proposals for change across a diverse range of scholarship, and organises these changes into specific categories. While many other models of teaching EIL are rather theoretical in nature, the GELT framework is underpinned by a substan-tial amount of classroom research, which was conducted by the authors when they worked as language teachers in Japanese higher education. Another appeal of the framework is that it is the product of more than 10 years of development. Earlier iterations of the framework appeared in Galloway (2011), having emerged from her doctoral research. A more fleshed out version of the framework then appeared in Galloway and Rose (2015), which incorporated updated theorisation and additional research. The framework appeared again in Galloway and Rose (2018), with slight alterations in terminology. Finally, an expanded version of the framework appeared in Rose and Galloway (2019), which drew on addi-tional curriculum perspectives, making it more relevant to inform class-room practices.

The current version of the GELT framework is displayed in Table 2.1. It is important to note that that the authors emphasise that even though items in the table are organised into columns, the framework labels of 'traditional ELT' and 'GELT' are conceptualised as being at either end of a continuum. The idea, then, is for teachers to work towards developing their curriculum to help them move more towards GELT typified practices. The authors also indicate that the framework does not embody an 'all-or-nothing' ideology. It might only be feasible for teach-ers to innovate some aspects of their curriculum at any given time. Indeed, this is the case for the authors themselves, who report on only some of the innovations they implemented in their own classrooms in

**Table 2.1** Global Englishes Language Teaching framework (adapted from Rose & Galloway, 2019: 21)

|  | Traditional ELT | GELT |
|---|---|---|
| Target interlocutors | Native English speakers | All English users |
| Ownership | Inner circle | Global |
| Target culture | Static NE cultures | Fluid cultures |
| Norms | Standard English | Diverse, flexible and multiple forms |
| Teachers | Non-NE speaking teachers (same L1) and NE speaking teachers | Qualified, competent teachers (same and different L1s) |
| Role-model | NE speakers | Expert users |
| Source of materials | NE and NE speakers | Salient English-speaking communities and contexts |
| Other languages and cultures | Seen as a hindrance and source of interference | Seen as a resource as with other languages in their linguistic repertoire |
| Needs | Inner Circle defined | Globally defined |
| Assessment criterion | Accuracy according to prescriptive standards | Communicative competence |
| Goals of learning | Native-like proficiency | Multicompetent user |
| Ideology | Underpinned by an exclusive and ethnocentric view of English | Underpinned by an inclusive Global Englishes perspective |
| Orientation | Monolingual | Multilingual/translingual |

Note: NE = Native English

Japan, with the hope that other researcher-practitioners will follow in their footsteps. So far, the authors' own work has addressed the following areas of the GELT framework:

(1) The classroom-based study in Galloway and Rose (2014) focuses on challenging *norms* in the classroom by increasing exposure to diverse English language forms by changing the *source of materials* used in a homework activity.
(2) The classroom-based study in Rose and Galloway (2017) focuses on shifting students' *ideology* on standards in English.
(3) The curriculum innovation in Galloway and Rose (2013) facilitates a shift in *teachers* through the hiring of teaching assistants of varied L1 backgrounds and, as a result, the *target interlocutors* with whom the students engaged.
(4) Innovations reported in Rose and Montakantiwong (2018) discuss ways in which teachers can influence views of *ownership* as well as *role models*.

(5)  The two experimental studies reported in Galloway (2013, 2017a) saw the creation of a new course, which re-assessed student *needs* and *goals of learning*, thus drawing in numerous other aspects of the framework during implementation.
(6)  Rosenhan and Galloway (2019) report on creative tasks to challenge ideologies surrounding *ownership* of English.

## What Does the Research Tell Us?

In this section, we introduce some of the classroom-based research which reports on putting EIL ideas into pedagogical practice. An overview of the studies is provided in Table 2.2.

The study by Sung (2015) reports on a pilot study phase of a larger project, where a Global Englishes component was integrated into the curriculum of a 13 week-long EAP course in a university in Hong Kong. Sung collected data from his participants via two focus group interviews with 25 students in total. His study found that students' perceptions of the added components were 'overwhelmingly positive' (2015: 44), although the activities did 'not result in a radical change in the students' attitudes' (2015: 47).

A further study by Sung (2018) reported on an out-of-class activity in Hong Kong, where 18 students in his EAP class were encouraged to seek out and engage in ELF communication for a homework assignment. Sung analysed students' written reflections, and logbooks in which they recorded the details of their ELF interaction. The author

**Table 2.2** Examples of studies that report on EIL classroom activities

| Researchers | Topic | Participants | Research design | Data collection method |
|---|---|---|---|---|
| Sung (2015) | Global Englishes exposure | University students in Hong Kong (N = 25) | Classroom interventions | Focus groups |
| Sung (2018) | Provision of ELF opportunities | University students in Hong Kong (N = 25) | Out-of-class intervention | Learner log, and reflection papers |
| Rose and Galloway (2017) | Global Englishes exposure | EFL learners in Japan (N = 108) | Classroom intervention | Reflection papers |
| Vettorel (2010, 2013, 2014) | Provision of ELF opportunities | School children in Italy, Poland, Latvia and Slovakia (N = 540) | Classroom intervention | Corpus analysis of exchanges |
| Baker (2012) | Raising intercultural awareness | Students (N = 31) and teachers (N = 6) in Thailand | Out-of-class intervention | Questionnaires and software usage tracking |

concludes that the activity provided students with new insights and a raised awareness of ELF.

The group of three studies by Galloway and Rose (Galloway & Rose, 2014, 2018; Rose & Galloway, 2017) represent a body of classroom intervention work, which the researchers conducted with 108 English language learners in a Japanese university. The first study reported on the use of a listening task where students were exposed to, and then reflected on, a variety of the World Englishes. The second study reported on a task which challenged students' perceptions of standard language by getting them to engage in a debate on issues surrounding the *Speak Good English Movement* in Singapore. The final study, with the same group of learners, reported on a presentation task, in which students researched and presented on the historical development of one variety of English. All studies reported positive results including heightened awareness of Global Englishes and self-reported increase in student confidence as L2 users of English. The researchers also reported that in some cases negative stereotypes were reinforced, which they attributed to superficial engagement with some of the tasks.

Vettorel's (2013) study was a longitudinal classroom intervention in which 540 school children in Italy, Poland, Latvia and Slovakia engaged in a long-lasting project where they engaged in ELF interactions with each other via written and online communication. The project analysed a corpus of these interactions and suggested the activities had good pedagogical value for the learners to develop their pragmatic strategies and linguistic resources in order to communicate with their peers. This is one of the largest ELF classroom intervention projects we have uncovered in the literature. Other aspects of the project are reported in Vettorel (2010, 2014).

The study reported in Baker (2012) sought to raise awareness of intercultural communication and Global Englishes in Thailand, via the introduction of a 15-hour independent study online course. The 31 students and six teachers who took part responded to the materials positively, reporting favourable attitudes towards the Global Englishes content of the course.

## Implications for Teachers in Global Contexts

EIL innovations do not mean that teachers must radically abandon their current teaching practices in order to adopt a different approach, but rather we encourage teachers to make modifications to their current practices to be more inclusive of EIL issues. Teachers, as educated professionals, understand the appropriate adaptations they can make within their own teaching contexts. In making each of the innovations outlined in the GELT framework accessible for teachers, we provide some example ideas of how small innovations may lead to positive steps towards teaching EIL in global classroom contexts. For example:

(1)   *Target interlocutors*: A good EIL curriculum could depict other L2 English users as target interlocuters for their learners to raise awareness that ELF communication may likely be a norm for their future English interactions.

(2)   *Ownership*: Materials in EIL curricula should be included to raise awareness that English is a global language in the form of readings, debates, or even assignments.

(3)   *Target culture*: Tasks and role-plays in the classroom should depict a diversity of English-using cultures, without always linking to native speakers and Anglophone contexts. For example, the role of an 'American' tourist could be re-assigned as L2-using tourist in a role play, or an assignment given to a learner in France requiring them to write an email in English to a fictitious host family in the UK, could be written to a fictitious host family in the Netherlands.

(4)   *Norms*: A good EIL curriculum should expose students to a diverse range of Englishes, thus instead of relying on audio materials provided by commercial textbooks, authentic examples could be drawn from TED talks and YouTube videos (discussed further in Chapter 4).

(5)   *Teachers*: EIL-oriented schools could evaluate their hiring practices and the language used in job advertisements to ensure they are targeting suitably qualified teachers, regardless of their L1 status. If teachers are part of a professional network, where jobs are advertised, they could ensure that no job advertisements are distributed which promote inequality for NNESTs.

(6)   *Role-models*: A good EIL curriculum will seek ways to introduce students to expert L2 users as potential role models, such as inviting competent L2 speakers to deliver guest lectures in an EAP course.

(7)   *Source of materials*: Materials could be drawn from both local and global origins to help learners understand that knowledge surrounding English language does not always need to emanate from 'native' English speakers.

(8)   *Other languages and cultures*: Teachers could permit the use of other languages in their class to fulfil certain pedagogical functions, without limiting opportunities for target language use.

(9)   *Needs*: Old curricula should be frequently re-assessed according to learners' needs for future English language use.

(10) *Goals of learning*: The goals of any curriculum should be communicated to learners in terms of 'can-do' statements, thus focusing on their linguistic development as opposed to linguistic deficiencies.

(11) *Assessment criterion*: Where appropriate to the goals of the curriculum, assessments should focus on the communicative competence of learners rather than adherence to grammatical standards.

(12) *Ideology and orientation*: A good EIL teacher should always be cognizant of their own ideologies and biases, which underpin their teaching decisions. Teachers could also directly engage in discussions with their learners to instil a global perspective of English, and raise their confidence as multilingual speakers.

This chapter has outlined key concepts surrounding the TESOL curriculum, as well as explored proposals and models for EIL innovations within such curricula. It has also introduced a handful of published research papers which have reported on EIL activities in classrooms around the world, while emphasising the fact that such research is currently scarce. This leads us to pose the questions: why is research into the teaching of EIL currently lacking, despite all of the calls for change? Is it because putting EIL research into practice is 'not immediately obvious' for teachers, as Dewey (2012: 162) has observed? Is it due to the theory–practice divide noted by many EIL scholars? Is it due to a lack of awareness among teachers of the various frameworks for innovation that have been proposed in recent years? Or is it due to a lack of reporting of innovations that are actually taking place in classrooms around the world?

We suspect that the lack may be a result of a combination of all of these, but for readers of this book, the final reason might be of particular relevance in terms of future pedagogical implications. We can assume that any teacher who is engaging with the content of this book is becoming acutely aware of the need to teach EIL and is developing ideas of how to teach EIL in their educational contexts. What is needed now is for teachers to report on these innovations to help build professional knowledge of what good EIL innovations might look like.

As Rose and Montakantiwong (2018) have observed, 'Although the Applied Linguistics research community has consistently voiced a growing need for a more EIL-oriented teaching approach, it is surprising how the very voices of the teachers who are supposed to be the megaphone for that message remain unheard' (2018: 99). This reporting needs not always be in the form of research papers in research journals, but also in professional journals, teacher newsletters, professional conferences, blog posts, or staff common room conversations. While research papers do help feed back practice into the research community to ensure research is teaching informed, other professional outlets can more quickly spread ideas within the teacher community. If innovation is to be achieved on a global scale, we will need both top-down and grassroots movements to operate with synchronicity to meet our aims.

## Post-reading Activities

### *Reflect*

Many EIL scholars point to a lack of research on teachers putting EIL activities into practice. Think about why this is lacking, and what can be done to fix the situation to bridge the noted theory-practice divide.

### *Discuss*

(1) All of the models of EIL innovation presented in this chapter (post-normative approach, WE-informed ELT, EIL curriculum blueprint, GELT framework) emphasise a need to increase exposure to a variety of Englishes in the classroom. How can exposure be provided by teachers, and at what stage in a learner's language development should this exposure begin?

(2) Vettorel's (2013) study used online communication to connect learners in different countries to provide real life ELF opportunities, which is something that teachers couldn't do 20 years ago. In what ways can technology facilitate the connection of learners on a global scale?

(3) In small groups, each choose a different study from Table 2.2 to read and critically evaluate, and to prepare a group discussion around its findings. First, provide an overview of what the researcher-practitioners did in their classrooms, and what they reported as a result of their intervention. Then lead a discussion on how feasible or effective the intervention might be for other EIL classroom contexts, and discuss ways in which the EIL activities could be improved to achieve better results or overcome any stated limitations.

### *Apply*

Looking at the GELT framework, and the example suggestions in the section 'implications for teachers in global contexts', apply this model to a specific teaching context or a curriculum that you are familiar with. If you do not have detailed knowledge of a real-life course, you may draw on an English language textbook to inform you of some elements of a hypothetical curriculum (most textbooks usually explicitly outline their goals, objectives, syllabus and sometimes a methodology). According to each of the dimensions in the framework, make an explicit suggestion for modifications which could help to transform the curriculum to better match the descriptions of GELT.

## Resources for Further Reading

Rose, H. and Galloway, N. (2019) *Global Englishes for Language Teaching*. Cambridge. Cambridge University Press.

This first four chapters of this book are entirely devoted to the topic of exploring Global Englishes innovations in language classrooms. The first chapter explores key constructs underpinning the field, and also contains a detailed overview of the most up-to-date version of the GELT framework. Chapter 2 adopts a highly accessible curriculum approach in its exploration of the implications of Global Englishes for TESOL, which our book summarises much of our content from. The fourth chapter in the book then explores educational innovation models, which will be of interest to teachers in management roles who are able to exert force to introduce top-down changes to curriculum within larger educational institutions. Overall, this book provides a state-of-the-art overview of the field. The second half of the book will also be of relevance to researcher-practitioners, as the focus moves from practice to research.

Selvi, A.F. and Yazan, B. (2015) *Teaching English as an International Language*. TESOL Press.

This book outlines the various facets of teaching EIL, including chapters on materials and methods, assessment, culture and curriculum development. It is published by *TESOL Press*, and accordingly squarely positions teachers as its target readers, making ideas very accessible. Much of the content in Selvi and Yazan's book is covered in similar books (including this one). However, one advantage of Selvi and Yazan's book is its concise format of just 50 pages. Thus, the book is likely to appeal to busy teachers, and may be a good resource to use in professional development workshops and short teacher-training courses.

Richards, J.C. (2017) *Curriculum Development in Language Teaching*. Cambridge: Cambridge University Press.

This is a new edition of Jack Richards' very popular book on curriculum development. Although it does not deal at length with many of the issues we have raised in this chapter on teaching EIL, it does go into considerable depth regarding the various facets and considerations for developing and innovating a curriculum. The book covers all of the various stages in the process of curriculum development including situation analysis, needs analysis, goal setting, syllabus design, materials development and adaptation, teaching and teacher support, and evaluation. Jack Richards has been the authoritative scholar on curriculum development for more than 40 years, and this book is a consolidation of that knowledge.

# Part 2

# Global Classrooms and Curricula

# 3 Language Norms in the Global TESOL Curriculum

## Pre-reading Activities

### *Think*

Kachru (1986) described English as 'the fabled Aladdin's lamp' (1986: 1). Think about why he explained the language this way and how you would describe English.

### *Discuss*

In small groups, discuss the following:

(1) What is Standard English? Why do some authors prefer to use the capitalised Standard English or 'standard' English instead of standard English?
(2) What role does Standard English have in English language classrooms worldwide?
(3) Who are native speakers and non-native speakers of English worldwide? What do you think about the native/non-native distinctions and why?

## Introduction

Historically speaking, language standards and language norms were dictated by those who held power such as royalty, the court and the upper classes (Galloway & Rose, 2015). For example, before the global spread of English, the Chancery Standard, based on the language of the courts, was established to enhance communication across the nation of England. These norms are increasingly challenged by the global spread of English, which has led to the emergence of a post-modern phenomenon where people with diverse linguistic and cultural backgrounds use the language to communicate in their own ways. It generates variations that are different from established language norms and causes destabilisation of those norms. This has been a challenge to people who seek to adhere the norms as linguistic benchmarks, including teachers (Seidlhofer, 2018). This chapter includes an examination of discussions surrounding the spread of English from social, political, economic and educational perspectives and effects these have had on language standards. Furthermore, the chapter offers an exploration of the implications of norm-bound beliefs within the context of English Language Teaching today. It also introduces examples of programmes and courses that promote EIL awareness and increase EIL experiences in English language classrooms. Finally, the chapter concludes by addressing future directions for the successful implementation of EIL-oriented pedagogic actions, as they pertain to language standards.

## Key Concepts

TESOL practitioners must be aware of these concepts associated with language norms because they are fundamental components of language and language teaching.

### Standard language

People tend to be open to the concept of a uniformed language, since they tend to see the imposed language uniformity via a one-and-only legitimate standard variety as necessary (Milroy, 1999, 2001) and to accept assumptions, such as the existence of uniformity in languages operating with notions of standards (Seidlhofer, 2018). As described in Jenkins (2015a), '[Language standards] are the prescriptive language rules which together constitute the standard and to which all members of a language community are exposed and urged to conform during education, regardless of their local variety' (Jenkins, 2015a: 22).

The variety of language considered to be the standard is called a Standard language. A Standard language is used as a yardstick against which other varieties of the language are measured. In this regard, a Standard language can be considered as a prestige variety within a society (Jenkins, 2015a).

Nevertheless, a Standard language, which is assumed to be uniform especially in its grammar and vocabulary, is never actually achieved. As language is always changing, uniformity is regarded as an idea in mind rather than a reality (Bhatt, 2001, 2005; Milroy & Milroy, 1999); and 'it seems appropriate to speak more abstractly of standardisation as an ideology' (Milroy & Milroy, 1999: 22–23). Lippi-Green (1997) defines the ideology as 'a bias toward an abstract, idealized homogenous spoken language, which is imposed and maintained by dominant bloc institutions and which names as its model the written language, but which is drawn primarily from the spoken language of the upper middle class' (Lippi-Green, 1997: 64).

As the previous two chapters have shown, in terms of TESOL, it is important to re-evaluate the use of a Standard English as a role model. We need to take into account the sociolinguistic reality that languages are unstable in nature because users utilise them in their own ways depending upon the contexts and aims. Moreover, as a result of constant changes in circumstances, especially globalisation, English has been spread globally; and the standards have been considerably shifting to keep up with those changes (Seidlhofer, 2018).

## Native speaker standards

Standards in TESOL are often attributed to the idea of a native speaker. That is, a native speaker is often positioned as a user of the correct or desirable norms and thus Standard English. However, as Chapter 1 explored, there are several approaches to define native speakers (e.g. Cook, 2008; Davies, 2003). The common one is based on birth: a person who learnt first in childhood; on knowledge: a person who has a subconscious knowledge of rules; or on identity: a person who has a sense of belonging in a language community (Cook, 2008). Although there are many different groupings of native speakers, a person who learnt English first in childhood is usually considered as a native speaker and often is used as a role model in English Language Teaching (Cook, 2008). However, taking into account the global spread of English and the current sociolinguistic reality (Graddol, 2006), the use of native speakers as role models for English language learners has been questioned (e.g. Cook, 1999, 2008, 2012, 2016; Davies, 1991, 1996, 2003, 2013; Medgyes, 1992; Paikeday, 1985; Rampton, 1990). Further to this, as native speakers (in the narrow definition of the term) are scattered in diverse linguistic communities around the world, the idea that all native speakers adhere to a uniform standard is a clear fantasy.

## The Global Spread of English

Standards attributed to English language are interconnected with push and pull factors associated with prestige and power. That is, English speakers are pulled to emulate the language used by powerful communities, which often develops the perceived standards. Furthermore, the standards are pushed onto other communities through the education system and other societal factors, thus strengthening their status as a standard. Thus, it is worth exploring further how push and pull factors were associated with the dispersion of English. The global spread of English has been attributed to various movements including colonialism, economic power and globalisation (Barnawi, 2018).

## Colonialism

Colonialism has played a crucial role in contributing to the spread of English, which peaked towards the end of the 19th century (Crystal, 2018; Pennycook, 1998). The growth of the British empire contributed to the strong ties between the use of English and power. In most colonies, the main institutions, such as the governing bodies, government agencies, the civil service, the law courts, national religious bodies, the schools and higher educational institutions, operated in English (Crystal, 2018), which saw powerful standards of English pushed into multiple parts of society. As a result, those who spoke Standard English had greater access to more and better jobs, leading to pull factors towards prestige varieties of English. This resulted in strong incentives to learn British English and created a preference towards British native speaking teachers and British English norms (McKay & Bokhorst-Heng, 2008). This historical perspective explains the continued prominence of British English in TESOL today.

## Economic power

As indicated in Chapter 1, the success in securing the status of English as a global language was attributed to the economic conditions that created commercial supremacy of the United Kingdom and especially the United States later in the 20th century (Brutt-Griffler, 2002; Crystal, 2018). Due to this dominant economic position, English became the language of international business and trade. As commerce expanded and English became a key to connect all parts of the world market, the use of native speaker English gave organisations access to international markets. Tourist and adverting industries were especially dependent upon English (Crystal, 2018). During this era, the United States contained nearly four times as many native English speakers as the United Kingdom, and these two countries grew to comprise 70% of all native speakers across the world (Crystal, 2018). Having the largest number of native speakers of English, economic and political underpinnings allowed the United States to influence global ideas of an English language standard. This economic power, and the pull of many speakers towards it, helped establish American English as a perceived standard in many parts of the world. Nevertheless, taking into consideration the growing number of non-native English speakers in rising economic powers, the United States' level of dominance has been changing (Graddol, 2006).

## Globalisation

In the era of globalisation, many people desire and think it is important to learn English because of a belief (sometimes unrealistic) in the power of the English language (McKay & Bokhorst-Heng, 2008). Knowledge of

English may bring economic, educational and social advantages (McKay, 2012); and English is often regarded as a key to personal success. Kachru (1986) used the term 'the alchemy of English' (1986: 1) and wrote 'knowing English is like possessing the fabled Aladdin's lamp, which permits one to open, as it were, the linguistic gates to international business, technology, science and travel. In short, English provides linguistic power' (1986: 1). As a result, there has been a rapid increase in the number of non-native speakers of English across the world, who were pulled towards the learning of English because of globalisation. Thus, a growing role of EIL can be seen in various fields. The fields more likely to be relevant to English language learners (education, international business, media and entertainment and technology) are explained in the following section.

## Education

The number of international students going to English-speaking countries is growing. At the same time there has been an increase in students who are taught in English, as more and more Outer Circle and Expanding Circle countries in Europe and Asia, are offering courses taught through the medium of English (Graddol, 2006; Galloway *et al.*, 2017). English is a means of attracting both international and domestic student communities, teaching staff and researchers in order to gain international experiences (Graddol, 2006; Galloway *et al.*, 2017). Furthermore, the use of English as a medium of instruction allows students to gain access to content knowledge as well as to improve English language proficiency and international competencies and to establish contacts ultimately contributing to their employability (Galloway *et al.*, 2017). Thus, there are more opportunities than ever before for non-native speakers to use EIL, which contributes to establishing new English language standards.

Education has been a powerful factor that has established the notion of a written academic English as a standard in this domain. In terms of academic publications, frequently popular handbooks and scholarly aids are available in English. The relevant terminology is often better established and recognised in English than in the local language. Thus, there has been a significant increase in the use of English in publications especially in science, such as biology, physics, medicine, mathematics and chemistry (Crystal, 2003). English is frequently used by non-native English speakers in order to maximise the potential readership. International scientific projects also are carried out by using English as a shared language (McKay, 2012). The establishment of a standardised English used in such publications, has seen the rise in courses that teach English for Academic Purposes (EAP). As academic English is nobody's native language, L1 and L2 speakers must learn the features of this perceived standard, giving rise to EAP-style courses in L2 classrooms, and composition-style or genre-informed courses in L1 classrooms.

## International business

Although native English facilitates the activities of many transnational corporations, especially for business outside of English-speaking countries, fewer interactions now involve native speakers (Graddol, 2006; Paradowski, 2008). The number of businesses outside English-speaking countries is on the rise and non-native speakers who use English to communicate with other non-native speakers are growing. For example, workers at Daimler-Chrysler are required to learn English as their working language. In the Czech Republic, Toyota Peugeot Citroën Automobile assembly plant workers have to use English as an in-house cooperate language of the Japanese, French and Czech staff. In these contexts, the standards used are often much more dynamic and emerge according to the communicative needs. To the extent that this trend continues, a working knowledge of English is essential to be employed in transnational corporations. The desirability of English is also seen in the outsourcing services, since most of the offshore contracts come from English-speaking corporations (Graddol, 2006). Call centres are in distant locations such as India because of the abundant supply of professionals with a high level of English language skills.

## Media and entertainment

A dominance of English language exists in satellite broadcasting, advertising, music and films (Crystal, 2003, 2018; McKay & Bokhorst-Heng, 2008; Paradowski, 2008). In the news media, English still remains the preferred and widely used language. English-language magazines, newspapers and broadcasting, such as *Time, Newsweek*, CNN and Reuters, are available around the world. Important to note is that Anglo-American cultures and values have an influence on many people around the world through the film industry (Hollywood), entertainment broadcasting, commercials, fashion, food, beverages, popular music, computers and high-tech as an incentive for learning and using the English language (Crystal, 2003). Recently American influence has declined, since cultural flows may no longer be unidirectional and are diversifying their directions and routes. As Graddol (2006) states, 'In East Asia, Chinese viewers are more interested in soap operas from Korea than the USA. Japanese Manga comics are being taken up in Europe and the USA. Hong Kong action movies have helped create a new Western film genre. "Bollywood" influence is being felt around the world' (2006: 112–113).

Media and entertainment have probably been the most powerful avenues to challenge the standards upheld in other sectors such as education. As learners are drawn to regionally based TV shows and movies, and to diverse Englishes in music such as hip-hop, their exposure to non-standard varieties has increased.

## Technology

Technology has also greatly contributed to the spread of English and the dissemination of knowledge (Graddol, 1997; McKay & Bokhorst-Heng, 2008; Warschauer & De Florio-Hansen, 2003). English has remained the dominant language, and over 80% of the world's electronic information is in English (Crystal, 2018; Galloway & Rose, 2015; Graddol, 2006; UNESCO, 2009), which is a powerful push factor of establishing global standards. In 2018, an estimated 25.4% of total internet globally was used by native and non-native English speakers followed by 19.3% by Chinese speakers, dropping to single digits for all other languages (Miniwatts Marketing Group, 2018). The current fast growth of internet usage among other languages, such as Chinese, Arabic and Russian, as well as the advent of powerful translation tools, may challenge the spread of English. Nevertheless, it is worth mentioning that many Outer Circle and Expanding Circle countries notably contribute to the production of Web content in English (UNESCO, 2009), which may disrupt current views of norms in the language as needing to adhere to native English. As a result of the continued dominance of English, upheld by these native and non-native users, English is likely to keep its status as a global language for some time (Ware *et al.*, 2012). In the current situation, it is legitimate to assume that there still are major incentives for learners to learn English to exchange information on the internet and to interact with internet users across the world (McKay, 2002; Ware *et al.*, 2012).

## Challenges to Established Norms in TESOL

In TESOL, there has been notable discussion about effects of the ever-growing role of English spoken by non-native speakers in challenging established norms. These include debates about Standard language, challenges to linguistic imperialism, user-based challenges to standards, leading to calls for revisiting current English language classroom practices.

### The debate about Standard English

Due to the global spread of English, a question has surfaced about the need to teach Standard English in language classrooms. This came to a head in the now historically famous debate between Quirk (1985, 1990) and Kachru (1985, 1991).

According to Quirk (1990), one common standard in English should be maintained because of a fear of English falling apart into different forms and functions, which are in danger of becoming too separated from standards. He believed learners of English need to learn Standard English for the sake of increased freedom and their career opportunities (Quirk, 1990). Quirk (1990) further mentions, 'If I were a foreign student paying good money in Tokyo or Madrid to be taught English, I would feel cheated by such tolerant pluralism. My goal would be to acquire English precisely because of its power as an instrument of international communication' (Quirk, 1990: 10). On the contrary, Kachru (1985, 1992) argues that the users of Standard English are expected to conform to local norms and speech strategies and claims the need for recognising and reflecting the realities of current multilingual societies including the linguistic, sociolinguistic, educational and pragmatic aspects of societies on teaching. Kachru (1991) also points out that Quirk's (1990) position emphasising the exclusive use of Standard English is unrealistic and questionable as it overlooks the sociolinguistic reality of the language. Thus, he called for re-examination of Standard English in TESOL.

In English Language Teaching, Standard English has been equated with English spoken by native speakers although the variation within Standard English has been ignored as it has been viewed as one uniform variety (Brutt-Griffler, 2002). Quirk (1990) claims that the varieties of English that are different from Standard English are considered as deficient, and English language teachers are recommended to focus on established native norms and native-like performance. In response to Quirk's (1990) view, Kachru (1992) argues that Quirk's approach is based on false assumptions about the users and uses of English. The assumptions include that English essentially is learnt as a tool to interact with the native speakers of the language, such as American and British. The international non-native varieties of English are essentially interlanguages striving to achieve native-like characteristics. English spoken by native speakers is considered an ideal standard of 'proper' or 'correct' linguistic behaviour for English language learners and non-native speakers' usage that varies from Standard English is perceived as defective and requires correction. As previously mentioned in this chapter, English should no longer be learned for communication only with native speakers and that non-native varieties are not considered deficit but serving localised communicative needs. In addition to Kachru (1992), the status of Standard English and speakers of the language and using them as a yardstick in TESOL have been questioned (e.g. Cook, 1999, 2016; Davies, 2003, 2013; Firth & Wagner, 1997; Rampton, 1990).

## Challenges to linguistic imperialism

According to Phillipson (1992), English attained its current prominent position due primarily to a political underpinning and actively promoting 'an instrument of the foreign policy of the major English-speaking states' (1992: 1). According to the concept of Linguistic Imperialism (Phillipson, 1992), the spread of English and the development of the current status of English by native English-speaking countries, such as the United Kingdom and the United States, are linguistic forms of imperialism through past and present colonial policies.

Regarding TESOL, Phillipson (1992) has also argued that a well-funded English teaching establishment such as British Council has helped spread a myth about the supremacy and necessity of learning native English over other languages worldwide. It has contributed to establishing a view of the language that presents English as a property of native speakers by promoting especially British and American English without providing students with equivalents from other varieties (Modiano, 2001; Phillipson, 1992). Deriving from this concept is the hegemony of native-speakerism (discussed in Chapter 1); that is, an ideology that native speakers are the best models and native English-speaking teachers are closely associated with 'superior' Western culture, has been problematised (Holliday, 2005; Swan *et al.*, 2015). The impact of native speakerism includes not only the supremacy of native English-speaking teachers but also native-speaker preferences leading to discriminatory hiring practices in TESOL. However, the superficially constructed ideology of the native speaker still dominates English Language Teaching discourse across the world (Holliday, 2005, 2015; Holliday & Aboshiha, 2009). Therefore, a call has been made for a quite drastic paradigm change, so that the ideology surrounding native English is revaluated and a removal of the native-non-native distinction within the TESOL profession is achieved (Holliday, 2005; Kubota, 2009; Kumaravadivelu, 2012a, 2016).

Despite its popularity and the existence of influence by native English-speaking countries through policies, it is worth noting that Philipson's theory of imperialism has been challenged for a number of reasons. One of the criticisms is that the theory ignores the agency of learners to choose studying English because of the incentives explained in the previous sections and focuses only on the agency of colonisers to impose English (Brutt-Griffler, 2002). Thus, the theory lacks consideration of how English is used in diverse contexts, how English is appropriated and used, or how to further their own cultural, social and educational interests in opposition to those that promote its spread (Canagarajah, 1999; Pennycook, 1994). In response to the criticism, Canagarajah (1999) reports an ethnographic study that investigates learners in a Tamil community inside and outside the classroom and articulates those who resist the learning of English due to their colonial history.

## Usage-based challenges to Standard English

Through use and appropriation in various contexts, diverse English varieties have emerged and have become equally valid to and independent from Standard English established by native speakers (Seidlhofer, 2004). English has been appropriated first by the Outer Circle countries where

English is used locally as a second language, such as India and Nigeria. The same kind of conceptual appraisal has been extended to Expanding Circle countries where English is used as a foreign language, such as Brazil, China or Germany. It has been assumed that they should use Standard English and learn those norms for contact purposes because those Englishes in Expanding Circle countries do not have their own established varieties of English. However, since globalisation has progressed, and English has been used as a lingua franca all over the world, people are constantly exposed to trans-local influences through media, education and commerce as explained in the previous sections. They develop local uses of English as well as increase the language use with other multilingual communities. Thus, House (2003) mentioned that ELF speakers' performance should be measuring against a successful ELF speaker who can communicate effectively in ELF contexts.

There has been an increase in the investigation of how English is used as an international language. Contrary to Quirk's (1985, 1990) fears of English becoming separate in different forms and functions for mutual intelligibility, research shows EIL speakers often succeed in communicating in EIL. The use of ELF necessarily does not impede communicative effectiveness (Firth, 1996; House, 2003; Meiekord, 2000; Seidlhofer, 2004) and rather facilitates communication in certain contexts (Cogo & Dewey, 2012). For example, the use of 'let it pass' concept (Firth, 1996) is commonly used in the ELF interaction. When the hearer faces problems in understanding the speaker's utterance, the hearer lets the unknown or unclear actions, words, or utterances 'pass' assuming that it will either become clear or redundant later. This procedure appears to give the impression of the talk 'being overtly consensus-oriented, cooperative and mutually supportive, and thus, fairly robust' (Seidlhofer, 2004: 218).

## A call for revisiting language norms in English language classroom practices

The decline in the power of Standard English, the ever-growing role of EIL, and its use lead to a call for revisiting current English language classroom practices by questioning some of the fundamental assumptions of English Language Teaching. As the previous chapter touched upon, one of those assumptions is the selection of an instructional variety. It is especially vital because which variety teachers use as a model affects material selection and assessment (Matsuda & Friedrich, 2012).

Regarding current approaches to the selection of instructional varieties, American or British English are predominantly, and unquestioningly, used because this maintains the status quo of previous practices (Matsuda & Friedrich, 2012). As discussed in Chapter 2, an EIL perspective suggests that an established variety that includes American, British English or Outer Circle varieties can be used alongside other varieties. This is especially relevant for classrooms in Expanding Circle contexts where the English varieties are less established than those of Outer Circle contexts (Honna & Takeshita, 2014; Matsuda & Friedrich, 2012). What is most important here is that the variety selected as a dominant model should be taught as simply one variety of English from among the many English varieties that the students will come across in the future, which may sound quite different (Matsuda & Friedrich, 2012). When using instructional varieties in the classroom, it is also important for teachers to include sociolinguistic discussions on language variation and norms.

Having chosen the instructional variety, it is then essential to consider how other varieties and EIL components can be implemented in a context sensitive manner. Mainly there have been three ways regarding how different English varieties and sociolinguistic underpinnings of English today can be taught in the classroom (e.g. Hino, 2012; Hino & Oda, 2015; Matsuda & Friedrich, 2012). The approaches tie in with the more macrolevel EIL models of English Language Teaching, which were presented in the previous chapters. These include:

- **Explicitly being exposed to the diversity of English** (e.g. Galloway, 2011, 2013, 2017; Hino, 2012; Hino & Oda, 2015; Lee, 2012; Sung, 2015): Learners are given opportunities to become accustomed to the linguistic and cultural varieties of EIL through exposure to different varieties of English. Teachers can use materials, such as CDs that accompany the textbooks and any materials that contain textual, audio and visual examples of other varieties of English.
- **Implicitly being exposed through authentic experience in EIL communication with appropriate support** (e.g. Vettorel, 2010, 2013, 2014): Learners are given opportunities to interact with English users from various cultural and linguistic backgrounds. Learners are not only exposed to different English varieties and users but also learn communication strategies and accommodation skills through EIL experience. They witness successful EIL communication that necessarily does not involve a native speaker. They can also learn strategies necessary for communicative effectiveness, such as 'let it pass' (Firth, 1996) and 'drawing on extralinguistic cues, identifying and building on shared knowledge, gauging and adjusting to interlocutors' linguistic repertoires, supportive listening, signalling non-comprehension in a face-saving way, asking for repetition, paraphrasing, and the like' (Seidlhofer, 2004: 227). In recent years various internet communities and social network services (SNS) have provided abundant opportunities for exposure to diverse English and EIL experience.
- **Explicit teaching about English diversity** (e.g. Bayyurt & Altinmakas, 2012; Baker, 2012; Galloway, 2013; Sung, 2015; Vettorel, 2010, 2013, 2014): Learners gain knowledge of EIL, such as the global spread of English today.

## What Does the Research Tell Us?

There has been a growing amount of research that proposed and implemented context-sensitive EIL-oriented programmes (see Table 3.1) and courses (see Table 3.2) incorporating these three approaches described above in order to increase students' awareness of the diversity of English. Although each case is context-specific, the detailed explanation of the specific institutional context and the rationale behind the pedagogical decision allow each reader to reflect on and to adopt to their teaching contexts (Matsuda, 2012, 2017). EIL-oriented awareness raising activity used in these courses and the impact on language attitudes are articulated in Chapter 6.

D'Angelo (2012) presented the undergraduate programme that included constantly providing opportunities to learn about Englishes and to examine critically their attitudes throughout the programme. Students

**Table 3.1** Examples of context-sensitive EIL-oriented programmes

| Researchers | Settings | Programme objectives |
|---|---|---|
| D'Angelo (2012) | A private university in Japan with over 13,000 students in 12 departments. The undergraduate EIL program admits approximately 96 freshmen per year. (Level = Mixed) | The objectives of the undergraduate programme include developing graduates who speak an educated Japanese English, exposing students to many cultures and Englishes, with a focus on Outer and Expanding Circle contexts, and fostering a deeper knowledge of their own culture. It also aims to develop autonomous, independent-thinking students who can contribute to their organisations and society and to foster international understanding. |
| Lee (2012) | A private high school in Japan that has a close connection with the university above. A separate World Englishes cohort of 40 students has been created. (Level = Intermediate) | The intensive programme is designed to enhance students' English communicative competence while helping them learn about going beyond native English-speaking cultures and to promote the English language as a tool for cross-cultural communication and mutual understanding across cultural boundaries. |
| Sharifian and Marlina (2012) | A public university in Australia with over 70,000 students and 10 faculties. 200 to 250 students (domestic and international students with different majors) in total enrolled in the undergraduate and postgraduate EIL programme. | The main objectives of the programme are to guide students to develop their knowledge of EIL/World Englishes to a professional level, to foster their ability to negotiate different Englishes and to gain intercultural communication skills and EIL/World Englishes-informed mindsets and attitudes. |

**Table 3.2** Examples of context-sensitive EIL-oriented courses

| Researchers | Participants | Course objectives |
|---|---|---|
| Bayyurt and Altinmakas (2012) | University EFL learners in Turkey (N = 64, Level = Upper-intermediate and advanced) | The course is set for fourteen weeks. The course is designed to uncovering embedded beliefs and ideas, enabling students to recognise and understand certain issues, and helping them re-evaluate their attitudes, beliefs and ideas. |
| Hino (2012); Hino and Oda (2015) | University EFL learners in Japan (N = 182 in 2010, Level = Mixed) | The course is designed for fifteen weeks to acquire identity as EIL users, to become familiar with linguistic and cultural diversity of EIL, to gain cross-cultural awareness needed for communication in EIL, to establish their own thinking to cope with the diverse values in EIL and to acquire mainly reading skills in EIL. |

also had an opportunity to study abroad in various countries. The programme hired teachers with different linguistic and cultural backgrounds. The faculty members were active in their professional programs in order to keep themselves updated in the field. According to the university's observation, the programme was successful in terms of changing how English was viewed in Japan, and their graduates had been placed in better jobs.

Lee (2012) explained how a World Englishes perspective could be incorporated into English language classrooms for a high school programme. Students came to the university once a week for a World Englishes-based communication class taught by the university department's faculty in tandem with teaching assistants from the master's program. The textbook selected for the course was about Japanese students' experiences of travelling overseas and of introducing Japanese traditional cultures to friends from foreign countries. Based on the textbook, various World English-oriented activities, such as discussions about different table manners from different cultures and questioning the stereotypes of certain cultures were included. The researcher's observation showed that the participants had become aware of different varieties of Englishes rooted in cultural and situational differences and had developed critical thinking skills.

Sharifian and Marlina (2012) introduced EIL/World Englishes-oriented undergraduate and postgraduate course in their university programme. The course included, but was not limited to, introducing the sociolinguistic reality of English today, international communication and, for postgraduates, issues with teaching EIL. They were not only exposed to the linguistic diversity of English and sociocultural differences but also asked to consider political issues that were associated with diversity and critically examine their experiences in terms of English use as well as English Language Teaching in various contexts. The programme hired instructors who were capable of teaching rich worldviews and cultural values from various countries. The programme evaluation was not yet conducted.

Bayyurt and Altinmakas (2012) implemented a World Englishes-based course that included discussions about stereotyping by using YouTube videos presenting varieties of English and a debate about Standard English and the existence of a 'Turkish English' variety. The researchers observed that the participants started to recognise and enjoyed exploring the variety of World Englishes.

Hino (2012) and Hino and Oda (2015) also conducted an EIL-oriented course by having students watch and critically analyse real-time news in English across the world, such as CNN (United States), BBC (UK), Channel NewsAsia (Singapore), ATV (Hong Kong), ABS-CBN (Philippines) and NHK World Daily News (Japan). Students were expected to maintain openness and flexibility for understanding different cultures. The researcher showed news in English from multiple sources and asked the students to read the same news in the Web pages. Comparisons of the views represented in the news media were followed by discussions on cultural differences and/or similarities observable in their news coverage. The questionnaire at the end of the term revealed that the students enjoyed learning diversity of English and developed global thinking.

## Implications for Teachers in Global Contexts

Although the EIL-oriented programmes and courses outlined above yielded promising results and successfully developed sensitivity towards EIL to a certain degree; some challenges and limitations were found. Most of the studies above acknowledged the existence of a strong preference for native English. As D'Angelo (2012) pointed out, there still were faculty members who were not convinced by the EIL paradigm, indicating the ideology of native speakerism remains deeply rooted (Holliday, 2015; Kumaravadivelu, 2016). Sharifian and Marlina (2012) also described 'We are still far away, we believe, from being fully successful in changing the mindset of many within the field who cherish what we see as "colonial" attitudes in ELT, such as native-speaker supremacy' (2012: 151). D'Angelo (2014) critically reflected on the programmes and found out that the students did not fully understand the notions of EIL. There have been more critical reflections of the changes that are already taking places, showing a difficulty and complexity of teaching EIL and some tensions and struggles that teachers and students experience inside and outside classrooms through the implementations of EIL pedagogic actions (Manara, 2014; Marlina & Giri, 2014; Marlina, 2014). Thus, more critical reflections are necessary to take one more step towards a drastic change.

Such continuing influence of native speaker norms and difficulty of teaching EIL show that implementation of change is not only about incorporating EIL components into classroom practice, such as teaching about EIL and increasing exposure to diverse varieties and ELF experiences in programmes and courses; but also changing societal attitudes toward EIL. In order to do so, development of more detailed and critical programme and course evaluations would be essential to confirm to what extent the programmes and courses are successful in terms of achieving their objectives so that practitioners in the field would be more likely to buy into the change.

Moreover, in the era of globalisation, teachers' roles are increasingly important especially in understanding the needs of students and guiding students to achieve the goal of the instruction taking into account the implications of the global spread of English (e.g. Seidlhofer, 2011). Thus, teacher preparation appears to be one of the key components to implement the changes in the English language classroom successfully (e.g. Galloway & Rose, 2015; Matsuda, 2017; Rose & Galloway, 2019).

Additionally, as indicated in Hino and Oda (2015), in English as a foreign-language contexts, there appears to be a lack of opportunities for real ELF experience. To provide sufficiently authentic and relevant learning opportunities, it is necessary to reach out and incorporate tasks and activities beyond the classroom. The use of web tools, such as e-mail, chat, forum, blog, Skype and WordPress have great pedagogical potential by creating a new multilingual and multicultural learning environment (Kohn, 2015; Ware et al., 2012; Vettorel, 2017). Some examples of such activities are presented in Chapter 6.

Still, the model of teaching and testing in many parts of the world is native-speaker English, particularly British and North American; and it rarely goes beyond traditional Standard language norms. The methodologies and materials that are used in most classrooms continue promoting native English varieties. Currently pervading communicative approaches often come with an emphasis on task-based language teaching, which is influenced by British and North American cultures (see Chapter 2), drawing on native English oriented materials (see Chapter 4). High-stakes tests continue to use traditional norms as a yardstick in order to measure learners' competence (see Chapter 5). Teachers may not be fully aware of EIL; or even if they acknowledge the notions, they may prefer teaching native-speaker English (see Chapter 8). Thus, current English language classroom practices tend to highlight and promote native speaker English as the one and only variety learners should strive to achieve. EIL-oriented pedagogy challenges the current norms used in TESOL, which need to be re-evaluated carefully (e.g. Dewey, 2012; Widdowson, 2012, 2015); and the selection of a dominant instructional variety should be made judiciously. All language learning and teaching needs, wants and situations are context-dependent. Thus, in order to make context-specific decisions on classroom practices, these needs must be taken into consideration (Kumaravadivelu, 2012a; McKay, 2012).

Overall, it is worth noting that the implementation is more likely to be a slow process mainly due to a strong native speaker propensity that leads to some resistance to the changes from students, teachers and programme administrators. Thus, we have to keep in mind that progress will be made gradually and successful implementation of the change generally is dependent on a sustained and consistent effort with evidence accumulation in shifting the current paradigm.

## Post-reading Activities

### Reflect

This chapter suggests that it is crucial to re-evaluate language norms in TESOL. Think about a teaching context you are familiar with, reflect on whether (and why) native-speaker standards are prevalent?

### Discuss

(1) This chapter discussed push and pull factors were associated with the global spread of English. In small groups, each choose a different factor and consider it in depth. Then discuss how such factors could affect English language teaching.

(2) In pairs, discuss whether you agree with the EIL perspective, suggesting that an established variety that includes, but is not limited to, American or British English, can be used alongside other varieties in classes. If so, what variety do you use mainly in your class and why? If not, why?

(3) This chapter introduced research that proposed and implemented innovative EIL-oriented programmes (see Table 3.1) and courses (see Table 3.2). In small groups, each choose a different study from Table 3.1 and Table 3.2. Read the programmes and courses very carefully and summarise the course objectives and course contents. Then address the challenges and limitations one is more likely to face and discuss how one can overcome those challenges and limitations.

### Apply

If you were to implement the study you chose in Discussion Three in your teaching context, what challenges and limitations do you think you are more likely to encounter? What can you do to overcome those challenges and limitations? In small groups, choose one specific context and design course objectives and a rough outline of an EIL-oriented course, feasible and suitable for the context. You can use Table 3.3 below. Then, share the completed course objectives and outline with other groups.

**Table 3.3** Post-reading activity

| Participants and setting | Course objectives | Course contents |
|---|---|---|
| … learners in …<br>(N = …, Level = …) | The course is set for …<br>The course is designed to … | The course includes … |

## Resources for Further Reading

Crystal, D. (2003) *English as a Global Language*. Cambridge: Cambridge University Press.

The book provides an overview of the spread of English and the development of the language. It includes the description not only of the current status but also of the future role of English as a global language. It also explores the characteristics of a global language and the influence of English as a global language. The reasons that English is the global language are examined from geographical-historical and socio-cultural perspectives. The former explains how English reached a position of pre-eminence by tracing the movement of English around the world, and the latter shows how English remains as a global language by looking at how people all over the world have become dependent economically and socially on the language. The descriptions of the current characteristics of English, such as varieties of English with different sounds, grammar and vocabulary, and the implications of current characteristics of English also are included.

Matsuda, A. (2012) *Principles and Practices of Teaching English as an International Language*. Bristol: Multilingual Matters.

This book offers theories regarding EIL and how they can be implemented in the classroom. It covers various aspects of theoretical and pedagogical concerns, such as choosing an instructional variety for an EIL-based curriculum, exploring Expanding Circle English varieties as an instructional model, evaluating communicative competence in ELF contexts, analysing political aspects of EIL, examining teaching materials and assessments and investigating teacher education for EIL. EIL-oriented programmes and courses implemented in various contexts, such as Japan, Turkey and Australia also are presented. Moreover, the book presents concrete, field-tested EIL-oriented lessons and activities for traditional English classrooms collected from all over the world. Those activities help learners raise awareness of EIL, foster their understanding of the concept and implications for international communication, and develop more open attitudes towards diverse English varieties.

# 4 Material Evaluation and Development in Teaching English as an International Language

**Pre-reading Activities**

> ### Think
>
> Think about the use of English as an international language. How does this affect the materials you would use in different ELT settings?
>
> ### Discuss
>
> (1) Do you think the textbooks you have been exposed to as a student and/or used as a teacher are adequate to teach EIL? Why? Why not?
> (2) Imagine teaching three different classes: a high school class in France, an academic English class for English-medium instruction in a university in Nigeria and a business English course in Taiwan. Could you use the same material in each setting? If not, how should the materials be different?
> (3) You want to expose your students to new varieties of English but there are no samples in the textbook you use. Where can you go to find alternative materials to expose your students to different varieties? What do you have to consider when using these materials?

## Introduction

Materials in language teaching can be 'anything used to facilitate language learning' (Tomlinson, 2012: 143). That means when we speak of materials we mean anything from commercially designed textbooks to real-world materials such as restaurant menus or movie tickets. Though teachers vary in the extent to which they bring real-world materials into the classroom, in most contexts the textbook is the main source of materials and the core of the program (McDonough *et al.*, 2013). Thus, as a major source of exposure to English in the ELT classroom and information about the language, textbooks are a key factor in teaching (Kachru & Nelson, 2001). Not only do they guide language teaching and teaching goals, but they also significantly shape how learners view the language (Matsuda, 2012). Given their considerable importance in the language learning process, it is crucial to carefully select a variety of teaching materials with the specific teaching context in mind to best support learners. Rose and Galloway (2019), however, point to the reality of most teachers, who are confined to using a limited variety of commercially produced materials. Thus, when addressing materials in teaching English as an international language, we have to start with a detailed look at those commercially produced materials. This chapter is therefore divided into two major parts: evaluation and utilizing alternative materials. The first part provides a guided framework with which ELT professionals can better understand their materials against an EIL backdrop. By discussing relevant parameters in which EIL materials differ from traditional ELT materials, the chapter guides readers through the evaluation of varieties, speakers, role models, culture and tasks. The second part takes the next step beyond evaluation by exploring potential materials with regards to particular learning outcomes. Addressing the goal of 'raising awareness', 'developing attitudes', and 'developing EIL skills', this part of the chapter investigates different real-world resources alongside relevant activities.

## Key Concepts

### Authenticity

Authenticity has been a chief concern in materials design for many decades, especially in the context of communicative language teaching. Most textbooks on ELT, material design and evaluation cover this term in one way or another, and it is not surprising that there are varying definitions that put focus on different elements of the classroom. This ambiguous term has been related to textbooks, classroom participants, the social and cultural situation of learning as well as the purpose of the communicative act (Gilmore, 2007). In the context of EIL, authenticity asks to what extent the materials used in ELT represent or mirror real-world English and English use. That is, the most relevant question of authenticity is whether or not the materials truly depict the diversity of the English language, its speakers and language use tasks and contexts.

### Hidden Curriculum

First introduced by Giroux (1988), the term Hidden Curriculum refers to the idea that textbooks and other materials have underlying norms and assumptions which are communicated to the students. This is especially relevant in EIL as the hegemony of the native speaker model is largely based on ideology. In other words, materials are assumed to have an underlying structure that is shaped by Inner Circle norms and standards of English use. Naturally, such an underlying structure is relayed to the learners exposed to the materials, and may thus greatly shape their beliefs and values regarding EIL and its speakers. Materials based on the native speaker model are likely to foster strong attachment to so-called standard language ideology, which is not conducive to using EIL with a variety of speakers. As a result, it is paramount for teachers and other ELT professionals to examine their materials closely in order to identify the potential hidden hegemony of the native speaker (Rashidi & Meihami, 2016). Closely evaluating ELT materials against EIL criteria is therefore crucial in moving towards a more EIL-oriented approach to English language teaching.

## Flexibility

The term flexibility is by no means specific to teaching materials or classroom teaching as such. Though being flexible seems an important part of everyday life in the 21st century, ELT classrooms' demands for standardization and objectivity alongside their reliance on established course books have created a rather inflexible atmosphere for ELT, it seems. As Bao (2015) points out, there are a number of definitions of flexibility, but essentially it means a teacher's ability to adapt and appropriate materials. In the majority of relevant literature, it seems that flexibility is treated as a quality of textbooks or materials, that is the extent to which these materials allow for adaption. In a slightly different manner, this chapter assumes that thorough evaluation based on EIL categories will allow teachers to be more flexible in using the textbooks regardless of the textbooks' inherent flexibility. In other words, we see guided evaluation that increases teachers' knowledge of the materials as key to flexibility in the ELT classroom.

## Material Evaluation

Evaluating materials in the context of EIL requires a detailed look at a variety of elements. Previous chapters have outlined how EIL requires rethinking fundamentals of language teaching, including the speakers and role models, culture, the target skill and even the language that is presented to the learners. Consequently, ELT professionals wishing to fully understand the hidden curriculum and evaluate the authenticity of their textbook and other materials should seek to evaluate each of these elements individually. There are different ways to guide evaluation, and in this context a checklist seems most appropriate as it allows in-depth guided analysis but at the same time creates a clear visual representation of the textbook's underlying frame of reference. So, we have created five individual checklists to guide ELT professionals through the evaluation of their textbooks with regards to the representation of English as in international language.

## Pluricentric language

Bringing the diversity of English into the classroom is one of the cornerstones in teaching EIL. As a pluricentric language, English has many codified forms, which follow their own standards, a state that has significant implications for what it means to speak and understand English. Varieties do not only differ in pronunciation, vocabulary or grammar, but as international communication tools they also embed local cultures and values. Portraying English in its plurality is thus crucial not merely for comprehension and familiarity but also for understanding the EIL using community. Pluricentricity of English raises two question when it comes to material design: Which varieties do we need to include? And how do we present varieties next to each other?

English users in different contexts will need to be familiar with a different range if varieties to facilitate communication. It is therefore impossible to say that a specific set of materials has the right balance between varieties or the most appropriate choices in presenting one variety as the normative model of instruction. What is found in a particular set of materials needs to be evaluated against the teaching context, based on specific learner needs. (Matsuda & Friedrich, 2012) make convincing arguments for using British or American English as the instructional model for Expanding Circle learning contexts, as these are well codified and offer a vast range of linguistic content. On the other hand, Outer Circle contexts should look towards their own use of English when finding the instructional model. It is specifically in Outer Circle contexts, where the representation of Outer Circle varieties as less valid, less prestigious and thus unequal, can be most damaging. Presenting a variety other than the local one as the normative model is likely to influence learners' self-esteem and confidence in using that local variety. It is therefore desirable to work with materials that present successful use of the local variety in many different contexts. Turning back to Expanding Circle contexts, it is important to present variety, so learners understand the pluricentric nature of English and develop a realistic image of real-world English use. Studies have shown that learners as well as teachers appreciate learning about diversity but consider varieties other than British and American English unsuitable for the ELT classroom. It is thus paramount to continue bringing diversity into the classroom and present different varieties as legitimate models of communication, so that learners' attitudes may change to match their needs as learners of a diverse language. If materials present one variety as 'the English language', as is too often the case, learners will develop a monolithic understanding of the language, and will have difficulty managing different varieties that they are bound to encounter outside of their classroom.

When wanting to evaluate pluricentricty in materials, the first step then is to investigate individual varieties in order to determine the range of Inner and Outer Circle varieties. By examining vocabulary, spelling, pronunciation and even grammar, it is possible to identify which varieties are included in the materials and thus to evaluate pluricentricity. For this, it is important to not only identify whether or not there are Outer Circle varieties, but also to establish the ratio of Inner vs Outer Circle varieties.

The more in-depth part of this analysis is to explore the manner in which varieties are presented, as this can influence students' attitudes towards different varieties and their speakers (see Table 4.1). Many materials contain vocabulary or pronunciation guides which may present information such as the following: Chair /tʃeə/. Learners are instructed to pronounce the word <chair> as /tʃeə/, with no reference to other possible pronunciations. Looking at descriptions of Outer Circle varieties, they may be referred to using words such as 'basic English', especially regarding pidgin varieties. Likewise, a particular variety may be referred to as 'English that corresponds to the dictionary' or even as 'standard English' or 'standard pronunciation'. Such different accounts of varieties or localized English use suggests that one variety is considered more normative than others. Such a hierarchy can also be created with specific activities, as oftentimes students are asked to translate words from one variety into the more dominant one (i.e. British or American English). It is thus important to investigate if varieties are presented as equal or whether some are presented as better, more correct, more normative, more prestigious than others. So, beyond the features of specific varieties, it is also helpful to consider descriptions, specific activities, or the context in which the varieties are presented to the learner.

**Table 4.1** Measuring varieties

| <u>Varieties</u> |
| --- |
| **Look at:** All written and spoken English language samples |
| **Look for:**<br>• Vocabulary, Spelling, Pronunciation, Grammar<br>• Variety status |
| (1) Only one Inner Circle variety |
| (2) Different Inner Circle varieties |
| (3) Predominantly Inner Circle varieties and Outer Circle varieties |
| (4) Mixed amount of Inner Circle varieties and Outer Circle varieties |
| (5) Outer Circle varieties as unequal |
| (6) Outer Circle varieties as equal |

## Speakers

Much more than varieties, English's diversity lies with its speakers. In EIL communication, learners will need to understand a range of different speakers from diverse linguistic backgrounds at different levels of competence. Native speakers are likely to constitute the minority among learners' future interlocutors and this should be reflected in the materials. Similar to varieties, the inclusion of particular nationalities in a given set of materials highly depends on the teaching context, and it obviously needs to be recognized that materials aiming to prepare learners for use in native speaker countries should favor those. However, materials to be used in Outer Circle contexts should highlight speakers from that country and its specific variety as well as surrounding countries. Ideally, these speakers should showcase different levels of the variety from basilects to acrolects, where commonly used. Similarly, Expanding Circle materials should present non-native speakers exhibiting non-native speaker accents that are relevant to the particular learning context. That means materials produced for Asia should mainly feature Asian speakers, whereas European materials should be based on speakers from European countries. Here too, it is desirable to have non-native speakers at different levels of linguistic skills. Though it is true that the non-native speaker is commonly presented in ELT materials, they are often stereotyped as learners of English or tourists to an English-speaking country. For EIL-oriented teaching, however, it is important to present all speakers as 'speakers in their own right' (Seidlhofer, 2011). This is important as it grants non-native speakers ownership of the language, acknowledging their rights and abilities to adapt and adjust the language to suit their communicative needs. If materials continue to favor native speakers from a small range of countries, it follows that learners may not be able to understand the majority of their future interlocutors or develop negative attitudes towards those speakers whose English differs from the native speakers they encountered in the classroom.

Understanding speakers within materials requires a look at everyone who is presented using English, and to analyze them in terms of their nationality and role. Identifying the speakers' nationalities makes it possible to evaluate the extent to which speakers from each circle are represented (Table 4.2). First, materials may only represent speakers from one Inner Circle country (1) or from different Inner Circle countries (2). While keeping their focus on the Inner Circle speaker, materials may also present a small amount of outer or Expanding Circle speakers (3). Lastly, materials can move away from the predominance of the native speaker (NS) and portray a mixed number of speakers from all three circles (4). Finally, materials can move on to presenting successful multilingual users of English as the speakers of the language (5). Next, it is important to consider how the outer and Expanding Circle speakers are presented. In the

**Table 4.2** Measuring speakers in materials

<u>Speakers</u>

| |
|---|
| **Look at:** Everyone who is presented using English |
| **Look for:**<br>  • Nationality<br>  • Speaker role |
| (1)  One Inner Circle country |
| (2)  Different Inner Circle countries |
| (3)  Predominantly Inner Circle Speakers and |
|      Outer Circle speakers |
|      Expanding Circle Speakers |
| (4)  Mixed amount of Inner Circle speakers and |
|      Outer Circle varieties |
|      Expanding Circle speakers |
| (5)  Multilingual users of English |
| (6)  Outer Circle speakers as learners |
| (7)  Outer Circle speakers as users |
| (8)  Expanding Circle speakers as learners |
| (9)  Expanding Circle speakers as users |

context of EIL one should distinguish between their representation as users of English (5,7) and their representation as learners of English (6,8). This distinction can be made based on the role that non-native speakers (NNS) take (e.g. tourist, student, business person etc.) and how they are positioned in comparison to the Inner Circle speakers. Finally, materials can move on to presenting successful multilingual users of English as the speakers of the language (9).

## Language use situations

EIL users will use English in a wide array of situations and have to develop a realistic role model of a successful English user in these situations. To allow them to do so, it is paramount for materials to display language use situations that highlight English medium interaction between Outer Circle and Expanding Circle speakers. Though most materials do depict non-native speakers, they are mostly presented in interaction with native speakers. In fact, many materials do not show any communication without a native speaker present. Learners of English needs to be exposed to a realistic representation of how speakers from all three circles use English successfully in communication with each other. This includes the importance of highlighting that English communication is not limited to Inner Circle contexts by favoring language use situations that take place in the Outer and Expanding Circle. If materials continue to portray English use situations in Inner Circle countries that focus on communication with the native speaker, learners will develop unrealistic aspirations and learning goals due to wrong role models.

By identifying all dialogues (i.e. language use situations between two or more people) and determining the nationality of interlocutors, it is possible to identify who uses English with whom (see Table 4.3). The first distinction in this section is made between intranational and international dialogues. Intranational dialogues are those in which all speakers are from the same country. The first two categories then comprise materials that present only intranational dialogues between speakers from the same Inner Circle country (1), and those that present intranational dialogues between speakers from the same Outer Circle country (2). Turning to international English use, according to circles, many different pairings of speakers are possible. For one, there is international use between speakers of different Inner Circle countries (3), and speakers of Inner and Outer Circle countries or Inner and Expanding Circle countries (4). Focusing on the Outer Circle, interlocutors may be from different Outer Circle countries as well as from Outer and Expanding Circle countries (5), though speakers may also be from different Expanding Circle countries (6). Lastly, materials may also include English

**Table 4.3** Measuring language use situations

**Language Use Situations**

| |
| --- |
| **Look at:** Dialogues |
| **Look for:**<br>• Nationality of interlocutor pairings<br>• Context |
| (1) Intranational Use in Inner Circle countries |
| (2) Intranational Use in Outer Circle countries |
| (3) International Use between only speakers of Inner Circle countries |
| (4) International Use between Inner Circle speaker and |
|     Outer Circle speaker |
|     Expanding Circle speaker |
| (5) International Use between Outer Circle speaker and |
|     Outer Circle speaker |
|     Expanding Circle speaker |
| (6) International Use between only Expanding Circle speakers |
| (7) International Use between speakers from all three circles |
| (8) Only Inner Circle context |
| (9) Inner Circle and |
|     Outer Circle context |
|     Expanding Circle context |

use situations featuring speakers from all three circles at the same time (7). Next, it is important to look at the context in which the language is used, i.e. in which country. Again, a distinction is made between materials that show English use only in Inner Circle contexts (8) or those that also show English use in Outer and Expanding Circle contexts (9).

## Culture

For successful EIL communication, ELT needs to develop Intercultural Awareness with regards to speakers from diverse cultural backgrounds, as EIL users have to negotiate a variety of socioculturally grounded language use situations (Baker, 2011). To that end, English needs to be disconnected from any specific national culture, especially those of Inner Circle countries. That means cultural content should be from the learners' cultures or sourced internationally. International cultural material refers to sourcing materials from all three circles, as well as utilizing materials referring to global cultural phenomena and issues. It is further important to approach culture dynamically. In that sense, it is not enough to learn a finite set of rules about behavioral etiquette and conventions. Rather, a dynamic approach to culture is necessary in which students develop an ability to negotiate and mediate 'emergent socioculturally grounded communication modes and frames of reference' (Baker, 2011) based on their understanding of the dynamic, fluid and hybrid character of intercultural communication. If materials continue to approach culture as a static concept connected to Inner Circle countries, learners will not be given opportunity to develop awareness of the relative nature of cultural norms and understanding that intercultural communication can and will be difficult (Friedrich, 2012).

Cultural references can be anything from referring to (famous) people, specific places, cultural products, cultural practice and perspectives. By identifying the countries to which these references are made allows exploring the scope of cultural references in terms of the three circles (see Table 4.4). That is, it is important to assess whether cultural references are made to only one Inner Circle country (1), different Inner Circle countries (2), predominantly Inner Circle but also Outer and/or Expanding Circle countries (3) or a mixed amount of references to Inner, Outer and Expanding Circle countries. Next, a closer look should be taken at cultural practice and perspectives, that is, customs and information about daily life as well as beliefs and world-views (Yuen, 2011), in order to understand whether or not culture is depicted as a static (5) or dynamic concept (6). Examples of static representation of culture are those where it is suggested that all people from a specific culture behave in a certain way based on their belonging to a certain culture or the assumption that cultural behavioral norms are determined by one specific interlocutor. In contrast to that, dynamic representation of culture allows learners to explore diversity within one culture or common ground between cultures.

**Table 4.4** Measuring culture

| Culture |
| --- |
| **Look at:** Information about cultures and (inter-) cultural behavior |
| **Look for:**<br>  • Countries<br>  • Dynamic vs static image |
| (1)  Culture from only one Inner Circle country |
| (2)  Inner Circle cultures only |
| (3)  Predominantly Inner Circle cultures and |
|     Outer Circle cultures |
|     Expanding Circle cultures |
| (4)  Mixed amount of Inner Circle cultures and |
|     Outer Circle cultures |
|     Expanding Circle cultures |
| (5)  Culture as static concept |
| (6)  Culture as dynamic concept |

## Proficiency

As EIL poses new demands to speakers and learners, ELT needs to focus on developing multiple forms of competency (Galloway & Rose, 2015). A focus on linguistic accuracy is no longer appropriate considering the extensive use of communication strategies among non-native speakers highlighted in ELF and EIL research (Björkman, 2014). It follows that classroom and textbook activities should represent this by providing sufficient opportunity for learners to practice relevant communication skills. Further, though a complete breakdown of communication is rare in EIL communication, materials should expose learners to instances of miscommunication, as they are likely to occur, and allow them room to explore successful strategies for resolution. Continuing to favor practicing Standard English and linguistic accuracy will not equip students with the skills necessary to negotiate meaning with their various interlocutors and put them at a disadvantage in international communication.

As our understanding of proficiency and subsequent learning goals has changed with regards to EIL, it is paramount to assess whether learners have sufficient opportunity to practice the necessary skills (see Table 4.5). To do so, the exercises and materials should be analyzed regarding their focus on 'Linguistic Accuracy' vs 'Communication Strategies'. Exercises that target linguistic accuracy practice linguistic elements such as grammar, spelling, pronunciation, whereas communication strategies refer to the strategies described above. In that sense, materials can be identified as practicing only linguistic accuracy (1), mainly linguistic accuracy but also communication strategies (2) or a mixed amount of both (3). Next, it is also interesting to consider where in the materials the activities are found

**Table 4.5** Measuring proficiency

| Proficiency |
| --- |
| **Look at:** Tasks and Exercises |
| **Look for:**<br>• Linguistics Accuracy: Grammar accuracy, Spelling accuracy, Pronunciation Accuracy<br>• Communication Strategies: Paraphrasing, Approximation, Circumlocution, Comprehension Check, Clarification Request, Confirmation Check |
| (1)  Only Linguistic Accuracy Practice |
| (2)  Mainly Linguistic Accuracy and Communication Strategies |
| (3)  Mixed amount of Linguistic Accuracy and Communication Strategies |
| (4)  Communication Strategies in: |
|     Vocabulary Practice |
|     Writing/Reading Practice |
|     Speaking Practice/Communication Practice |
|     Listening Practice |
| (5)  Portrayal of Miscommunication |
| (6)  Successful Resolution of Miscommunication |

that practice communication strategies (4), as this can help determine whether or not communication strategies are actually targeted. In that sense, it can be useful to distinguish whether communication strategies are practiced within vocabulary practice, writing and reading practice, speaking practice or listening practice. For example, an exercise to practice finding synonyms as a reading exercise suggests a vocabulary target, whereas the same activity within a speaking or communication part of a textbook indicates a communication strategies target. Lastly, in EIL miscommunication is likely and it is therefore of interest whether any instances of miscommunication are portrayed in the materials (5) and if learners are presented with strategies for their successful resolution (6).

## What Does the Research Tell Us?

The following parts offers an overview of research into the extent to which teaching materials are underpinned by a native speaker model vs EIL orientation (see Table 4.6).

Caleffi (2016) looked at ELF and textbooks, specifically the way in which listening and speaking activities foster ELF communication by examining recent ELT textbooks for upper secondary and adult learners of English. Listening activities were examined regarding their exposure and potential for reflection of authentic NNS accents and NNS – NNS communication and speaking activities were analyzed according to their active engagement of communication strategies, cross-cultural topics and ELF use. Caleffi found Standard British English to be the majority accent,

**Table 4.6** Example studies that report of materials research

| Researchers | Topic | Evaluation method | Material |
|---|---|---|---|
| Caleffi (2016) | ELF-oriented approaches | Qualitative Analysis | Recent ELT textbooks |
| Matsuda (2002) | English users and uses | Quantitative and qualitative analysis | Seven Japanese 7th grade ELT textbooks |
| Naji Meidani and Pishghadam (2012) | Country-specific references and representation of English as a Lingua Franca | Qualitative and quantitative content analysis | New American Streamline Cambridge English for Schools Interchange Series Third Edition<br><br>Top Notch |
| Rose and Galloway (2019) | English varieties, speakers, ownership | Holistic evaluation | New Heady: Upper Intermediate<br><br>Interchange 3<br><br>Market Leader: Upper Intermediate<br><br>International Express: Upper Intermediate<br><br>Global: Upper Intermediate<br><br>English Unlimited: Upper Intermediate |
| Syrbe and Rose (2016) | Global orientation of textbooks | Qualitative analysis | Camden Town, volume 6; Green Line, volume 6 and English G21, volume 5 |
| Vettorel (2018) | Communication strategies | Qualitative analysis | Italian upper secondary school textbooks |
| Yuen (2011) | Foreign cultures | Content analysis | Longman Elect, Treasure Plus |

as most of the interaction in the audio material was between native speakers only. In line with that, she found few opportunities for learners to utilize all their linguistic resources creatively or communication strategies, as well as ELF interaction.

Matsuda (2002) examined Japanese 7th grade textbooks sanctioned by the Japanese Ministry of Education according to their representation of English, its users, and its use contexts. In terms of English varieties, she found a strong reliance on American English, which was positioned as the standard throughout all books. In fact, she only found one chapter among all seven textbooks that presented a small number of Outer and Expanding Circle speakers. Matsuda further found that native speakers were not only the majority but also tended to speak more words and played more important roles within the dialogues. The same is true for the use contexts, in which she found that the majority of dialogues were between native speakers from the same country or native speakers from different countries. Only two textbooks also portrayed a small amount of English use exclusively between non-native speakers, for example tourists visiting Japan.

Naji Meidani and Pishghadam (2012) carried out a detailed analysis of four textbooks published at different points in time to evaluate the extent to which the international status of English is represented. The textbooks were evaluated according to their references to Inner Circle countries, references to Outer and Expanding Circle countries, non-native accents dialogues in non-English speaking countries, place of home culture and famous people. Though they revealed a strong reliance on the native speaker and Inner Circle, they did find gradual change towards a stronger representation of EIL in more recent publications.

Rose and Galloway (2019) investigated six globally used textbooks to represent a variety of teaching contexts. Specifically, they asked what models were used, who the target interlocutors were, how ownership is depicted and what linguistic orientation is promoted. For each question, each book was given a score out of five depending on the extent to which they represented a traditional vs global orientation. When it comes to language norms, all books promoted British or American standards, only one book was found to challenge these norms for pronunciation. The analysis found a wider range when it comes to ownership, which was evaluated based on cultural references. Though one book still had predominantly Inner Circle references, all other books included global cultural references, and references to Outer and Expanding Circle cultures. Regarding the target interlocutor, a similar range was found with numbers ranging from 1–4, with most books depicting global target interlocutors.

Syrbe and Rose (2016) explored Camden Town, volume 6; Green Line, volume 6 and English G21, volume 5, the three textbooks used in Germany's most populous state. In order to examine the global orientation of the textbooks they investigated them according to the owners of English, target interlocutors, models and norms, culture, concepts related to the global use of English. Though all textbooks were dominated by native speakers from the UK or the US, there was also a visible number of speakers from Australia and South Africa, where some of the real-world materials were taken from. Though the textbooks also featured some Expanding Circle speakers, for example from Germany, all of the dialogues featured at least one native speaker, suggesting the native speaker as unquestioned target interlocutor. Similarly, when it comes to intercultural communication, the advice given to students focused exclusively on the UK and US. In accordance with that, native speaker English, specifically Received Pronunciation, was positioned as a desired learning target.

Vettorel (2018) analyzed 20 textbooks used in the Italian upper secondary school context between 1990 and 2015 regarding their incorporation of communication strategies. Dividing these into four main areas (appeal for help, meaning negotiation, responses, achievement strategies), she identified tasks that allowed learners to practice individual communication strategies. Overall, the older textbooks tended to include less communication strategies, though only three were found to not include any.

She further found at least one activity for each of the four examined areas, most activities however were to practice meaning negotiation.

Yuen (2011) investigated two series of junior secondary English language textbooks in Hong Kong regarding their representation of foreign cultures. To this end, Yuen identified all cultural references and analyzed them according to their type (Person, Product, Practice, Perspective) and their region (Western countries, Asia, Africa). Overall, she found references of the Product category most frequently, and found an overemphasis on Western, specifically English-speaking countries.

## Implications for Teachers in Global Contexts

The research that has been done so far paints a fairly clear picture of the still very prevalent native speaker model in local as well as globally used and produced materials. Accordingly, teachers who undertake an analysis of their own materials as suggested earlier in this chapter are likely to find a similar picture for the textbooks they use. It is thus paramount for teachers to have access to a variety of teaching materials to take an EIL-oriented approach. As major publishers have thus far not taken this route, it seems teachers have to rely on using alternative resources for the time being.

### Utilizing alternative resources

When searching for advice on which materials to use, there is an array of publications that mention various materials or discusses the usefulness of individual material choices and activities. Though this suggests that there is a large number of supplementation materials available, it is important to keep in mind that not all of these are suited for the same learning outcomes and activities. In fact, choosing or creating suitable materials strongly depends on the learning goal as well as on the teaching context. On the whole, there are three main learning outcomes in EIL-oriented teaching:

- **Raising awareness**: Increasing students' knowledge about the role and forms of EIL and diversity among EIL speakers.
- **Developing attitudes**: Developing students' attitudes towards all varieties and speakers of English in a positive way.
- **Fostering EIL skills**: Developing and practicing individual skills required for EIL communication.

#### Raising awareness

Awareness-raising activities directly teach about the language's diversity, its role, its speakers and their cultures. Such activities allow learners to explore the sociolinguistic and sociocultural elements of different Englishes and their speakers.

Rather than learning about a great number of varieties or learning to understand diverse non-native speaker accents, raising awareness is about allowing students to understand why and how English developed into a pluricentric language and who its contemporary speakers are. One way to raise students' awareness is to communicate meta-knowledge about the language's diversity. Depending on students' level of proficiency, adapted textbook materials are well-suited for this. Especially introductory books such as Gramley's (2012) *The History of English* or McIntyre's (2009) *History of English* can offer adaptable materials to improve learners' understanding of the pluralistic nature of English. In more advanced classes, teachers can also explore different models used to explain and map the language's variety such as Kachru's Three Circle model, McArthur's Circle of World Englishes or Modiano's English as an International Language. For teachers wishing to explore this even further, it is also possible to draw on models of the spread of English or investigate different colonies in terms of their English language development. It might be useful, for example to investigate the differences between former settlement colonies (Schneider, 2012) such as the US or Australia, in which English became the native language, and so-called former exploitation colonies (Schneider, 2012), in which English now is used as a second language (e.g. East African or South East Asia). Likewise, the Four Channels of English Spread (Galloway & Rose, 2015), provides a valuable resource based on which learners can do their own research and explore how English came to a particular country and how this specific channel has influenced the development of that variety.

Turning to the speakers of English, awareness-raising materials should provide students with demographic information about who uses English in the 21st century. Specifically, learners should gain awareness of the fact that non-native speakers now greatly outnumber native speakers. Beyond (adapted) textbook materials, reports about non-native speakers' language usage and ability can be utilized to allow students to explore where English is learned in the world and to what extent the language is used by its non-native speakers. An example for the European context is the so-called Eurobarometer (Commissie, 2012), a report providing detailed data about second language use and learning among the citizens of EU member states. Where this material is too challenging for students, it can serve as an excellent resource for teachers to create their own materials, be it handouts or presentations.

Expanding on this, awareness-raising should further focus on the contexts in which English is used by its outer and Expanding Circle speakers and what this communication entails; in other words, the language use situations. Again, the aforementioned reports on language use offer a starting point for learners to explore the domains in which non-native speakers use English most frequently. Beyond that, learners should develop an understanding of how ELF communication differs from English use between native speakers, namely the increased use of communication strategies and the higher likelihood for miscommunication. Unfortunately, to our knowledge there are no real-world materials that would showcase this and that could be used to exploit these strategies in more detail. There are, however, individual accounts, that highlight native speakers' struggle in EIL settings due to their inability to accommodate and adjust their language (Hazel, 2016; Morrison, 2016) which could be used as reading materials. Yet, there is a significant lack of alternative materials, and thus the need for material writers and EIL researchers to work together closely, as Galloway and Rose (2017) point out.

Activities with these materials can range from reading comprehension to discussion to asking students to conduct their own research into the diversity of English. When working with models of English spread, one activity could be to discuss language needs in different contexts. For example, Galloway and Rose (2015) divide English spread into four different contexts, each of which has unique language histories (compare settler colonization vs slavery). Students could be given adapted reading materials about each context and then discuss and collect language use situations for English and compare differences and similarities in each context. Utilizing adapted textbook materials, this could be extended as research activity in which students find specific countries that fit each context and compare their ideas of language use situations. Building on this, the discussion can go further into how the language use situations have resulted in vastly different roles of English in these regions. With more advanced students and specifically in multilingual contexts, another possible research activity is to focus on influences from other languages and research how English has changed with regards to specific locally spoken languages. With lower level students, reading and research activities could focus on mapping the English-speaking world, for example by color coding maps according to which circle the country belongs to. Similarly, learners could be asked to research numbers of English speakers in different parts of the world. Focusing more on specific varieties, another activity could give students a number of words specifically used in different new Englishes, and ask them to match these to a specific country based on readings they do. Lastly, the two previously mentioned newspaper articles about native speakers' struggles in EIL settings can be used for reading comprehension and a basis for discussion. Discussions should focus on why native speakers struggle and whether some non-native speakers may struggle in the same way, leading them to the question how native speakers could be educated to better communicate in EIL settings.

### Developing positive attitudes

Attitudes influence the way we approach speakers of different varieties and our ability to communicate, as explained in Chapter 6. Changing attitudes is also important as they are a major barrier to the necessary changes in ELT. With teaching EIL, the goal is for learners to understand different varieties as expression of local identity. In other words, varieties are approached as an expression of local culture and local communication needs. To achieve this, teachers should take a qualitative approach and explore one or two varieties and their context in-depth, or focus on a particular group of speakers. In Outer Circle contexts it would obviously be ideal to explore the local variety not only to positively influence learners' attitudes but also to increase their confidence in using that variety. In Expanding Circle contexts, teachers can choose geographically relevant varieties, or make a practical choice based on availability of resources.

In terms of materials, a lot of the resources suggested for awareness raising can also be used to develop student attitudes, as you cannot influence students' attitudes without increasing their knowledge and awareness of how English is used globally. When using textbook materials, the focus should shift from the spread of English to studying the sociolinguistic context of individual varieties or language use contexts. This can be in the form of a specific type of colonization or following the development and rise of one particular variety. A type resource particularly suited to develop positive attitudes is postcolonial writing. Here, teachers can exploit written books or audio books. Postcolonial writing is well-suited as it expresses not only linguistic elements of new varieties but also carries sociocultural knowledge that can be explored in many ways. Choosing appropriate writers depends on the context of learning and the level of students. For example, if the curriculum includes a unit on India, this is a good opportunity to bring postcolonial respective postcolonial literature into the classroom. Recently, the BBC has started publishing news in West African Pidgin English, providing a major resource for teachers. Teachers and learners can explore the variety but also local culture and people by identifying topics of importance. More so, BBC has great prestige and authority attached to it, which can positively influence students' attitudes towards pidgin Englishes. This is further substantiated by the fact that BBC Pidgin discusses and reports news stories at the same level of importance as the other BBC services, which showcases to students that highly important matters or global politics or culture can be discussed in pidgin English as well. A resource from the South African context is Trevor Noah, a well-known comedian, who has written and recorded three books describing his life growing up in South African under Apartheid. In his audiobooks, he speaks different South African English accents as well as a variety of other languages spoken in the country, providing a great resource to explore multilingualism. He further addresses issues such as English as medium of education and how languages shape identity. In that sense, his narratives are highly relevant to better understand postcolonial contexts and their relationship with English.

Activities can focus on language form or the sociocultural elements of postcolonial contexts. In case of the former, learners could be asked to identify particular vocabulary or grammatical features of a given variety. Teachers may encourage students' creativity by asking them to translate a standard English text into a particular variety. Doing so would acknowledge this variety as valid means of communication, positively influencing student attitudes towards new varieties. If materials are available from different points in time, it would also be interesting for students to track specific language developments that have shaped the variety, for instance, by identifying to what extent and in what features the language differs from standard English, those this would require a lot of preparatory work from the teacher. Other activities could focus on identifying different degrees of standardization of a particular variety within one variety by looking at language use in different contexts, such as the court house and the market. This would also lend itself to a discussion about appropriacy of different ways to use English and thus move into sociocultural questions. Further activities of the latter type should mostly focus on reading-based discussions as well as research of particular varieties or postcolonial contexts.

### EIL skills: Comprehension

When it comes to practicing comprehension, the focus is clearly on the form of particular varieties, as the goal is to improve students' practical ability to interact with speakers of different varieties. Naturally, it is impossible to bring all varieties into the classroom to the same extent, so variety choice strongly depends on the learning context, that is, which varieties are relevant to the learners' real world and future use of English. Though it is true that many materials now contain more than one variety, the Englishes that are included tend to be limited to Inner Circle varieties. Additionally, where Outer Circle varieties are represented, they often only exhibit few of the characteristics and speakers are highly standardized. To truly allow students to practice comprehension of different varieties, teachers will have to supplement with outside materials.

There is an array of print, audio, video and internet sources that teachers can exploit in order to make their ELT classrooms more diverse. First, there are databases showcasing different varieties such as the Introducing Global Englishes website or Macmillan's English around the world series. Especially the first one is very well suited to first introducing learners to different varieties as they can hear the same text spoken by speakers of different varieties. However, to foster real comprehension learners require continuous exposure, which cannot be provided using such databases as their content is limited. Audiobooks provide an excellent resource to build on initial exposure due to their length and the many activities one can design around an audiobook. It can also be assumed that students are more inclined to listen to audiobooks than to read a book. Audiobooks are often aimed at in international audience and can thus be expected to exhibit a certain degree of standardization, which makes them well-suited for less advanced learners. The same applies to movies, which offer another valuable resource to bring different varieties into the classroom. Movie activities can take a focus on language or content, and can be used with learners at all levels. However, teachers need to keep in mind though that actors are oftentimes no native speakers of the particular variety they are portraying, so there may be an issue of authenticity.

TED Talks offer another excellent resource considering the number of available topics and varieties. By focusing on the content of a TED Talk, learners can practice their ability to understand a particular variety while at the same time learning about an area of interest. As TEDX diversifies and continues to offer a group of talks focused on a specific country, they will increasingly offer new materials of great relevance to students from related geographical contexts. Similarly, news and newspapers offer an opportunity to focus on learning content while being exposed to different varieties. Many news websites offer written as well as spoken information, both of which may exhibit the local variety to a certain degree. Most recently, BBC has started offering news in pidgin English to cater to their African readership. Further, TV shows produced in Outer Circle countries can also be used with more advanced students. This includes fiction shows as well as non-fiction. In fact, reality TV shows may be best suited to get a genuine insight into how locals use their language. Naturally, teachers will have to pay close attention to whether or not the content is appropriate for their learners.

Arguably the best exposure to different varieties are its authentic speakers, and it seems obvious that bringing in speakers of a particular variety would be a great resource for the students (Matsuda, 2003b). Where this is realistic, it should be utilized as much possible not only to provide exposure but also opportunity for interaction. Unfortunately, this is not possible for many ELT classrooms, especially in areas where most countries belong to the Expanding Circle, such as Europe. In those cases, it might still be possible to utilize native speakers of those varieties where teachers have access to them. For example, they record language samples, and specifically focus on distinctive language and pronunciation patterns of that variety, or with a thematic focus to supplement the topics students encounter during their course. They might also be able to search for and find samples of specific varieties on websites such as YouTube.

When supplementing materials in order to bring diversity into the classroom, teachers need to remember that familiarity with a specific variety positively correlates to comprehension (Field, 2003). In other words, the more students are exposed to a particular variety, the better they will be able to understand its speakers. That means it is not enough to just use a specific variety for one or two activities throughout the course as is often done in mainstream textbooks materials. Variety and diversity should be a constant element of ELT, exploited with all topics in order to truly develop learners' comprehension skills with regards to a pluricentric English.

Though initial activities may focus specifically on pronunciation features, further activities do not have to differ from commonly used comprehension tasks. In fact, a focus on the content will naturally further students' ability to understand that particular variety and their success in dealing with content comprehension activities will show their progress in that respect. Some have, rightfully, claimed that a number of films displaying a particular variety do so by using actors who are not native speakers of that variety and whose imitation is not authentic. However, identifying such inauthentic features could be turned into activity itself, with learners who are well familiar with that particular variety.

### EIL skills: Communication

Regarding communication strategies, it is often pointed out that learners practice these naturally within the classroom. Though this is true for many classrooms, teachers can do a more to create additional opportunities for learners to practice these skills. Generally speaking, communicative activities that focus on reaching a communicative goal, without any specific language focus, are well suited to allow learners to use communication strategies freely, especially in multilingual classrooms. In monolingual classrooms learners are more likely to fall back on their first language when encountering linguistic difficulties. Especially in those classrooms, teachers may want to choose materials and activities that help learners develop particular individual communication strategies.

Most textbooks do not emphasize practicing those skills, and teachers will have to find alternative materials, though those are scarce. On the whole, these activities should focus on achievement and compensatory strategies; in other words, strategies learners can use when they lack vocabulary. For circumlocution practice, for example, games such as taboo or crossword puzzles can be utilized to practice describing an item without making the actual word. The same games may be used for approximation practice, additionally teachers can create word pairs, so that learners can practice finding an alternative term for a vocabulary item. These activities can easily be incorporated into vocabulary practice, and do not have to take up much time. Another commonly observed strategy is 'word coinage', a process where speakers create a new word in English that may not exist based on a particular language rule. Often, this process includes adding specific morphemes such as -ist, -ism or de- to a known word. By creating activities that specifically focus on the function of these morphemes, teachers can support this process. The challenge with this activity is not only for teachers to allow usage of linguistically 'wrong' words, but also to make a distinction between teaching existing words and allowing learners to play creatively with the language and its structure. The most challenging part, however, is creating materials that foster negotiation of meaning.

### EIL skills: Intercultural communication

Again, intercultural communication is something that can be practiced naturally in intercultural and multilingual classrooms, but actual materials are few. For one, exposure to a larger variety of intercultural communication or intercultural misunderstandings, and subsequent analysis can foster learners' intercultural communication skills. There are, for example, some cases in advertising where even large companies such as Coca Cola did not consider particular cultural elements when creating their adverts. Analyzing these mistakes could be a fun and engaging way into creating greater awareness off the importance of culture. A lot of textbooks and other culturally influences materials operate with rather strict stereotypes, so another possibility to create greater awareness of the fluid and complex nature of culture is comparing these stereotypes with each other or with learners' experience. For example, tourist books are still very prevalent among travelers and they usually give a variety of information about the host culture. This information tends to be static and simplistic, which could be analyzed in itself, but it might also be interesting to analyze the perception of one culture from within different cultures (e.g. description of Japan from a German or an American guidebook). However, all these activities focus on awareness rather than active participation in intercultural communication, which is almost impossible to recreate in monocultural classrooms. One possibility to do so is to make greater use of technology by creating networking opportunities between learners in different countries. One such project is carried out in Germany, the Telecollaboration Project for Intercultural Language Acquisition (Hoffstaedter & Kohn, 2014), which is more closely examined in Chapter 6 of this book. Their website offers tools and resources for teachers to help foster learners' intercultural communication skills.

## Post-reading Activities

### Reflect

This chapter suggests that most commonly used materials are inapt to teach EIL. Do you agree with this?

### Discuss

(1) This chapter has covered many elements in which EIL differs from the traditional native speaker model. Which of these do you think requires the most immediate change?
(2) This chapter suggests that teaching EIL requires a significant reconsideration of teaching and materials. How do you think this affects the teaching of different levels?
(3) What do you think is the biggest barrier to using more EIL-oriented materials?

### Apply

Choose one of the resources proposed in this chapter and design a lesson utilizing this resource to teach EIL.

## Resources for Further Reading

McKay, S.L. (2012) Teaching materials for English as an International Language. In A. Matsuda (ed.) *Principles and Practices of Teaching English as an International Language*. Bristol: Multilingual Matters.

This book features contributions by a variety of scholars in the field, of which of which two chapters are relevant for EIL materials. Chapter 5, authored by Sandra Lee McKay, offers a thorough discussion of the implications the macro-level spread of EIL has for materials development, focusing on its function as communication device between non-native speakers. Large parts of this chapter deal with existing materials and highlight their shortcomings, while offering advice how to critically exploit those shortcomings in the classroom. She further offers insight into how existing materials should be changed to better represent EIL, as well as suggesting some ways to supplement and to conduct social-based research with the students to broaden their understanding of EIL. The chapter concludes with guiding questions for the material design process which can be utilized by teachers as well as professional material writers. Overall, this chapter offers a lot of insight into relevant issues with current materials; however, discussion remain largely on a meta level. In that sense, this chapter is mostly recommended for scholars wishing to broaden their theoretical understanding but less suitable for teachers and ELT professionals seeking practical guidance. The last chapter of this book presents EIL activities for traditional ELT classrooms and provides a number of ready-made lessons to teach about World Englishes along with the materials and teacher instructions. The lessons are divided into Introduction to World Englishes, Language Attitudes, Local Creativity, Culture and Writing. Though this chapter does not offer direct instructions for materials design, the ready-made lessons show useful examples which can be followed by ELT professionals wishing to create their own materials.

Rose, H. and Galloway, N. (2019) *Global Englishes for Language Teaching*. Chapter 6. Cambridge: Cambridge University Press.

This book's chapter on teaching materials has a strong focus on research and evaluation of existing materials. By taking stock of the extent to which textbooks.

# 5 Testing and Assessing a Global Language

## Pre-reading Activities

### Think

What skills and knowledge makes a person proficient in English? How would one go about assessing these skills and knowledge?

### Discuss

In small groups, discuss:

(1) Think of different English tests you have taken or administered. How do they compare to each other? Do these tests serve different purposes in terms of the skills or knowledge they assess?
(2) Do you think current assessment practices reinforce prescriptive language standards? What are the positive and negative benefits of adhering to standards in tests?
(3) Are traditional assessment practices appropriate to testing EIL? Why? Why not? How should they change to be more inclusive of the ideas presented in previous chapters?

## Introduction

Language testing has a significant influence on English language classrooms as tests often determine learning goals, and they are seen as indicator for language proficiency (Coombe, 2018). Many educational contexts use tests and other forms of assessment to determine achievement in learning and many learners study for one or more of the commercial proficiency tests such as TOEFL or IELTS. In that sense, the desire to perform well on a particular form of assessment acts as a motivator for, if not a sole purpose of, learning. Equally important is the fact that successful performance on a language test is seen by many people as proof for someone's proficiency in that language. In other words, high test scores are assumed to equate to a high level of proficiency. Accordingly, good test performance is an important criterion for successful completion of a class or course and is often a key factor to entering university, or to gaining access to jobs and visas. This is why major proficiency tests are considered *high stakes* tests. To maintain their function in a variety of domains, a test's so-called *face validity*, which is the extent to which we trust a specific test's results, is a major concern of their publishers. Their influence on learner motivation and their acceptance as measures of proficiency mean that language tests have a considerable influence on learning content, as teachers are likely to want to prepare their learners for those tests as best as they can.

But tests not only influence the learning process; they also have a strong impact in various social domains as they function in a gatekeeper role (Rose & Syrbe, 2018), especially in large-scale international tests of which the results often determine the test-taker's access to employment or admission to university, domestic or abroad. As English is the medium of instruction for many international programs, gaining a certain IELTS or TOEFL score is the requirement for most students seeking to study abroad. Moreover, an increasing number of programs also require their domestic students to show a certain level of English proficiency either through particular testing or through their high school diploma (Rose & Syrbe, 2018). Especially in many countries in Asia, university entrance examinations contain a specific English language section. A famous example is China's National College Entrance Examination, in which the English section is equal to the Chinese section. In Japan and South Korea, English has replaced 'Foreign Languages' on entrance examinations. Other countries such as Hong Kong make passing an English test compulsory to graduate high school. Though most countries in Europe do have a foreign language section as part of their high school graduation tests, English is the only compulsory foreign language within many European countries and thus constitutes a major part of high school examination.

In the context of English language teaching, language assessment is one of the areas in which the monolithic understanding of English is most visible and thus one that requires substantial changes (Hall, 2014). Generally speaking, language tests are tools used to collect information based on which inferences are made about someone's performance in a real-world setting. It follows that test characteristics need to match the characteristics of said real-world settings for the inferences to be valid (Hu, 2012). To give a simple example, testing someone's driving ability by having them drive in a small town limits the inferences one can make about this person's ability to navigate major city traffic as the characteristics of the test setting (small town) do not mirror those of the real-world setting of a major city. The same holds true for English language assessment, an area that received heavy criticism for their adherence to native speakers as providing the norms and benchmark for successful uses. Testing someone's English proficiency by having them do a test based on the native speaker model limits the inferences that we can make about the test-taker's ability to use EIL, as the test characteristics (native speaker model) do not mirror the real-world setting that is EIL. In other words, assessment based on only the native speaker model is insufficient in addressing English speaker's needs in the 21st century. To provide a valid measure of someone's ability to use EIL in a globalized world, it is crucial to radically re-think the function and nature of language tests and our understanding of proficiency, a process that affects test design as well as use of test scores (Canagarajah, 2006).

## Key Concepts

### EIL as target language use domain

English language tests are designed to evaluate someone's ability to use English in a particular real-world context, which guides test design and application of test scores. This real-world context is referred to as the criterion (McNamara, 2000) or the target language use domain (Bachman & Palmer, 2010). This target language use domain is by no means the same for all English language tests, and the process of test creation should start with recording the particular characteristics of the specific target language use domain with regards to which test is to be designed (Hu, 2012). Considering EIL, the target language use domain may be a localized Outer Circle context, specific Expanding Circle context as well as the whole global English-using community (Canagarajah, 2006). In the 21st century, tests of English proficiency have to be designed with regards to the EIL community as the target language use domain in order to provide a valid and relevant measurement tool of English proficiency.

In terms of target language use domain, EIL differs from native speaker contexts in terms of speakers, varieties, culture, skills and language use tasks. In the majority of EIL contexts, non-native speakers outnumber native speakers (Seidlhofer, 2011). That is, English speakers are more likely to talk to other non-native speakers than native speakers. This means that English speakers have to accommodate their communication to users of diverse cultural backgrounds and varying levels of English proficiency and accents. In many global contexts, English speakers are further confronted with the need to understand different varieties that might differ greatly from the English used in Inner Circle contexts and taught in most EFL classrooms. This diversity means today's English speakers are required to understand a large number of varieties and be able to shift between varying local and emergent norms (Canagarajah, 2006).

### Test design – construct and content

The test construct is the definition of particular skills the test aims to measure and how to measure them, and is sometimes referred to as operationalization (McNamara, 2000). As English tests are designed for different purposes, the skills they measure can also vary greatly (Hu, 2012). Think, for example, of the different skills required to translate medical texts from Japanese into English compared to those skills needed to communicate in English for tourism purposes. This means that constructs can be defined in many ways, depending on the specific skills being assessed. It follows then that construct validity is not in the construct itself but the extent to which the test measures the skills necessary for successful performance in the relevant *Target Language Use Domain*. Most English test constructs are defined so that they measure conformity with external language norms (Canagarajah, 2006). For example, the IELTS speaking test construct is described and measured in terms of fluency and coherence, (precision of) lexical resource, grammatical accuracy and (precision of) pronunciation. The idealized native speaker serves as a benchmark for precision, accuracy and successful performance (Hall, 2014). Such a test can only allow valid inferences about Target Language Use Domains in which such accuracy and precision is the determining factor for successful communication. This, however, is not true for EIL, in which speakers rely on strategies rather than follow prescribed standards (Rose & Syrbe, 2018). In fact, studies have observed standard Englishes to have little relevance to successful EIL, as users employ communication strategies, pragmatic skills and intercultural skills. With regards to EIL as the Target Language Use Domain, tests based on constructs that measure accuracy only address a small part of the skills required for successful performance (Canagarajah, 2006), in which case we speak of *construct underrepresentation*.

Test content refers to the actual language that test-takers are exposed to in the test as well as the specific activities they are asked to do. These two should be directly sampled from the Target Language Use Domain to ensure content validity (Rose & Syrbe, 2018). With regards to EIL, the key issue for language content is the emergence of new varieties in the Outer Circle. New varieties differ from Inner Circle varieties in terms of pronunciation, vocabulary, spelling and also grammar (Schneider, 2012). Naturally, the relevance of being able to understand a particular variety depends on the testing context and the purpose for which results are to be used. Despite the current range of varieties, most tests only sample language from speakers of highly standardized native varieties of English from the Inner Circle (Hu, 2012). However, this type of constrained test content is insufficient to gather information about a test-taker's ability to understand speakers of any other varieties. As native speakers and their Englishes are the minority of English speakers today, this point is particular problematic and greatly affects the test's content validity. In assessment, the activities of a test need to link directly with what test-takers do with the language and who they communicate with, which is particularly interesting when assessing speaking skills (Elder & Davies, 2006). That is, test developers need to reconsider what the communicative goal of a specific task or exercise is, and consider who the target interlocutor should be.

## Testing EIL

Despite such obvious shortcomings of common testing practice, there is disagreement about the extent to which English language assessment needs to be, and already has been, adapted (Canagarajah, 2006). While standardized tests are often criticized for their lack of EIL incorporation, the test companies themselves make opposite claims. ETS, the administering body of the TOEFL, for example, recognizes the role of EIL and specifically states that the test meets the demands of testing English in a global world (Educational Testing Service, 2013). Even where there is agreement that testing has not responded to EIL for the most part, there are many different ideas and opinions about the extent to which testing practices need to change. That is why Elder and Davies (2006) speak of strong and weak approaches to testing EIL. A weak approach does not require a substantial change of testing practice but rather eliminates certain elements. For one, texts are vetted to exclude specific items and expressions which are particularly rooted in Inner Circle native speaker Englishes such as sports metaphors. Further, highly proficient non-native speakers can serve as interlocutors and only those errors that result in miscommunication are penalized. A strong approach, on the other hand, advocates a complete reconceptualization of the way we assess English. It is important to note that these are not two mutually exclusive approaches but rather should be seen as a continuum, in which the degree to which assessment needs to be adapted towards EIL and the specific changes that are necessary depend on the particular context in which the test is administered and for which the scores are used.

Contextualizing language assessment requires a thorough understanding of the Target Language Use Domain (Bachman & Palmer, 2010). In local contexts, specifically within the Outer Circle, language input can be chosen from specific, relevant geographical areas and the activities and skills should be based on the domains in which English is used in that particular Outer Circle context. As the Target Language Use domain is rather small and more clearly defined, creating responsive and relevant language assessment is a comparatively easy task from a test design point of view. However, it should be noted that the lack of prestige for certain varieties creates a great barrier to the design of such tests. The question of how assessment should address EIL becomes particularly difficult when looking at global contexts and standardized testing (Hu, 2012). This is because, unlike testing in local contexts, globally administered assessment tools tend to be used for a variety of Target Language Use Domains which makes it more challenging to sample relevant language and activities, and to define the proficiency construct. While many standardized tests are taken in order to study in Inner Circle countries, even in those contexts most students will encounter native and non-native speakers from diverse contexts, so that it seems far more relevant for generalized standardized tests to assess EIL.

Assessing EIL requires a complete reconceptualization of our under-standing of proficiency (Canagarajah, 2006), which should start by recon-sidering who we consider role models of successful English use. As an international language with far more non-native than native speakers, L2 speakers of the language seem an appropriate choice of role model, specifi-cally successful multilingual speakers of English (Kirkpatrick, 2006). By examining what these speakers do when they use English in global contexts, it becomes clear that a usage-based approach is most relevant to testing EIL (Hall, 2014). Instead of conformity with language norms, communicative effectiveness or performance should be the ultimate mea-sure of proficiency (Canagarajah, 2006). In other words, assessing gram-matical accuracy makes room for assessment of strategic competence (Elder & Davies, 2006). Ideally, such a usage-based approach would examine how test-takers use English in specific contexts whose character-istics should be congruent with EIL as Target Language Use Domain. This means a move away from testing discrete items and towards assess-ment of proficiency based on the extent to which they successfully carry out the specific task and reach a particular communicative goal, which is specifically important as different communication contexts require an application of diverse skills sets.

Designing such usage-based assessment has to start by identifying the characteristics of the particular language tasks in the relevant Target Language Use Domain. Those characteristics then determine the so-called test specifications, based on which actual test items are written. Writing test specifications requires determining the topics, task types and language skills (Bachman & Palmer, 2010). Topics for EIL assessments can vary from particular academic fields to everyday life. Task types, on the other hand, are very specific to EIL. In a usage-based approach, tasks should generally be performance tasks, in which students have to demon-strate their ability to use English to achieve a communicative goal. This is in contrast to the commonly used selected response items (e.g. multiple choice), which measure knowledge of a language. In contrast, perfor-mance tasks allow test-takers to show what they can do with the language and not what they know about it.

As assessing EIL is a matter of assessing someone's ability to use English to communicate with various L1 and L2 speakers, a variety of group tasks rather than individual tasks seems most appropriate. In such tasks, test-takers would be confronted with a particular situation in which they need to use English to achieve a specific desired outcome. Successful achievement of this outcome would then be considered proof of English ability. This could, for example, be negotiating a business deal or conversing in an academic context or other work-related areas, all depending on the topics chosen for the assessment and its intended purpose (Elder & Davies, 2006). In terms of standardized assessments, the key step to selecting meaningful and relevant performance tasks is to identify the types of interaction that EIL users carry out most frequently.

In terms of language skills, it seems clear that the construct of proficiency needs to be redefined to include strategic competence as well as intercultural competence. Specific communication strategies, such as paraphrasing, describing unknown items, confirming or checking comprehension, or asking for clarification, have been identified as particularly common in EIL communication and are thus essential to an EIL test construct. The next step is choosing the language content and input to expose the test-takers to. Regarding EIL, it is essential to include a variety of Englishes, including other L2 speakers to truly test learners' ability to understand their diverse future interlocutors. Though some might argue that it is unfair to test people based on a variety they have not been exposed to before, one has to keep in mind that in the 21st century English speaker are very likely to encounter unfamiliar varieties. It is therefore essential to test their ability to cope with these varieties in order to gain meaningful information about their proficiency in EIL.

## Recent Developments in Testing Practices

Though the debate around language assessment and EIL is still largely theoretical, some changes in testing practices can be identified. Overall, changes have taken place more rapidly in local contexts as there is a higher degree of teacher autonomy and there tends to be a clearer and more easily definable Target Language Use Domain. In fact, there are a number of university and high school programs that take an EIL approach to teaching and testing English (Hu, 2012).

When it comes to large-scale standardized tests, less change can be found. Though test designers and publishers have recognized the role and plurality of EIL, actual change is minimal to this date and tests such as the IELTS and TOEFL still reinforce the native speaker language norms (Hall, 2009, 2014). The IELTS has included more variation in the backgrounds of L1 speakers in their listening section alongside highly proficient L2 speakers, and employed writers from a more diverse range of countries. They have also decreased the importance of cultural knowledge in their test tasks, in order to prevent disadvantaging test-takers from different cultural backgrounds. In addition, the descriptors for the different skills level now use the term 'expert user' instead of native speaker. The TOEFL, too, has started including a small number of L2 speakers in their listening section, and also employed L2 English speakers as raters. Further, the rubrics for rating test-taker performance include some emphasis on intelligibility and effective use of grammar, rather than solely referring to accuracy-based criteria.

## What Does the Research Tell Us?

In this section, we present six empirical studies that explore notions of language testing in relation to EIL. Table 5.1 outlines each of these in terms of their overall design and topic focus.

Abeywickrama (2013) investigated the impact of using non-native speakers in listening tests for academic purposes. Using speakers from three countries (Brazil, Korea, Sri Lanka), she examined test-takers' comprehension of these accents and performance in the listening tests. She found that the accent of the speaker had no effect on test performance, even when test-takers were from the same L1 background. Despite this, the test-takers favor a native speaker variety for test use.

Chalhoub-Deville and Wigglesworth (2005) examined judgement of speaking proficiency by native speaker raters from different Inner Circle countries. These raters judged international test-takers' responses to the speaking section of the TOEFL. Rating variation was analyzed according to the raters' nationality, among other factors. Overall, differences according to country of origin were small, however, they found a tendency for American teachers to rate highly, and for UK teachers to give the lowest scores.

Davies *et al.* (2003) examined bias in international English tests against test-takers who had not been exposed to standard varieties of English. By comparing test-takers' scores on international (TOEFL and IELTS) as well as local tests in different contexts in Asia, they closely examined the norms applied in different proficiency tests. While their results are not very conclusive, they do argue for a stronger inclination of IELTS towards standard English norms, potentially putting test-takers who have not been exposed to those at a disadvantage.

**Table 5.1** Studies related to language testing and EIL

| Study | Design | Focus |
|---|---|---|
| Abeywickrama (2013) | Comparative study of rater behavior | Effect of non-native speaker accents on listening comprehension |
| Chalhoub-Deville and Wigglesworth (2005) | Comparative study of rater behavior | Different native speaker raters |
| Davies *et al.* (2003) | Comparative study of local and international tests | Acceptability of local norms |
| Hamp-Lyons, Davies (2008) | Content analysis | Native vs non-native speaker raters |
| Khan (2009) | Interview-based case study | TOEFL in higher education |
| Ockey *et al.* (2016) | Survey study | Accent strength and familiarity effect on comprehension |
| Uysal (2009) | Critical analysis | IELTS Writing section |

Hamp-Lyons and Davies' (2008) study explored the extent to which speakers of non-standard English varieties are at a disadvantage when taking international tests of English that are based on a standard variety. Exploring test-takers' written responses alongside raters from their own and American English-speaking backgrounds, they were unable to identify statistically significant group differences. In other words, they were unable to support the claim that those test-takers are at a disadvantage but also found no results to the contrary.

Khan (2009) investigated the use of TOEFL as entrance test for a university in Saudi Arabia. She conducted interviews with students and teachers regarding the reasons why TOEFL is used in such a way, and their opinions on TOEFL's potential to facilitate the teaching and learning of EIL. Students and teachers agree that TOEFL is used as entrance test in Saudi Arabia as it constitutes the norm for testing English proficiency in international tertiary education. They further state that TOEFL is used by the university to signal the adherence to international standards, and that its use is part of a larger process of Americanization. Students and teachers in this study showed awareness of the use of EIL mostly between non-native speakers in local contexts, and they recognize the discrepancy between this use and TOEFL's focus on American English. In fact, students express anxiety about and difficulties with American English, especially in the listening section of the test.

Ockey *et al.*'s (2016) study examines the extent to which test-takers listening performance is influenced by the strength of and their familiarity with the speaker's accent. This study was motivated by the ongoing debate about test fairness with regards to using unfamiliar accents, specifically those of L2 speakers. After purposefully sampling native speakers with different accent strength for the listening section, they analyzed TOEFL test-takers responses to the listening tasks and assessed their familiarity with these accents based on a survey. Indeed, they found that even light accents affect comprehension alongside familiarity.

Uysal's (2009) critical review of the IELTS writing test focuses on a number of elements, one of which is the degree to which it truly is an international test. Examining this in more details, she finds that the test only utilizes varieties from the Inner Circle. She further finds that the writing construct does not acknowledge variety in rhetoric conventions in different global and local contexts. However, she notes the inclusion of non-native speakers as raters is a step towards internationalization of the test.

## Implications for Teachers in Global Contexts

### Test washback

Test washback refers to the effect, positive or negative, that testing has on the classroom, including learner attitudes, teaching content and program design. Testing practices influence the choices that teachers and learners make, as they both focus on ways to better prepare for different tests the learners have to take, and help teachers evaluate the success of their teaching (Sadeghi & Ghaderi, 2018). This is especially visible when it comes to deciding what language content to teach and which materials to select. Naturally, this affects learners the most as these decisions have considerable effect on their learning progress and the desired learning outcomes.

When it comes to test washback and EIL, the main concern is with the way standardized tests uphold Inner Circle native speaker norms (McKinley & Thompson, 2018). As test content influences classroom content, it seems obvious that tests based on Inner Circle Englishes will lead to their overrepresentation in the English language classroom. By the same token, Inner Circle-based testing will hinder learners' acceptance of other varieties of English, as tests set the norms for acceptable and desired language. Changes in testing can thus positively influence the acceptance of local standards in global contexts (Hu, 2012).

Likewise, teachers wishing to best prepare their students to take tests that are based on such restricted norms are likely to focus exclusively on these norms in their teaching, elevating them even further. In other words, if testing practices do not change, it is very unlikely that teaching practices will ever change. Maintaining restricted L1 norms in testing significantly impedes the development of EIL teaching materials. It also acts as a barrier to EIL innovation which aims to foster changes in attitudes and the acceptance of local varieties. Thus, changes in testing practices are necessary not only to create more meaningful tests but also to allow teaching practices to move more easily towards EIL.

## Local assessment of EIL

While large-scale standardized tests take up a huge portion of the discussion around assessment, the majority of assessment takes place in local classrooms. These tests are mostly designed by teachers or the school and fitted for their students' specific learning goals and needs. This means that local assessment and test designers are in a position to make their assessments more meaningful and relevant with regards to EIL, where necessary (Hall, 2014). In the classroom, tests can have many functions, and the degree to which teachers and school are able to design their tests around EIL depends on the test purpose. A common type of assessment, achievement tests, for example, should be closely connected to the materials, skills and knowledge taught in the classroom. If English was not taught as an international language, it would not be fair and valid to test it as such as testing and teaching are closely intertwined. Test washback shows the effect testing has on teaching, but this example shows that testing principles are also unlikely to change without considerable changes in teaching practices. The most predominant type of test that learners encounter in the classroom is an English proficiency test and here, changes towards EIL are most needed.

When it comes to designing relevant EIL tests for the classroom, the two major questions teachers need to ask are 'who are my students going to use English with?' and 'in what situations are they going to use English?'. In other words, the focus is on designing meaningful tests for that specific purpose (Hu, 2012). From a quick literature review on assessment and EIL, it becomes apparent that there are a large number of ideas and proposals, creating a difficult field to navigate especially for TESOL professionals with limited time, resources and prior knowledge. Though these ideas and proposals are important in their own right, not all of them are immediately relevant to the local English language classroom. Presumably, the goal of most local classrooms is for learners to develop a reasonable level of English proficiency that allows them to successfully manage common English language encounters they will have in the future, such as for travel or work-related communication. To this end, local test designers need to consider their learners' future interlocutors as well their contexts of language use.

The question of future interlocutors, or who learners are going to use English with outside the classroom, is especially important for EIL, because today the heterogeneity of the English-speaking community is unparalleled. Not only does this mean English users will encounter diverse interlocutors, it also means that one cannot assume the importance of the native speaker (or particular non-native speakers) for all learners. As a result, teachers wishing to create relevant assessments need to carefully consider the potential future interlocutors of their learners as this determines the accents and varieties they have to understand. Naturally, this reality should be represented in the accents and varieties incorporated in assessment. Students learning English in Europe, for example, are most likely to use the language with other European L2 speakers, whereas Asian learners may be more likely to encounter other Asian speakers of English. By the same token, African learners are likely to use English with L1 and L2 speakers from their own and other African countries. Naturally, an English proficiency test in each context should be constructed with these particular future interlocutors in mind and thus include relevant speakers and varieties.

Contexts of language use refers to specific communicative interactions. Commonly, many English assessments are pen and paper based, often focusing on reading skills using multiple choice questions. However, this format is only relevant for a small number of learners. As a teacher, it is paramount to consider the kinds of activities students will carry out through English in the real world in the 21st century, and their success in these activities often depends on communicative competence, rather than accuracy. This means teachers need to step out of their comfort zone when it comes to creating tests, as EIL assessment should be based on communicative activities, not pen and paper tests of linguistic knowledge. Doing so, tests can assess learners' abilities to use English (creatively) to achieve a communicative goal. Most activities used in the context of communicative language teaching can be utilized as assessment tools. For lower level learners, activities might be used where partners have to overcome content gaps by conversing with each other to share knowledge (i.e. information gap activities). More advanced learners can be assessed within the context of group activities such as role-playing specific scenarios, in which the successful completion depends on the resolution of a task or issue.

## Post-reading Activities

### Reflect

Do you agree that current assessment practices are insufficient in evaluating English proficiency in the 21st century?

### Discuss

In small groups, discuss the following questions:

(1) This chapter has discussed a number of potential changes to current assessment practices. Which do you think are most important and why?
(2) Some argue that it is sufficient for Anglophone university entrance tests to be based on the native speaker model. Do you agree or disagree?
(3) Considering the diversity of EIL as a Target Language Use Domain, do you think it is feasible and possible to have standardized general proficiency tests? What is the alternative?

### Apply

Imagine you have been asked to design an English speaking proficiency test for people who need to use English for international business communication. Write the test specifications for three different activities. Consider:

- the topics
- task types
- language skills
- language to be sampled

## Resources for Further Reading

Hu, G. (2012) Assessing English as an international language. In L. Alsagoff, S.L. McKay, G. Hu and W.A. Renandya (eds) *Principles and Practices for Teaching English as an International Language* (pp. 123–144). New York: Routledge.

The usefulness of this chapter is in its comprehensiveness. The author offers a thorough review of established practices with regards to EIL, but also summarizes recent changes and changes demanded in the relevant literature. Most importantly, however, he goes one step further and proposes five principles for meaningful EIL assessment. The chapter is thus a key reading for TESOL professionals wanting to create EIL assessments as well as those wanting to analyze and review existing assessments. In his summary, he makes the distinction between a weak and strong approach to EIL assessment, which differs in the extent to which the actual test construct has been changed. The key tenets of his principles are that multiple native as well as non-native varieties should be used and that linguistic norms should only be set with regards to the specific context of use. Further, he proposes that intercultural competence should be incorporated into the test construct.

McKay, S.L. and Brown, J.D. (2016) *Teaching and Assessing EIL in Local Contexts Around the World.* Routledge.

This book is written for TESOL professionals and provides a useful resource for local teachers wishing to create more EIL-oriented assessment. As the title suggests, this book addresses teaching and assessment alike and highlights their interrelated relationship, both guided by the idea that goals and standards are defined within the local teaching context. While the authors' claim of a Global English standard may be debatable, their intelligibility principle is highly relevant in the context of EIL. In this they argue that the main goal of teaching and thus object of assessment should be learners' ability to be understandable. These principles are laid out in Chapter 3, which serves as a basis to their ideas about assessing grammar (Chapter 4), oracy (Chapter 5) and literacy (Chapter 6). Though Chapter 5 mainly consists of a literature review, Chapter 6 outlines a rubric for assessing EIL that can serve as valuable point of reference for teachers in any local context.

Fulcher, G. and Davidson, F. (2006) *Language Testing and Assessment: An advanced Resource Book.* London: Routledge.

This book can be used as a practical step-by-step manual for designing language tests and assessments in all contexts. Though it does not address EIL in any way, it provides useful guidance for those who wish to create EIL-oriented assessments. Each unit addresses a specific step in the design and implementation of language tests based on theoretical input but always accompanied by practical application activities. The section on classroom assessment is particularly useful to TESOL practitioners. For those who want to further explore particular areas of language assessment, the book also offers additional readings by experts in the field and additional activities and suggestions for future research in part C.

# Part 3

# Teachers and Learners of a Global Language

# 6 Learners' Attitudes and EIL-oriented Activities

## Pre-reading Activities

*Think*

Recall and reflect on any experiences during which you used English to communicate with people from different lingua-cultural backgrounds. Think about these experiences and how they affected your ideas about English and its usage.

*Discuss*

In small groups, discuss the following:

(1) What are language attitudes? Think of a few examples of language attitudes. Why do you think language attitudes are important in terms of EIL?
(2) How can you measure language attitudes? Think of as many ways as possible of measuring language attitudes and evaluate each approach indicating its strengths and weaknesses.

## Introduction

The ratio of people who speak English as a second/foreign language (non-native speakers) to those who speak English as a native/first language (native speakers) is in a period of rapid growth. Crystal (2018) estimates that the total number of English speakers in the world approached 2.3 billion in 2017. Graddol (2006) has predicted that by the year 2050 the number of English speakers shall have surpassed 4 billion, of which a little more than 0.5 billion will be defined as native speakers. Accompanying the global spread and diversification of English, the power and status of native speakers have been eclipsed by the rapid expansion of English language learning policies in parts of the world where English is spoken as a second/foreign language (Crystal, 2018; Graddol, 1999, 2006).

In TESOL, scrutiny has increased over the native speaker reference model (discussed in Chapter 3) from different facets that includes, but is not limited to, learners' attitudes. This chapter describes English learners' attitudes, focusing on the extent to which English language learners are aware of and understand the implications of these phenomena, and their attitudes towards English varieties and speakers of these varieties. The chapter introduces the notion of language attitudes. In order to examine the language attitudes, three different approaches are presented. Using these approaches, empirical studies that investigated current learners' attitudes also are described. Lastly, based on the findings of the empirical studies conducted on language attitudes of current English language learners, the emerging research studies of the influence of EIL-oriented activities on learners' language attitudes are introduced.

## Key Concept

Language attitudes is a crucial concept in order to investigate the influence of the current dispersion of English on English language learners.

## Language attitudes

Baker (1992) and Cargile *et al.* (1994) emphasise that the investigation of attitudes toward language is especially important, since it provides a macro-sociological indicator that reviews current community thoughts, beliefs, preferences and desires. Attitude surveys provide social indicators of changing beliefs and inform policy implementation, as a favourable attitude towards the subject of language is crucial for the successful implementation of foreign language policy and practice (Baker, 1992). As such, a great deal of language attitude studies related to language education have been conducted (Baker, 1992; Garrett, 2010). Furthermore, second language and foreign language acquisition research regarding social psychological approaches to motivation (e.g. Dörnyei, 2005; Dörnyei & Ryan, 2015; Gardner, 1985, 2010; Gardner & Lambert, 1959, 1972) have consistently shown language attitude as playing an important role in the attainment of a second language/foreign language. That is, positive attitudes toward the language, its speakers and its target community are observed as contributing to a learner's motivation, which has an impact on successful second-language development. In contrast, negative attitudes toward the language especially a learner's own variety may have a negative impact on their language attainment.

Although attitudes are considered a critical concept in many fields such as sociolinguistics and social psychology, it is not easily defined (Edwards, 1982; Garrett, 2010). Nevertheless, Garrett (2010) indicates that Sarnoff's (1970) definition of attitudes is widely cited by researchers; that is, 'a disposition to react favourably or unfavourably to a class of objects' (1970: 279). Gardner (1985) describes language attitude as the language learners' views of the target language, target language speakers and sociocultural and pragmatic benefits related to the target language. While Gardner's (1985) construct works for most foreign languages, the growth of EIL challenges many of the attitude studies' foundations.

Since the attitudinal objects, languages, become hybrid as well as diverse and unstable by being used so broadly within and across such diverse linguistic communities, we must increasingly question: to which form of the target language do we refer?; who are the target language speakers?; and to which sociocultural aspects tied to the language do we infer?

## Research Techniques for Language-Attitude Research

Since the early 1960s, language-attitude research has been increasing dramatically, making use of investigative techniques that include matched and verbal-guise techniques, questionnaires and interviews, and societal treatments (Cargile & Bradac, 2001). Among those research techniques, the verbal-guise technique has dominated the social scientific approach to the study of language attitudes (Cargile *et al.*, 1994; Cargile & Bradac, 2001; Jenkins, 2007).

### Matched and verbal-guise techniques

The matched-guise technique used in the study of language attitudes relies on measures that require participants to evaluate audiotaped speakers without any social group labels attached. The various speech samples are obtained by one speaker who is able to switch between the language varieties in order to eliminate potential confounding variables, such as vocal qualities. The evaluations can cover a range of items. For example, listeners may be asked to indicate whether they think the speaker is friendly or intelligent. Because other linguistic factors supposedly are controlled, speaker evaluations are believed to reflect the listeners' underlying attitudes toward the target language variety. However, this paradigm has been criticised, since there are problems with the authenticity of the language varieties that are produced by one speaker and with the lack of contextualisation for each presented variety (Garrett, 2010). Due to the limitation of the authenticity, a modified version has been developed: the verbal-guise technique. The verbal-guise technique involves using speech samples that are produced by authentic speakers of each variety instead of having one speaker produce all varieties.

### Questionnaires and interviews

Questionnaires and interviews involve asking people directly what their attitudes are concerning various language behaviours through the use of interviews and questionnaires, the advantage of which is that information about specific attitudes can be obtained. Since the approach asks directly about language attitudes, it is subject to reflection and social desirability biases which can be reduced in the verbal-guise techniques by distracting respondents from the real intent of the research questions (Cargile *et al.*, 1994; Garrett, 2010). There has been an increase number of studies that employed folk-linguistic approaches developed by Preston and his colleagues (e.g. Niedzielski & Preston, 2000; Preston, 1989). The studies have focused on folk perceptions of English varieties (perceptual dialectology), using various kinds of map tasks (e.g. McKenzie, 2008a, 2008b, 2010).

## Societal treatments

Societal treatments have been conducted on the treatment of language in the public domain according to language varieties through content analysis. Techniques here include observational and ethnographic studies and analyses of government and educational language policies as well as literature and business documents and media output. The relatively minor mention in the attitudes literature of this approach may be attributed to the fact that considerable attitudinal data are in ethnographic studies and they have not been incorporated into mainstream attitudinal reviews (Garrett, 2007). Many attitude researchers view this approach as a preliminary study for more sociolinguistic and psychological studies (Galloway & Rose, 2015; Garrett, 2010). An example of a study that used a societal treatment approach was conducted by Haarmann (1986) who investigated the characteristics of stereotypes by focusing on the use of English in television advertising in Japan. A total of 2919 Japanese television commercials were examined through content analysis. The findings revealed that English was used for positive features, such as high prestige, almost exclusively for commercial purposes, making the images of the products advertised more appealing to customers. The study concluded that the frequent use of English due to its prestige functions in the mass media appeared to have been affected by the attitudes of Japanese toward foreign cultures in general.

## Studies About English Language Learners' Attitudes Toward English Varieties

As Seidlhofer (2004) and Jenkins (2007) observed, although there have been several studies identifying the importance of English as a lingua franca, there still are relatively few empirical studies focusing on attitudes toward it, especially in the Expanding Circle contexts. In the extant studies, the verbal-guise technique was mainly used in Japanese contexts (e.g. Cargile *et al.*, 2006; Chiba *et al.*, 1995; Fraser, 2006; Matsuura *et al.*, 1994;

McKenzie, 2008a, 2008b, 2010; McKenzie & Gilmore, 2017; Sasayama, 2013), Korean contexts (e.g. Yook & Lindeman, 2013), Austrian contexts (e.g. Dalton-Puffer *et al.*, 1997) and Danish contexts (e.g. Ladegaard & Sachdev, 2006). The questionnaires and interviews were used in Japanese contexts (e.g. Evans & Imai, 2011; Galloway, 2011, 2013, 2017a; Matsuda, 2003b), Chinese contexts (e.g. He & Li, 2009; He & Zhang, 2010; Hu & Lindeman, 2009; Kirkpatrick & Xu, 2002; Kuo, 2006; Wang, 2013, 2015; Wang & Jenkins, 2016), Brazilian contexts (e.g. Friedrich, 2000), German contexts (e.g. Grau, 2005) and multiple contexts (e.g. Timmis, 2002; Tokumoto & Shibata, 2011). A few examples of these studies from each approach are presented in the following narrative.

## Examples of studies about learners' attitudes toward English varieties mainly using a verbal-guise technique

Chiba *et al.*'s study (1995) addressed the issue that most studies that employed a verbal-guise technique focused on the attitudes of English language learners toward native English speaker's speech. Due to the lack of language attitude research focusing on non-native English speaker varieties, the researchers conducted a study using a verbal-guise technique and questionnaire to investigate attitudes of 169 Japanese university students majoring in English and international business toward English accents: British, American, Japanese, Hong Kongese, Malaysian and Sri Lankan. The participants perceived two native accents, American and British, more positively than the non-native accents that included Japanese, Hong Kongese, Malaysian and Sri Lankan. The participants tended to recognise native accents more readily than non-native accents although they had difficulty identifying whether the native accents were American or British. The study suggested that their preference towards native accents seemed due to familiarity although their familiarity with their own variety did not contribute to their approval of English spoken by Japanese native speakers. The study results supported speculation that the Japanese students gained an impression that American/British English was the ideal, since American or British English usually was used as a role model in classrooms. Furthermore, in the English as a foreign language context, they lacked exposure to other varieties of English.

The questionnaire about the extent to which students agreed with general ideas about foreign languages and language learning, consisted of 21 items that included 'I study English because it is required for graduation' and 'I am interested in the English of Singapore and India.' A statistical analysis (principal component analysis) was conducted and yielded seven factors. The relationship between these factors and the participants' ratings were examined. The correlation analysis confirmed that the students who had a strong interest in American or British people, culture and language showed more negative attitudes toward the non-native accents. One of the major limitations of this study was that it included university students whose majors were English or international business only. Although the participants' characteristic is interesting because they were more likely to use English with native and non-native speakers in the future, they might not have been typical of Japanese university students.

More recently, McKenzie and Gilmore (2017) examined 158 Japanese university students' attitudes toward seven English accents: Southern American, Standard Mid-West American, Scottish Standard, Japanese, Thai, Chinese and Indian by using a verbal-guise technique and an open-ended question asking the participants to describe speakers of non-native English and non-native English speech. All the speakers in the verbal-guise studies were female. Prototypical speech samples were chosen. The findings showed that, similar to Chiba et al.'s (1995) study, the participants rated American and British English varieties higher than Asian English varieties with a particular preference for Standard and non-Standard American English regarding prestige and correctness of the speech. These attitudes also were confirmed by the qualitative study: Half of the participants indicated that non-native English speech was incorrect and lacked intelligibility. The study attributed the results to greater levels of exposure among Japanese students to American English at all levels of the Japanese educational system. Yet, Standard British English, to which the participants might have been exposed, was not included in the study, which might have contributed to the participants' positive attitudes toward British English.

In a European English as a lingua franca context, Ladegaard and Sachdev (2006) examined attitudes of 96 Danish high-school and university students toward five English accents: Standard American, General Australian, Standard British, Scottish Standard and Cockney. The verbal-guise experiment was controlled carefully in terms of speakers and content. A questionnaire also was used to measure the participants' attitudes toward American and British language and culture. The data indicated that the participants perceived the Standard British speaker as favourable in terms of status and the most appealing role model of pronunciation despite their strong preference towards American culture. This may have been due to their exposure to Standard British English as a model for pronunciation in Danish English language classrooms. It is worth noting that the low ratings on the measures might have been attributable to the young females who made up the majority of participants rating older male foreign speakers as indicated in the study; that is, the participants'/speakers' gender might have been a potential confounding variable.

## Examples of studies about learners' attitudes toward English varieties using a questionnaire and interview

Timmis (2002) conducted a questionnaire survey and 15 interviews in order to examine attitudes toward native-speaker norms of 400 students from various countries. The study indicated that the majority of the students showed a strong preference towards native English in terms of pronunciation and grammar usage. One of the most apparent reasons for their attitudes mentioned in the interviews was using native-speaker pronunciation and grammar as benchmarks of achievement.

Matsuda (2003b) conducted a qualitative study to investigate Japanese private high school students' attitudes toward English varieties by using a questionnaire with 34 students, conducting interviews with 10 students and observing English classes for 36 hours. All data were combined and analysed using thematic analysis. The findings revealed that the students perceived English as a symbol of internationalisation and an important tool for international communication and showed an interest in international understanding and communication. Nevertheless, they viewed English speakers as those from America and Britain and used these English varieties as a yardstick as indicated in Timmis's (2002) study. A lack of awareness about other English varieties was also evident. Regarding their own variety of English, they perceived it as incorrect and lacking intelligibility.

Evans and Imai (2011) also investigated 98 Japanese university students' attitudes toward English varieties. They were asked to answer two open-ended questions: 'name countries around the world where you know English is spoken as a native language' and 'what kind of impression do you get when you hear these varieties?' The participants indicated that America, Britain, Canada and Australia were English-speaking countries. Canadian and Australian English often were evaluated in relation to American and British English indicating that the participants were less familiar with Canadian and Australian varieties. American English was perceived more positively with regard to status comprised of features, such as 'correct' and 'standard.' British English was perceived as more socially appealing and consisted of social attractiveness aspects, such as 'beautiful', 'courteous,' and 'gentle.' The findings might have been because of the close relationship between Japan and America in politics and economy and exposure to American English in the English language classrooms in Japan.

More recently, Wang and Jenkins (2016) distributed a questionnaire to 502 Chinese university students and 267 professionals in China working for foreign trade companies, international marketing departments in Chinese enterprises, international liaison offices of some China-based organisations and institutions, and Chinese-foreign joint ventures. Twelve English major and 12 non-English major students from a Chinese university and 11 Chinese professionals were recruited for interview. Some professionals had used and expected to use English to communicate with non-native English speakers who did not share a first language, and very few students showed a lack of awareness for English as a lingua franca. The interview data revealed that, although the assumption about the native-speaker norm-reference model was found, those who encountered English as a lingua franca tended to challenge this assumption and to think that native-speaker norms were not necessary to communicate effectively. The study concluded that the participants' English as a lingua franca experience played an important role in their attitudes toward native-speaker English, and it allowed the participants to be more open to different varieties of English. Thus, the increase of English as a lingua franca experience in language classrooms proved crucial to develop learners' understanding of English as a lingua franca and foster positive attitudes toward diverse English varieties.

## Implications of the research related to learners' attitudes toward English varieties

Caution should be exercised regarding the interpretations of the obtained results from most studies. First, these studies are very narrow in scope, as only phonological features tend to be researched and analysed in the studies, thus ignoring other dimensions of variation. Second, studies which use the verbal-guise techniques and extant questionnaires inform whether learners prefer one narrowly defined dialect over another narrowly defined dialect with no ability to measure attitudes beyond these dialectal boundaries. Third, the current research techniques are out of touch with the current sociolinguistic reality of how English is used in the 21st century (Rose & Galloway, 2019). Pennycook (2010) argues that the nationalist core of the World Englishes framework, with its identification of distinct varieties of English based on geographic boundaries, is severely outdated in its lack of ability to capture fluid uses of English. Likewise, the verbal-guise technique, with its narrow focus on specific and constrained versions of English, does little to represent attitudes related to the fluid ways in which English is used in global contexts. Pennycook (2010) further argues that linguists need to move beyond state-bound representations and explore globalised linguascapes in order to 'avoid the national circles and boxes that have constrained World Englishes and, indeed, linguists more generally' (2010: 685). Finally, most studies tend to be cross-sectional with limitations in sampling assigned as a specific case to a particular context. Thus, the development of research tools reflecting the sociolinguistic reality is necessary (see Chapter 10). Also, more systematic large-scale longitudinal research is recommended to capture not only learners' current language attitudes but also their attitude change (Galloway, 2017; Sung, 2015). More detailed descriptions of the sample of the research is necessary to increase the applicability of the findings.

Despite the limitations in the current approaches to examine language attitudes, most studies using a verbal-guise technique, and questionnaires and interviews have revealed a strong preference towards the native speaker English varieties from the Inner Circle. The native speaker varieties were also seen as benchmarks against which other varieties can be measured and evaluated. Although current EIL can no longer be seen as a discrete entity with linguistic stability, shared expectations and identifiable social groupings, learners continue to hold norm-bound orientations, such as accepting the superiority of native-speaker English and perceiving other varieties of English negatively. Learners were less familiar with non-native speaker varieties. These attitudes are more likely to be affected by how the learners are exposed to learning language in the classroom. More precisely, a lack of EIL awareness due to exclusive exposure to native-speaker English in the classroom appear to be associated with the learners' less positive attitudes toward non-native speaker varieties. Thus, in order to increase English as a lingua franca exposure and awareness, incorporating EIL-oriented activities into classrooms is a key. An increasing number of studies in the field have called for the implementation of such activities in the classrooms (e.g. Bowles & Cogo, 2015; Matsuda, 2012).

## What Does the Research Tell Us?

In response to the need for incorporating EIL-oriented activities into classroom practices as described in this chapter, there have been a growing number of studies that implemented EIL-oriented activities and critically examined the influence of the course on learners' attitudes. Furthermore, given the limited time which can be spent on EIL elements in general English language courses and given the environments (e.g. English as a foreign language contexts) where the exposure to EIL communication is limited, some studies explored the possibility of implementing EIL activities outside the classroom and its impact on learners' attitudes. Table 6.1 presents the EIL-oriented activities in the classroom and the out-of-class EIL-oriented activities are included in Table 6.2.

Galloway and Rose (2018) implemented presentation tasks, and students were asked to choose, study and prepare a 10-minute presentation about a regional variety of English and/or the use of English as a lingua franca in a specific context by using the library and self-access centre, and search on the internet for information. They perceived the activity positively and also thought that it helped them to understand the features of a variety of EIL-oriented activities and to challenge their preconceived notions of the varieties.

As introduced in Chapter 2, Rose and Galloway (2017) instructed students to debate as a part of the Speak Good English Movement in Singapore (SGEM). They received some guidance in order to conduct some research on the SGEM through different sources. Comments from the reflection papers revealed that students thought that the debate helped them to raise awareness and provided an opportunity to explore English use in Singapore. The students' reflections revealed that 76.5% were against the SGEM.

**Table 6.1** Examples of EIL-oriented activities in the classroom and its influence on learners' attitudes

| Researchers | Participants | Activities (Duration) | Main attitudinal data |
|---|---|---|---|
| Galloway and Rose (2018) | University English as a foreign language (EFL) learners (N = 108, averaging 27 students per class, Level = Intermediate) | Presentation tasks in the classroom (two weeks) | Hand-written reflections |
| Rose and Galloway (2017) | University EFL learners (N = 108, averaging 27 students per class, Level = Intermediate) | A debate on the Speak Good English Movement (SGEM) in Singapore in the classroom (one week) | Hand-written reflections |
| Grazzi (2015); Grazzi and Maranzana (2016) | High school EFL learners in Italy (N = 10, Level = Intermediate), University learners of Italian (N = 10, Level = Intermediate) | Telecollaboration exchanges in the classroom (nine weeks, written computer-mediated communication) | Online survey |

**Table 6.2** Examples of EIL-oriented activities outside the classroom and their influence on learners' attitudes

| Researchers | Participants | Activities (Duration) | Main attitudinal data |
|---|---|---|---|
| Galloway and Rose (2014) | University EFL learners (N = 108; averaging 27 students per class, Level = Intermediate) | Listening journals outside the classroom (thirteen weeks) | Journal entry reflections, interviews |
| Sung (2018) | University English as a second language learners (N = 18, Level = upper-intermediate to advanced) | English communication with exchange and/ or international students (or students from a different lingua-cultural background) outside the classroom (thirteen weeks) | Learner log, written reflections |
| Hoffstaedter and Kohn (2015); Kohn and Hoffstaedter (2015) | Secondary school EFL from European countries (Germany, N = 7, Spain, N = 7, Netherlands, N = 2, France, N = 2, Turkey, N = 2, Bulgaria, N = 3, Portugal, N = 1, Level = Mixed) | Telecollaboration exchanges from the pupils' home (20 mins–70 mins, 3D virtual worlds in OpenSim, video communication in BigBlueButton and Skype as well as text chat in Moodle.) | Performance observations, feedback comments |

The study also pointed out that the activity enabled students to reflect not only on the Singaporean case study but also on their stereotypes and beliefs about standard language ideology.

Grazzi (2015) and Grazzi and Maranzana (2016) conducted a telecollaboration activity. The two groups of Italian and American students were randomly paired into 10 dyads. They were asked to choose among the various topics and to produce and upload a text regarding the topics onto a webpage. They were allowed to add audio-visual materials (e.g. pictures and videos) and links to other websites (e.g. YouTube and Wikipedia) to share additional information. They engaged in asynchronous written conversations by using their foreign languages. The Italian students used English as a lingua franca in the activity that functioned as a vehicular language among the speakers who did not share a first language. In questionnaires the Italian students indicated that they thought that they were able to improve their English to some extent and showed positive attitudes toward the various aspects of the activity such as the use of digital multimedia facilities, the social contacts, and the exchange of ideas and personal views from another country. Nevertheless, some students did not think that the activity contributed to their improvement of language and cultural knowledge. Some students suggested the use of synchronous videoconferencing in addition to the asynchronous text-based communication.

Galloway and Rose (2014) instructed students to keep listening journals, and they asked students to listen to speakers with different backgrounds or listen to English as a lingua franca interactions for about ten minutes once a week. The students were able to choose from various sources that included, but were not limited to, CDs, online corpora and online media. They also were asked to keep records on the information, such as the speakers' nationality, reasons for their choices, and reflective comments on each listening session. Although students were exposed to different English varieties, the activity was less likely to help students reflect on their English as a lingua franca interactions. In some cases, the journal activity reinforced existing stereotypes about native speaker English and non-native speaker English. However, the interviews with students at the end of the Global Englishes-oriented course showed a change in opinions.

Sung (2018), as discussed in Chapter 2, employed out-of-class activities; students were asked to engage in English communication with students from different lingua-cultural backgrounds outside the classroom on campus for 10 to 20 minutes each week during the term. Students also were asked to take notes during the weekly activities throughout the term and to write two reflection papers on their communication experiences. Based on the self-reports of the activities, the students have been noted to become more aware of the role of English as a global language that includes appreciation of the diversity of English, questioning of the relevance of native-speaker norms, recognition of the importance of communicative strategies, and awareness of the value of multilingual resources. At the completion of the study, the students reported that the activities prepared them for English as a lingua franca communication in the future.

Hoffstaedter and Kohn (2015) and Kohn and Hoffstaedter (2015) explored how telecollaboration tools and environments could be used to improve foreign language learning and teaching. The tools included synchronous spoken and written communication via videoconferencing, 3D virtual worlds and chat. Students were less worried about making mistakes and made an effort to communicate with each other. They often addressed personal topics instead of task-related topics showing that they turned the activities into a real-life experience.

## Implications for Teachers in Global Contexts

The classroom activities described above have contributed to raising learners' awareness of English as a global language. Nevertheless, as addressed in Galloway and Rose's (2014) and Rose and Galloway's (2017) studies, simply exposing learners to different English varieties may not lead learners to challenge the current norms. They tended to see the varieties through the lens of their own existing perceptions. Since the language attitude studies showed that learners still showed a strong preference towards native English, it would be essential for learners to engage meaningfully with the varieties that include encouraging them to think about the varieties in use and why they are used in a certain way within a specific context. Not only first-hand EIL communication experiences but also the presentation and debate activities were successful in giving learners such opportunities, and these activities allowed learners to reflect deeply and critically on their communication experiences or attitudes toward English in global contexts. As Sung (2018) pointed out, all these types of activities were more likely to be complementary. Activities that increase exposure to different English varieties and EIL interactions can be accompanied by teaching about EIL explicitly in the classroom addressing the sociolinguistic reality and issues associated with EIL. Further investigations of suitable combinations of these different types of activities are recommended in order to maximise their pedagogical potential.

Important to note is that the levels of learners' proficiencies in the activities above tend to be high. Thus, more studies implementing EIL-oriented activities with lower proficiency learners and their impact on learners' attitudes are recommended. For lower proficiency learners, more support is necessary (Galloway & Rose, 2018), such as providing them with some presentation and debate templates in English and allowing them to explore the role of English in global contexts not only by using English but also by using their native/first language. Additionally, prior to active engagement in authentic EIL communication, teachers are able to give learners opportunities to practice how to communicate meaningfully in global contexts through role-plays in EIL interactions.

The learners' direct exposure to and active engagement in authentic and meaningful EIL communication scenarios of their choice could allow learners to experience EIL in action and challenge traditional notions of 'variety' and geographically defined 'communities'. In cases where learners' encounters with speakers with different lingua-cultural backgrounds are limited, teachers could use digital media that enables learners to engage in real-life EIL interactions with people from anywhere in the world outside and beyond the traditional classroom, such as telecollaboration with the use of videoconferencing, Skype and chat (e.g. Kohn, 2015). These provide various options for autonomous, authenticated and collaborative language learning. The multimedia nature of the web allows combining texts, images, sound and video to facilitate communication. The activities above show that digital media may be used as valuable learning tools to experience EIL in real life. The selection of telecollaboration tools involves availability, communication support and personal preferences. Thus, the flexible use of available telecollaboration facilities would be desirable, and more investigations are needed regarding how to select and make use of the various tools in order to increase opportunities for EIL interactions.

## Post-reading Activities

### Reflect

This chapter suggests that current learners' attitudes towards English are less likely to reflect sociolinguistic reality. How about current learners in your context? What attitudes do they have towards English in your context and why?

### Discuss

(1) In small groups, each choose one different attitude study that was not described in detail in this chapter and read the study carefully. Summarise it and address its challenges and limitations. Discuss these and how you could do it differently in order to investigate attitudes more precisely.

(2) In small groups each choose one EIL oriented activity from Table 6.1 or Table 6.2 and read the study carefully. Summarise it and address its challenges and limitations. Discuss these and indicate how you could do it differently, in order to change the participants' language attitudes more effectively.

(3) As indicated in this chapter, more studies implementing EIL-oriented activities with lower proficiency learners and their impact on learners' attitudes are recommended. In small groups, discuss how you can adapt the activities chosen in Discussion Two for low-proficiency learners?

## *Apply*

(1) In small groups, each choose one specific context and create a plan for language attitude research. You can use the table below. Then, share the completed plan with other groups.

| Challenges and limitations of previous related language attitude studies | Participants and setting | Research techniques | Expected results |
|---|---|---|---|
| | ... learners in ....<br>(N = ..., Level = ...) | | |

(2) In small groups, each choose one specific context and design an EIL-oriented activity feasible and suitable in the context. You can use the table below. Then, share the completed activities with other groups.

| Participants and setting | Activity aims | Activities | Main attitudinal data |
|---|---|---|---|
| ... learners in ....<br>(N = ..., Level = ...) | | | |

## Resources for Further Reading

Galloway, N. (2017) *Global Englishes and Change in English Language Teaching.* Abingdon: Routledge.

This book provides an overview of the field of Global Englishes that includes relevant concepts, such as World Englishes, English as a lingua franca, English as an international language and Translanguaging and implications of work in these fields in English language teaching. The issues, such as the dominance of native speakers and standard language ideology are critically examined. It also covers various studies of English language attitudes towards English varieties, English in English language teaching, English language teachers and the role of Global Englishes. Additionally, an empirical study of language attitudes in a Japanese university context conducted by the author (Galloway, 2017a) is presented. The study builds on a previous study (Galloway, 2013) and is part of a larger study (Galloway, 2011). Some practical suggestions such as how Global Englishes components can be incorporated into different courses in various contexts also are included.

Garrett, P. (2010) *Attitudes to Language: Key Topics in Sociolinguistics*. Cambridge: Cambridge University Press.

The book covers most important topics related to attitudes towards language and offers comprehensive analyses of attitudes from various aspects at all its levels, such as words, grammar, accent as well as attitudes toward 'whole' languages, codeswitching and standard language ideology. It includes a review of the main theoretical issues pertaining to attitudes, such as facets and manifestations of attitudes, attitude structure and stability and durability of attitudes. The book includes descriptions of three main approaches in attitudinal studies addressing the relative advantages and disadvantages through the exploration of empirical studies. It addresses the methodological issues of the empirical studies and the external factors potentially having an impact on language attitudes. Issues concerning language attitudes in the four professional fields of law, health, education and employment also are discussed. The book includes a large-scale study undertaken in Wales of language attitudes demonstrating how methods can complement each other, and how a project can benefit from each of these methods.

# 7 Teachers of a Global Language

## Pre-reading Activities

### Think

Bring in an artefact (e.g. photographs) that best represents your belief of what an English language teacher is. Ideally, the item you bring should contain no word or description. Place it on the table with a blank sheet of paper on the side, then walk around the room to look at each of your classmates' object. Write down on the piece of paper your own interpretation of the object. After everyone has finished, go back to your seat and read your classmates' interpretations of your artefact. Are they in line with your own interpretation? What are areas of similarity? Where do they diverge?

### Discuss

(1) To what extent do you think our prior language learning experience contributes to what we do in a language classroom as a teacher?
(2) What are your key beliefs about the English language and how people learn? Can you identify some of your past experiences that might influence those beliefs?
(3) What are some factors (personal or contextual) that you think might promote or hinder your effectiveness as a teacher of English as a global language?

## Introduction

As the use of English expands globally, simultaneously bringing speakers of recognised English varieties from every conceivable corner of the world into closer contact with one another, the goal of promoting mutual comprehensibility among interlocutors, especially learners of English, has become increasingly apropos. This challenging task inevitably lies in the hands of none other than the teachers. Whether and how such a goal can be fully realised impinges so much on the sense and use teachers make of both theoretical as well as pedagogical suggestions offered by scholars in the interrelated fields within the Global Englishes paradigm. In other words, for any initiative to take root and sustain, it is crucial that 'what language teachers think, know and believe and of its relationship to teachers' classroom practices' (Borg, 2015: 1) are taken into account.

This chapter examines what it means for L2 English language teachers to be teaching English in an era where it claims the status of a global language. Using the language teacher cognition framework as theoretical lens, it seeks to shed light on the teachers' cognitions and practices with regard to the shift in goals of English as a Second Language (ESL) and English as a Foreign language (EFL) education away from the native-like proficiency model toward equipping the learners with intercultural awareness and competences. It begins by explaining how language teacher cognition has been defined followed by discussion of current understandings of L2 English teachers' cognition of today's TESOL. This sets the stage for an exploration of L2 English teachers' cognition of English as an International Language (EIL) in teacher education programmes and different challenges faced by L2 English teachers in incorporating EIL in their in-service teaching practices. The chapter concludes with how teacher education can contribute to the changing role of these teachers.

## Key Concept: Language Teacher Cognition

To make sense of the language learning and teaching experience in the language classrooms, knowing what is happening in the minds of teachers is necessary. In this chapter, we draw on the much-cited definition by Borg (2015) who defines the term 'language teacher cognition' as 'what teachers think, know, and believe and of its relationships to teachers' practices' (2015: 1). He used it as an inclusive term to describe a dynamic system of knowledge, thoughts, beliefs and attitudes personally held by language teachers. Complex yet practical, personal yet contextualised, language teacher cognition configures diverse mental events which are continually refined throughout the teacher's educational and professional lives.

Language teacher cognition encompasses cognitive constructs such as the teachers' *knowledge, beliefs, conceptions and attitudes* upon which language teachers draw in all aspects of their work, especially in their actual classroom practices within a particular context. Language teachers have cognitions about all aspects of their work from generic issues (e.g. lesson planning, classroom management) to specific curricular areas (e.g. grammar teaching, literacy instruction, or literature). English language teacher cognition has been extensively explored in several areas of L2

English instruction such as grammar teaching (e.g. Hos & Kekec, 2014; Nishimuro & Borg, 2013; Underwood, 2012; Watson, 2015), reading instruction (e.g. Hammond, 2015; McNeill & Kirk, 2014), writing instruction (e.g. Gaitas & Alves Martins, 2015; Nguyen & Hudson, 2010) or speaking instruction (e.g. Farrell & Yang, 2017).

However robust the field may seem to be, this newly emerging line of inquiry still lays subject to terminological variability and lack of a unified framework within which programmatic research agendas are conceived (Borg, 2015). To tackle this, a theoretical framework of language teacher cognition was proposed, which has come to serve as a conceptual tool and a springboard for other conceptual or empirical research that share similar endeavours. The framework outlines the relationship among language teacher cognition and other elements from prior language learning experience ('schooling'), pre-service teacher education ('professional coursework'), to in-service teaching experience ('classroom practice') (see Borg, 2015 for more details). In this sense, language teacher cognition can be understood as a collection of all experiences related to the learning and teaching of a language one has constructed from the earliest experience of the language to the pedagogical practices in which one is engaged at the present moment and throughout their professional career.

While having long been subject to numerous explorations in educational psychology, the notions of knowledge and beliefs are gaining wider recognition among applied linguists and scholars in the field of second language learning and teaching. Teacher beliefs, for example, are found to feature prominently in language teacher education (e.g. Johnson, 1994) and in-service teaching experiences (e.g. Li & Walsh, 2011) where their classroom behaviours are affected, although discrepancies between beliefs and behaviours can also be observed (e.g. Farrel & Ng, 2003). This suggests that what the teachers do in the classroom is deeply intertwined with what they know and believe. Another closely related concept is L2 teachers' emotions, which has begun to receive more research attention (see edited volume by Martínez Agudo (2018) for detailed discussions of the topic). Given that teachers are not only imparters of knowledge but also feeling human beings, the role of teachers' emotions, the influence they have on the teachers' practices, and how the teachers can deal with positive and negative emotions warrant a systematic exploration.

If we are to fully understand the teachers and why they do what they do, the teachers' beliefs, thoughts, knowledge and emotions that informed their practice must be attended to. Without addressing these teachers' preexisting beliefs, it could be difficult, if not impossible, for any changes we wish to cultivate in a language classroom to happen. Language teacher cognition may thus provide valuable insights into what underpins the teachers' cognitive and emotional aspects about certain elements, the extent to which these cognitions have come about, and the way they get displayed in their pedagogical practices.

The next section looks at the L2 English teachers' cognition of English and the ways it is addressed in today's TESOL programmes around the world. Despite its much-touted status as a 'global' means of communication, English may not always be treated as such.

## Current TESOL Situation: What Does it Look Like Now?

### Traditional TESOL perspectives on English and English language teaching

TESOL as a field has long been predominated by native-speakerism – the conception that a native speaker represents the ideal teacher of English (see Chapters 1 and 3 for more detailed discussion). Past and recent research have provided useful insight into the attitudinal aspects of the L2 English teachers regarding native speaker norms and other non-Inner Circle varieties studying/working both in Inner Circle countries (e.g. Selvi, 2013) and in Outer and Expanding Circle countries (e.g. Decke-Cornhill, 2003 (Germany); Sifakis & Sougari, 2005 (Greece); Atay, 2008 (Turkey); Mahboob & Talaat, 2008 (Pakistan); Wu & VanderBroek, 2008 (Ghana); Koskun, 2011 (Turkey); Braine, 2013 (China); Zacharias, 2014 (Indonesia); Young et al., 2016; Sadeghpour & Sharifian, 2017 (Asia-Pacific); Baker & Jarunthawatchai, 2017 (Thailand); Lim & Burns, 2018 (Cambodia); Monfared & Khatib, 2018 (India and Iran)). Consistently found from these studies had been that native-speaker norms as a preferred language learning choice are not limited to learners but also acknowledged in language teachers themselves. Across different global English teaching contexts, teachers predominantly and consistently express a preference for standardised English such as American or British English over other English varieties, including their own localised English varieties as well as other local languages and cultures. Wherever our fingers touch on the world map, be it Asia (e.g. Braine, 2013) or Europe (Modiano, 2009), these attitudes in favour of the native speaker norms are still very much present. While some teachers display positive attitudes towards the idea and concurred that the so-called 'perfect' English was ungrounded, the native English model still prevailed. Even over a decade later into the 21st century, a clear preference for Inner Circle varieties over those spoken in other circles remains the general trend.

The spread of this ideology was exacerbated by globalisation, which has seen an exponential growth in the number of international students pursuing higher education abroad (outside of their home country), especially in English-speaking countries. Many higher education institutions, in an attempt to internationalise their image as a global learning community, have invested massive amount of time and money to attract international students and staff. However, in spite of the growing awareness of English with its current function as the world's lingua franca, these institutions who claimed their 'international' orientation are often characterised by an emphasis on the Western-borne, native speakers' norms with scarce attention to other varieties of English. This is especially relevant for the English language teaching industry worldwide. A vast majority of TESOL programmes in different teaching contexts and cultures remain heavily and inadvertently unaware of their role in circulating the long-outdated dichotomy of the superior Self vs the inferior Other (Pennycook, 1998) via course content, materials, assessments and curricular documents.

While often regarded as experts in their own contexts, pre- and in-service TESOL practitioners are re-positioned merely as passive adopters of the dominant English-speaking West philosophies (Dewey & Patsko, 2018; Ilieva & Waterstone, 2013; Kamhi-Stein, 2009). In some cases, as exemplified in studies by Inoue and Stracke (2013), this Western superiority is not forced upon but actively embraced by many students themselves. Some students learning English as a second or foreign language choose to pursue their TESOL education in Inner Circle countries fully aware of the competitive edge they would afford by obtaining a degree qualification deemed as more privileged in their home countries. In many parts of Asia, as a result of native-English speaker fallacy, teaching English means teaching standardised versions of English along with the cultural information associated with Anglo-white, native Inner Circle English users with middle-class values. Instead of being judged against their qualifications and ability to equip learners with much-needed capability 'to shuttle between different varieties of English and different speech communities' (Canagarajah, 2013: 6), teachers' competence is still based on their proficiency in standard English (Braine, 2013).

## Negative impact of Nativespeakerism on student teachers

L2 English learners and teachers are often framed in discourses in which their linguistic, cultural and other differences are characterised as problematic. Often labelled as 'non-native', students and teachers participating in North American TESOL programmes and whose first language is not English are identified as 'weak' and having problems with English language skills (Llurda, 2005).

Studies exploring the experiences of international teaching assistants in English-speaking countries (e.g. Braine, 2010; Jenkins, 2014; Hebbani & Hendrix, 2014; Reis, 2011) have described challenges international students face, one of which being trying to remediate their nonnative English speaker status while adjusting their linguistic practices to accommodate the local native speakers in their respective educational settings. This is highlighted in Hebbani and Hendrix's (2014) online survey of international teaching assistants, teaching communication courses in American universities who were faced with resistance from their US students simply because they are not native English instructors. Communicative breakdowns were attributed to the foreignness of these international teaching assistants, ignoring the fact that communication is a matter of 'it takes two to tango' and that it should be the responsibilities of every party to adapt and accommodate in order to communicate successfully with individuals from diverse backgrounds.

Many international teaching assistants feel insecure about their English, an experience similar to that of other non-native English-speaking teachers. Due to the internalised belief that native speakers are better users and teachers of English, these teachers may experience linguistic and professional insecurities. With the presumed linguistic deficiencies imposed upon them, these teachers' knowledge of their own local English varieties and cultures is often regarded as a deficit. For example, Canagarajah (2012) shared his in-service teacher training experience with the United States Information Agency in Sri Lanka. Using Sri Lankan English while also codeswitching between English and Tamil during the lesson, he felt devasted when his English was questioned and ridiculed by the so-called US experts: 'I was left with a poor image of myself as a teacher. ... I had never thought my teaching practice or English proficiency was questionable' (2012: 259). These experiences of low self-esteem and professionally induced anxiety are shared by many L2 English teachers (e.g. Galloway, 2014; Hammad & Ghali, 2015; Park, 2012; Takahashi, 2014; Tum, 2013), which have also found to have negative impact on the teachers' performance and cognition of their intended practices in the future language classrooms.

## EIL teaching: Objection?

Such inherent negative repercussions of the long-established native speaker standards on L2 English teachers have given rise to a paradigm shift in the English language teaching industry whereby EIL teaching are advocated as another alternative way to approach the L2 English pedagogy. Recurring among early studies on L2 English teachers' cognition of EIL and its pedagogical implication is one of general objection, however. Although EIL has received a growing awareness from both the learners and teachers, partly due to the realisation that English is now, in most cases, spoken as a lingua franca among speakers of other languages, ELF speakers' Englishes are still seen as deficient versions of native speaker models. Jenkins (2007), for example, found in her study using group discussion method that teacher participants, native and non-native English alike, felt that ELF generated a sense of fragmentation, which could act as a potential cause leading to a lower or loss of the standard that one may use as a shared point of reference. ELF was also mentioned by some participants as sounding unnatural and therefore a tendency for causing unintelligibility among non-native English speakers.

While initially faced with resistance, the perceived benefits of the new paradigm did not go unnoticed. Findings of many studies also revealed that teachers and learners of English were 'acutely aware of World Englishes' (Young *et al.*, 2016: 17) and found EIL conceptually appealing. The study concluded by suggesting that future research take further steps in discovering the complex relationship between teacher cognitions of language variety and the extent to which those cognitions inform classroom practice. One particular insight drawn from the study was that students' propensities towards a particular variety seem to depend largely on exposure, either through the artefacts outside (such as media) or the teachers and what happens inside the classroom itself. The next section thus carries on with a deeper investigation into TESOL teacher education where EIL ideas have started to be implemented in the language classroom.

## Language Teacher Cognition of EIL-oriented TESOL Teacher Education

The arrival of EIL in educational environments characterised by multilingual and multicultural orientation has led to reconceptualisation of the English language teacher education. In response to these emerging new scenarios where both learners' and teachers' needs must be taken into account, many English language teacher educators have begun to reflect on their own assumptions and beliefs about language education. They are exploring ways to introduce and engender teachers' awareness of a perspective shift in the teaching principles underlying English language pedagogy within language teacher education programmes.

Despite a continuing trend in the American and British English, the wind of change is in the air. In recent years, as exemplified in a steady growth in publications that discuss English teaching from an EIL perspective (e.g. Bayyurt & Akcan, 2015; Bowles & Cogo, 2015; Marlina & Giri, 2014; Matsuda, 2017; Sifakis & Tsantila, 2018; Vettorel, 2015; Zacharias & Manara, 2013), an increasing number of postgraduate TESOL and applied linguistics practitioner educations around the world have started to include EIL perspectives education programmes at varying degrees from stand-alone lesson activities to the entire course dedicated to the topic.

Several studies regarding EIL teacher education (e.g. Bayyurt & Sefakis, 2015a, 2015b; Dewey, 2015a; Pedrazzini, 2015) make a strong case for the importance and inclusion of ELF in pre-service teacher education programmes and continuing in-service teacher professional development. Pedrazzini (2015), for instance, found in her study that ELF-aware activities offer teacher trainees' another perspective into the sorts of variations typically found in ELF communication even if in the end these teacher trainees may return to the 'safety net' of established native Inner Circle varieties in their teaching contexts. The consensus among these teachers who have reported on their attempt to incorporate EIL in their classroom seems to be the importance and priority of EIL-oriented instruction and myriad ways in which these priorities can be practically addressed in teacher education.

While student teachers' professional insecurities (and many other negative impacts of monolingual TESOL programmes) should provide sufficiently reasonable ground on which calls for change are warranted, one key issue that runs through all the studies is incongruence in beliefs and practices. Teachers' stated beliefs do not always parallel their observed practices. Teachers often reported they felt it was necessary to be more open about the needs to move away from the so-called standard English, recognising that this approach may not reflect the actual usage of English in the current world. However, though teachers have been reported to find proposals for using English as a lingua franca as a basis for L2 English instruction conceptually attractive, actual implementation of the proposed instructional alternative remains scarce. ELF as an actual and doable English language teaching model was inconceivable. EIL ideas are interesting and worth knowing but no study has ever reported on TESOL teacher education programme's successful attempt in changing the teachers' beliefs and practices of native speaker models to those advocated by EIL. This incongruence has been attributed to various contextual factors in their workplace which have to be taken into account when one aims to arrive at a deep understanding of the teacher cognition and practices.

Whether the perceived benefits of the new paradigm are brought into pedagogical realities hinges on the very decision the language teachers themselves make, and these decisions are determined by a number of factors. Many studies have reported on some difficulties encountered by teachers when designing and delivering EIL-tailored activities or tasks in their language classroom. These implementational challenges include:

## Course design and delivery challenge

Some TESOL programmes are EIL-oriented only by name. Issues surrounding EIL may be superficially addressed, gravitating toward theories, while empirically based suggestions for teachers to actually try it out in their real-life classroom remain few and far between. Even when EIL/ELF/Global Englishes were mentioned in the course or programme descriptions (e.g. syllabus), its presence remained superficial without any associated guideline for pedagogical application (Dewey, 2014; Dewey & Patsko, 2018; Matsuda, 2009).

## Contextual constraints

The kind of limitations teachers may experience can be macro (e.g. nature and status of the course, curriculum) or micro. Micro problems are classroom-based, revolving around time and learners (e.g. a particular student population, students' limited proficiency, frustration when facing classroom realities, overwhelming reading loads). Teacher educators in Matsuda's (2017b) publication offered honest and open accounts of the difficulties they experienced and of the lessons they have learnt from these experiences. The difficulties included context-specific ones such as the elective status of a course, the composition of a particular student population or a course deemed too theoretical by the participants. Authors also mentioned time and curricular constraints; students' lack of proficiency and the frustration students feel when leaving the idealistic and safe environment of the course and encountering the reality of teaching. In addition, students were often overwhelmed by the amount of reading they had to do. Some of the authors also had to deal with the doubts and reluctance of the students who resist change. What is really interesting in these accounts is the authors' realisation of the flaws of their work, the subsequent amendments they made to the courses and the benefits of reflection and retrospection which accompanied the task of writing up their papers.

## Ideological challenges (Language teacher beliefs and attitudes)

Resorting to a critical reflective narrative approach, some teachers reflected on their experience of incorporating EIL elements in various teaching contexts. As a result of this contemplation, attachment to native speaker norms entertained by both teacher trainers and student teachers along with resistance to the EIL principles was consistently found to be a recurring theme (Giri & Foo, 2014; Manara, 2014; Tanghe, 2014). Many L2 English teachers have expressed qualms about the effectiveness of EIL and what will be required of them in its implementation. This may be due to the fact that the English language curriculum, as well as learners' expectation, dictates that they follow the 'native speaker' English model, which learners and teachers alike aspire to replicate despite the well-attested difficulties of the conceptualisation of such varieties.

Of all these challenges, teacher cognition is perhaps the crucial disabler that stops change from truly happening. Therefore, it is worth looking at those elements that have been found to account for it.

## Impact of EIL Teacher Education on Language Teacher Cognition

Given that the implications brought about by the teachers' underlying beliefs about what English as a subject means for them have a wide impact on a number of areas, from the students' learning experiences to the teachers' own classroom practices to language curricular design to material writing, it is important that these teachers' experiences be told and their voices heard. Mentioned as a catalyst for change (Rose & Montakantiwong, 2018), teacher education affords such kind of opportunity for teachers to make themselves heard. A number of studies have reported on the impact of pre-service language teacher education and continuing professional trainings for in-service teachers on their beliefs and practices. Through several aspects of the teachers' pre-service education such as courses in the programme, teacher educators and the practicum experience that are often positioned at the centre of these language teachers' cognition, teachers are given the opportunity to engage with EIL principles and challenge their pre-existing language ideology.

Advance has also been made in EIL teacher education as evidenced in publications that showcase how L2 English teachers across learning contexts interpret EIL, resulting in a variety of EIL-inspired teaching practices at all levels and in every form (see Table 7.1 for sample topics related to EIL teacher education). While scholars have noted the urgency of reconceptualising teachers' cognition of the subject they teach, and that this sort of conceptual change must come from the teachers themselves, what studies on EIL and its pedagogy have in common is that they emphasise how teacher education and professional development play a key role in language teachers' conceptual transformation. It is during the process of teacher education that the teachers' prior expectations and personally held beliefs are either unwavering or transformed by the programme agenda, the effect of which can last throughout their entire career (Borg, 2015).

To challenge native-speakerism, EIL teacher education programmes can help student teachers in three ways: looking inward, looking around and looking forward/ahead. This discovery could bring about not only eye-opening insights but also new horizons on which your practices can be transformed.

## Looking inward: Stay aware of prior learning experiences through self-reflection

Many studies showed that prior language learning experiences constitute one of the main sources of the teachers' cognition on language teaching. Evidence have shown that the experiences teachers have when they were language learners, or what Lortie (1975) called 'the apprenticeship of observation,' (1975: 61) can influence teachers' beliefs not only about language teaching and learning but also their pedagogical approach. Since it is usually one of the earliest times to be exposed to a form of education for the teacher, this type of learning experience plays a powerful role in those formative years leading up to their career. With a lot of time spent observing and interacting with their teachers, teachers have inevitably come to their own conclusion what education should look like.

One way to foreground our prior belief is through self-reflection (e.g. Richards & Lockhart, 1994; Schön, 1983; Wallace, 1991). Originally developed in mainstream teacher education, the reflective approach as one of the educational tools for teacher professional development has begun to gain popularity in language teacher education. By facilitating teachers to voice their thoughts about their teaching choices and beliefs, self-reflection proves an effective tool to engage teachers and teachers-to-be in revisiting English and its teaching.

Language teachers should pay attention to prior language learning experience on the teacher's conception of English as a global language and its pedagogical implications. Pre-service teachers take in new information regarding learning and teaching based on personal experiences strongly shaped by perceptions held before entering the programme. This suggests that the prior beliefs the teachers bring to their teacher education and career can either promote or hinder the degree to which new concepts may be internalised and adopted in practices. Numrich's (1996) diary studies of pre-service teachers discovered that some of them avoided grammar teaching or giving corrective feedback because of their negative experience as learners. Some teachers who enjoyed the cultural components during their own learning experience reported having tried to do just the same with their classroom. Also relevant is the study by Johnson (1994) who pointed out how the pre-service teachers' prior beliefs formed as learners can affect their instructional decisions. These decisions in terms of what constitutes the most appropriate images of teachers, materials and class-room activities, she explained, are formed on the basis of their first-hand experience as L2 learners. Emerging from her data was also 'the apparent power that images from prior experience within formal language class-rooms had on these teachers' images of themselves as teachers' (1994: 449). This also resonates with the in-service EFL teachers in Öztürk and Gürbüz's (2017) study in Turkish contexts whose initial conceptualisations on how English should be taught or what a good English teacher should look like were rooted in their language learning habits and by observing their own teachers in the past.

One illustrative example comes from the case of Zeynap who was one of the English teacher participants in Öztürk and Gürbüz's (2017) study, in which she wrote in her reflection report how she had asked her students to keep a vocabulary notebook because it had worked for her in the past as a learner and so should it be for her current students. Clearly, the teacher's classroom practices can be affected by the belief in the effectiveness of certain activities formed in her prior learning experience. What was your experience learning English as a child? In which sort of settings did you come across English? What was your motivation to learn English? These questions are at the heart of our discussion so far of how important it is to be vigilant of our own personal past as a learner of the language.

## Looking around: Stay informed of the current sociolinguistic landscapes

What has become the role of the English teachers in this globalised world? In responding to the changing learning landscape of the 21st century, L2 teachers are urged to critically reflect not only on their own past learning experiences and the underlying beliefs (they have or used to have) about the subject but also on their role as a teacher of the very subject which has now become a global language with multiple varieties used by different speech communities. With the continually growing research literature under the Global Englishes paradigm, teachers are invited to see oneself as a reflective practitioner. To be a mindful EIL practitioner means to be in constant awareness of both their internal state (who they used to be, who they are, who they would like to be, overall emotional states) and external surroundings (who their learners are and what kind of teaching environments, micro and macro, they are in). Teachers engaged in such mindful, EIL-oriented practices are not only well-informed of the principles emerging from the scholarly realm but also able as well as willing to 'develop instructional sequences, lesson adaptations, policies and tests that make sense of ELF while being relevant to and appropriate for each local teaching and learning context, its needs, its wants and idiosyncrasies' (Sifakis *et al.*, 2018: 157).

In line with this view of language teacher as a mindful practitioner is a recent development in translingual pedagogy (Canagarajah, 2013, 2016; Zheng, 2017) where language teachers are encouraged to embrace one's own professional trajectory as a translingual language teacher. With the goal of equipping learners with communicative strategies vital to a successful sense-making across sociolinguistic boundaries, translingual teachers endeavour to expand their learners' as well as their own repertoires of linguistic, social and cultural resources. As suggested by Canagarajah (2013), instead of fostering mastery of grammatical rules of a single variety, teachers are best positioned to cultivate language awareness and pragmatic strategies in learners, which can be achieved in several ways such as awareness-raising activities or critical examination of relevant theories in the field (see Matsuda, 2017 for sample EIL lessons, activities and tasks).

## Looking ahead: Visualise future in-service teaching context

Conflicts between prior beliefs attained during the course of teacher education and real-life practices among novice in-service teachers are common. These teachers often find themselves struggle over applying the content they are taught and trained during their TESOL programme in the real practice. Taking Swan's (2015) study of English teachers from seven different countries as example, it was discovered that participants' desires to follow what they were taught were sometime at odds with their classroom reality. In similar manner, teachers in Johnson's (1994) study realised through reflection how they rushed through the lesson plans instead of providing authentic input, something which they had been trained to do. It may be difficult for these teachers to come to term with why they do what they do unless they understand who they are as teachers as well as what their teaching environments look like. Fullan (1993) noted the powerful role the wider context to which the teachers belong such as that of each educational institution culture plays in the teachers' attitudes. Some studies have discovered that although some TESOL practitioners were trained under Western-based TESOL education they adapted their pedagogical approaches in ways that they deemed fit with the local students' needs while bearing in mind contextual factors such as students' first language (Barnawi & Phan, 2015; Li & Edwards, 2013). To meet the shifting needs of learners, the decisions regarding 'which English' and 'whose English' to be taught should be considered in relation to a realistic, close-up picture of one's teaching environments (Young & Walsh, 2010). In other words, teachers must first have a clear understanding of their own local contexts, both external and internal.

External contexts refer to variables that make up the teaching/learning environments surrounding the teachers' professional life. Teachers are advised to carefully consider contextual factors influential on the way they learn to teach the language throughout their professional trajectory. Within a newly proposed model of Clusters of Language Teacher Cognition (Öztürk & Gürbüz, 2017), the learner profile and institutional factors such as organisational atmosphere, testing and curriculum policies were delineated as determinants of teachers' practices. With regards to the learner profiles, teachers may look into the learner's view of themselves – how they see themselves now and would like to see in the future (see Chapter 6 for more detailed discussion).

Also worth taking into consideration is the teaching context. In which curricular level (elementary, secondary, higher education, or vocational school) will I be teaching? What type of institution (government/state or private) am I planning to get involved? What kind of policies will I be required to adopt (e.g. Am I required to use English as the only medium of instruction? To what extent am I allowed to use other languages, if at all possible?)? At the start of our teaching career, most of us are likely to be welcomed with the 'challenging realities' where we experience a process in which what we had learned from our teacher education about language teaching had to be (somewhat or completely) revised. There is nothing wrong about wanting to apply everything we know about in our classroom and hoping that all will go as planned, but we also need to bear in mind that, due to various contextual factors, our practices may have to change in accordance with the kind of reality we are facing. Adapting our teaching approach that best responds to the teaching context is not an option but a necessity.

While centralised language teaching is becoming less relevant in a neo-liberal time, policies still affect teachers' daily practice to a certain degree as evidenced in the universal implementation of standards concerning learners' language proficiencies in most countries. Thus, it is equally important for teachers to stay informed of relevant language policies (e.g. institutional and national curriculum guidelines) and the potential effect they may have on their practices. Only in this spirit will the teachers be positioned to bring about a well-balanced policy–practice compromise in which regulated policies are met and students' learning experiences transformed for the better (e.g. Menken & García, 2010).

In addition to the external context, we also need to consider our internal context – the level of autonomy or agency we may have. What EIL strives for is to offer an alternative pedagogical framework of going about conducting one's teaching practices. Suggested ideas are put forward, instead of imposed upon, for interested teachers to think about and decide whether (and in what ways) those ideas can play part in reinventing their classroom that better aligns with today's sociolinguistic reality. Given that an appropriate degree of reflexivity, responsibility and autonomy are applied, teachers can take liberty to integrate EIL principles in the course of lesson design and implementation that suit their ELT context the most.

In summary, each individual teacher possesses 'a system of interwoven beliefs, assumptions and knowledge' which, when interacting with experience, will have 'evolved in an individual and organic fashion' (Woods, 1996: 248). Since these cognitions are shaped by 'the totality of teachers' lived experience' (Borg, 2015: 126), to fully understand teachers' cognitions on any aspects of their work, the experiences they have had in the past as learners and in the present as teachers must be thoroughly accounted for.

## What Does the Research Tell Us?

Li's (2017) article puts forward a three-step EIL-oriented pedagogy for TESOL teacher education courses and programmes that aims to foster teachers' linguistic self-respect, build their pedagogical competence for plurilingual teaching, and transform their classrooms. The author describes in elaborate details how a series of inquiries (carried out in three stages through course assignments) which was built on these teachers' authentic knowledge about language and culture, allows teachers to learn more about themselves and their students as cultural beings.

Bayyurt and Sifakis (2015a, 2015b) presents their findings of a research study in which they designed and implemented an 'ELF-aware teacher education programme' based on ELF and WE principles and contextual information in a Greek-Turkish teacher education programme. Through ELF-aware lessons (such as relevant readings and discussion questions), it was clear from the findings that the programme played a role in raising the teachers' awareness of EIL and enhancing their reflection on the relevance of ELF for their own classrooms throughout the course of the study.

**Table 7.1** Example research topics relevant to EIL teacher education

| Researchers | Topic | Participants | Research design | Data collection method |
|---|---|---|---|---|
| Li (2017) | EIL pedagogical activities | Pre-service and In-service in a North American TESOL programme | Qualitative, action research | Autobiographies, series of written in-course assignments |
| Bayyurt and Sifakis (2015a, 2015b) | EIL pedagogical activities | In-service English language teachers (N = 12) | Qualitative, action research | Autobiographies, answers to questions from course content, document analysis (e.g. lesson plans) submitted online, face-to-face focus group interviews |
| Rose and Montakantiwong (2018) | Reflective practices | English language teachers teaching in Japan and Thailand (N = 2) | Duoethnography | Individually constructed narratives followed by a critical dialogue of each other's stories through questions and feedback |
| Lee (2018) | Teacher as agent of Change | English major university students enrolled in a 14-week English education pedagogy course (N = 17) | Grounded theory | reflective essays, semi-structured interviews, and in-class observations |
| Lee and Lee (2018) | Learners' perception of EIL in informal digital learning of English (IDLE) environments | Korean EFL students (N = 317) | Quantitative survey | A three-section questionnaire |

Rose and Montakantiwong (2018) recount their experiences in integrating EIL ideas in their respective instructional contexts (Japan and Thailand). Adopting an innovative duoethnographic approach, the tales of these two teachers highlight not only challenges and successes encountered during their attempt to realise research-based EIL pedagogical suggestions in real-life language classroom but also the need for incorporating individual and collaborative reflective practices in the teacher education programmes, which they see as an integral element to the successful implementation of innovative ideas. Their less than conventional adoption of duo-ethnography as a method of inquiry 'provides a promising new avenue for teacher-researchers to explore their own practices in relation to "the Other" and to share these experiences within a wider professional community' (2018: 99).

Lee's (2018) study found that EIL learning tasks (e.g. interaction with English users from diverse sociolinguistic background, reflective tasks) coupled with instructional support provided by language teachers play a vital role in transforming students' EIL experiences and bringing about attitude changes in relation to varieties of English. Teacher practitioners wishing to make a difference in the learners' TESOL experience can entertain these various roles by introducing different perspectives and issues surrounding English used as an international mean of communication (disseminator); sharing with students practical EIL experiences and providing resources for EIL tasks (resource); giving constructive guidelines and feedback (facilitator); and encouraging students to carry out activities using EIL mindset (supporter).

Lee and Lee's (2018) empirical study discovered how engagement in Informal Digital Learning of English (IDLE) practices can enhance students' perception of EIL, suggesting that EIL education may potentially be realised without any teacher-driven, structured EIL intervention outside of a traditional EFL classroom. In line with previous research which have found students' EIL-related performance to be positively affected by greater exposure to or use of diverse English inside and outside the classroom, this study offers a new pedagogical insight for teachers who wish to combine technology and EIL curriculum in their practices.

## Implications for Teachers in Global Contexts

A recent call for re-drawing the boundaries of the field of language teacher cognition (Burns et al., 2015) points to the fact that teachers need to be equipped with a comprehensive understanding of how their cognition regarding the language and its pedagogy affect who they are and what they do as a language professional. The 21st century has so far been subject to the effect of globalisation, which has altered the face of social, cultural and linguistic diversity in societies all over the world, and the TESOL industry is by no means an exception. In keeping with this new reality, practitioners partaking in the practice of language education are expected to acknowledge the full range of linguistic diversity presented in their classrooms. Teachers are in the best position to ensure that learning success is within reach for students from a wide range of backgrounds and that their classroom remains a safe space where students feel a sense of communal participation and belonging. However, any positive changes we hope to initiate in the classroom cannot happen unless the thoughts, knowledge and beliefs that guide what teachers do are not fully understood.

Teachers' perceptions of the notion 'Global Englishes' or EIL and whether they are translated into language classroom practices suggests a fruitful area of investigation for understanding the complex yet intriguing operation of the teachers' mental lives. Building on previous language teacher cognition studies together with research conducted in the realm of Global Englishes, this chapter emphasises the importance of language teacher cognition on the major issues underlying the English as an International Language paradigm and the extent to which these EIL-related mental activities are mirrored in their professional experience. While much work remains to be done to enrich our understandings of the matter as well as its practicality in diverse contexts, we cannot afford to take the teachers out of the equation as what the teachers think and believe must ultimately be considered in terms of its effects on their students' learning as well as their own. We believe that the notion of language teacher cognition could even be further examined in relation to identity-related issues in different contexts, a topic we turn to in the next chapter.

## Post-reading Activities

### *Reflect*

Self-reflection has been emphasised as a vital component of teachers' professional growth and improved learning experiences of the students. Now think back on your experience as a learner of English in whatever context you have been brought up in. Are there any questions you have about your own language learning histories you would like to probe after reading this chapter? If so, what are they? Process this list by sharing it with your classmates and/or by reflecting on it in your own journal. What have you discovered?

### *Discuss*

(1) Common research findings have indicated that teachers' attitudes toward EIL and its potential classroom applications are characterised by ambivalence. That is, although teachers seem to be familiar with the plurality of English and the role it plays in international communication, they are still reluctant to regard forms deviating from the 'good' (standard) English as acceptable. What do you think could be underlying reasons for this?

(2) The chapter mentions a variety of challenges cited by teachers who have attempted to infuse EIL in their instructional practices (e.g. design and delivery challenge, contextual constraints, ideological issues). To what extent does each of these limiting factors impact EIL implementation in your teaching contexts (current of future)? What are some other factors that you can anticipate?

(3) What aspect of your personal biographies would you say has most shaped your pedagogical principles/philosophies as an L2 English teacher?

### *Apply*

(Adapted from Brown & Barrett, 2017)

**Duoethnography: (Re-) discovering our stories**

(1) Pair up with your classmate with whom you think you share some educational backgrounds (e.g. went to the same or similar (types of) school; registered for the same courses; etc.) but also someone who differs from you in a significant way. This person will be your story co-/de-constructor.

(2) Together come up with a list of topics or questions for a one-hour (or shorter if needs be) dialogue about each other's experiences learning and teaching English. Sample topics can include memorable experiences related to learning English, motivation to become an English teacher, perceived strengths and weaknesses as a student, learning strategies, learning role models, the role the family plays in one's educational experience, and so on. Engage in a conversation using the topics you come up as prompts. Record the conversation.

(3) Separately, transcribe the conversation and take notes on what you think provides insights into your beliefs about learning and teaching English.

(4) Then write a summary of your story about your English learning and/or teaching experiences. Do the same for your dialogue partner. Note that this will be your interpretation of what you heard in the conversation.

(5) Share the story with each other. Discuss the accuracy and consistency of your interpretations. To what extent does each of your stories correspond or diverge with the ways you had intended it to be perceived by the other person?

(6) Once you have shared your interpretations, search in your stories for aspects or elements that may have an impact on your current preparation as a language teacher and your effectiveness in your future classroom. Can you identify existing beliefs or ideas about the English language and/or the teacher of the language you might bring to your future classroom that could be beneficial or detrimental to your practices and your students' learning? How might your own experiences be used to help you understand and meet the needs of your future students?

## Resources for Further Reading

Kubanyiova, M. and Feryok, A. (ed.) (2015) Language teacher cognition in applied linguistics research: revisiting the territory, redrawing the boundaries, reclaiming the relevance [Special issue]. *Modern Language Journal* 99 (3), 435–636.

An essential collection of research effort and critical insights drawn from the field of Language Teacher Cognition (LTC). In attempt to redraw the boundaries of LTC, this volume showcases eight published research papers on language teachers' beliefs, knowledge, attitudes and related concepts and on how these concepts relate to teacher learning and what teachers do in the classroom. Serving as exemplary research directions, this is a good place to start if you are thinking of doing research in this field.

Farrell, T. (2018) *Reflective Language Teaching: Practical Applications for TESOL Teachers* (2nd edn). London: Bloomsbury Academic.

A highly accessible resource book for language teachers and educators interested to enhance their professional practices through self-initiated reflection, a practice which has increasingly become an essential element of teacher education programmes. In this book, the author urges language teachers to approach reflection critically, building on information grounded in research and applying the practice in ways that best suit their contexts. Reflective strategies are presented in a comprehensible manner with several illustrative case studies and reflective discussion questions to help readers see more clearly its practical adaptation to real-life teaching scenarios.

# 8  Global Language and Identity

## Pre-reading Activities

### Think

Imagine being asked to describe yourself as an English language teacher (or practitioner or any other addressing terms appropriate to your teaching context). What metaphor would you choose to describe how you see yourself in that role? (e.g. Teaching English in a Japanese secondary school is (like) ...) Write down your answer. When finished, share your thoughts about why the metaphor is appropriate.

### Discuss

(1) What are identity categories (e.g. race, ethnicity, gender, social class, language, nationality) that people use to describe language teacher identities? To what extent and in what ways do you think each of these categories can affect a teacher's behaviour in a classroom?

(2) How does the native/non-native dichotomy shape the perception of a teacher's professional self? What do you think could be the relationship between one's language ideology and one's sense of self?

## Introduction

In the 21st century, the topics of identity, selfhood, or 'subjectivity' have become 'today's talk of the town and the most commonly played game in town' (Bauman, 2001: 16). The *self*, as reference to one's own perceived sense of identity, has been a topic of preoccupation in both academic and popular literature. For the general public, the obsession manifests itself in a growing trend in self-help culture, a huge multi-billion business that proposes different self-improvement advice to all walks of life. On academic front, recent research articles and scholarly books on the topic of 'the self' are well underway and proliferating. The rise of interest in the self (or selves) points to the fact that possession of knowledge about 'who we are' is clearly a crucial and abiding pursuit of curiosity to countless many in our globalised society. Globalisation has also led our quest of self-knowledge to extend beyond our geographically defined concept of nation, as identities are no longer bound by nation-states. Globalisation has brought about an increase in use of English for intercultural communication. This spotlight cast upon English as a global means of international communication subverts traditional identity of L2 English learners and teachers in a language classroom (Lamb, 2004; Ryan, 2006). As one engages in ELF communication, opportunities to re-conceive our available linguistic resources are brought to the forefront, engendering a new platform for identity construction. This has led some learners to develop a greater sense of global identity (e.g. becoming global citizens) and had led others to tighten a stronger grip on one's local identity.

This chapter discusses how L2 English learners and teachers develop and enact identities in the era of globalisation from an EIL perspective. Based on various theoretical perspectives on identity, the chapter opens with a brief overview of multiple ways in which self/identity has been conceptualised and empirically investigated. In particular, we will look at the facets which are closely connected to L2 English learner and teacher identities in the changing sociolinguistic landscape of English learning and teaching. The chapter also explores the pedagogical insights that these different perspectives have generated. We will then explain why learning about the self is important for both teachers and learners to cultivate a healthy sense of their L2 selves. This chapter concludes by reflecting on what EIL teachers can do to promote a healthy sense of L2 self in both our learners and ourselves.

## Defining the Self

### Self vs identity

The self makes a fascinating topic of study from a wide ambit of disciplines. This diversity explains why research on self or identity is rather fragmented and why a multitude of self-related terms has proliferated in an attempt to capture and describe this construct. One illustrative example is an overlapping usage of the term 'self' and 'identity', both of which are often used interchangeably, inconsistently and without clearly defined characterisation. For the concept of the self to make sense (or at least manageable), the self is broken up into different components to which separate terms are given. When self is conceptualised in relation to specific areas of our life such as contexts or certain roles in social groups, real or imagined, the term 'identity' is adopted. Our language identity, for example, refers to our sense of self with respect to a particular language (e.g. English), a specific learning setting (e.g. English as a foreign language), language use (e.g. English for tourism), or other social factors such as geographical regions (e.g. Geordie, Texan English), social class (e.g. Posh English) or social groups (e.g. football speak). Our sense of self can also be defined in terms of particular types of thoughts or emotions such as self-efficacy, which refers to our beliefs or expectations about our competence to perform certain tasks or actions (Mills, 2014). L2 linguistic self-confidence is another construct related to our sense of self, which refers more specifically to learners' beliefs in their capability to communicate in a second language (Sampasivam & Clément, 2014). As with other areas of life, we move across a multifaceted volume of self-constructs on our journey from language learner selves towards language teacher selves.

## Self-concept

In answering the pre-reading questions at the start of this chapter, you may have mentioned several self-related constructs, from personal attributes, perceived strengths and weaknesses, to preferences and dislikes. Key experiences in your past as well as people who have been influential or acted as a role model for you along your life journey might also have been alluded to. You might perhaps find yourself thinking about your hopes, motivations and professional aspirations for the future. All of these represent your sense of self – your self-concept or identity as a teacher. Seemingly distinct, these elements of self are constantly in interaction, contributing to our overall sense of who we are (or who believes ourselves to be). This self-concept also guides our behaviours in the classroom. Clearly, even the ostensibly simple task of imagining yourself as a teacher is a complex undertaking, even for those with substantial teaching experience. The challenge is further complicated if other roles are drawn into the sense of our teacher selves, as teachers often adopt multiple roles such as a parent, partner, carer, researcher, or learner, each of which comes with distinct expectations and responsibilities. It becomes even more complicated when, as teachers, we have to extend our consideration to the domain of our language learners and the complexity that accompanies each and every one of them as individual learners.

## Multiple Ways of Understanding the Self: Different Views of L2 Learner and Teacher Identity

Applied linguistics (and social sciences in general) has observed the shifts in views on identity from structuralist and essentialist perspectives, where identity was seen as a definitive set of genetically inherent characteristics possessed by an individual in a fixed and static inner core, to post-structuralist perspectives in which the self has come to be seen as a complex and multi-layered construct (Joseph, 2016). Early descriptions of identity emphasised a stable and fixed nature of identity and its construction. That is, once constructed, identity remains unchanged. With the advent of constructivism, emphasis has been on the dynamic nature of identity and social contexts under which identity is constructed. Arriving at a single unified definition is, thus, a rather futile quest.

Research on L2 learner and teacher identities has been conducted within and across disciplines from educational psychology to language education, each from different theoretical premises. L2 self-concepts and identities are therefore defined from these many possible perspectives. In social psychology literature, L2 self-concept has been theorised as individuals' cognitive beliefs about their abilities and affective appraisal of their competence in learning a second language (e.g. L2 English learner self), or specific skills (e.g. L2 Academic English writer/learner self) (Williams *et al.*, 2015). From a post-structuralist perspective, a popular stance embraced by the majority in the field, L2 teacher identity is seen as complex, multifaceted, dynamic, socially situated and a process or way of being and becoming (Barkhuizen, 2017).

## Key themes associated with the post-structuralist approach to identity

This section explores five key themes associated with current approaches to identity. These are positioning identity: as socially constructed; as discursively constructed; as multidimensional; as part of a power relationship; and as shaped and negotiated by past, present and future. Each of these are explored in turn.

### Identities as socially constructed/situated/contextualised

Identity work always is constructed in the company of others. Nobody becomes who they are in a vacuum, separate and distinct from the community in which they have been socialised and therefore influenced to varying degrees by a pre-packed cultural and contextual values. As people grow up, they develop their understanding of their sense of self by picking up various clues from the people and the environment surrounding them, either face-to-face or in an electronically mediated mode. Norton (1997, 2000) has classically defined identity as the ways people construct and make sense of their relationship to the world across time and space, as well as their possibilities for the future. For instance, L2 language learner's self-concept has been discussed in connection with the concept of 'community of practice' (Wenger, 1998), which refers to communities of which learners seek to become 'legitimate members' such as a proficient user of English in an English-speaking country. These communities can be an actual, physical space or an imagined one. We can think of our English learners as seeking to become (or simply be recognised as) members of international community of practice where they exert effort in learning the behaviours and the lingua franca needed to be successful in such international communities. Research suggests that learners' perceptions of the relationship between their existing cultural identity and feelings about its compatibility with an imagined English culture have implications for the learners' enthusiasm in learning the language (Ryan, 2006). In a nutshell, the teacher's sense of self essentially reflects their interaction with, and interpretation of, the social contexts where they live and learn. The self cannot be conceived without taking into account its relationship with the wider social context.

### Identity as discursively constructed

Identity is formed, negotiated and transformed through discourses where individuals not only engage in identity work by taking up subject positions (i.e. ways of being someone or something) but also play a role in maintaining and circulating particular ways of viewing the world (ideologies) in society (Baxter, 2016; Block, 2007). Teachers develop their professional identity by participating in various genres of discourse, which help them to form a meaningful engagement with their students, teacher colleagues, other classroom stakeholders, as well as internal identity construction with their personal subjectivities or ideologies (Alsup, 2006).

### Identity as multi-dimensional

Identity is enacted through our utterances, signalling different dimensions of identity (race, ethnicity, gender, social class, etc.). Critical dialogues around social identity categories such as race, gender, ethnicity, language, class and 'native-status' have started to gain attention in the field of TESOL (e.g. Block & Corona, 2014; Kubota, 2015, 2019). To understand identities, it is important that we realise how identities are always a convergence of different social categories. As L2 learners and teachers navigate the fast-shifting social landscape of home, school, local and international communities, issues of racial, ethnic, gender and class identities will always come up. Park (2015) argued that self-perceived marginalisation experienced by non-native English-speaking learners and teachers may occur due to their visible minority racial and linguistic identities in scenarios where pervasive attitudes and behaviours in English language teaching (ELT) enterprise and the worldwide presence of English language are closely associated with 'whiteness' identities. The interconnectedness among language, race and other social categories was illustrated in a body of scholarly work (e.g. Kubota, 2019; Kubota & Lin, 2006; Motha, 2006; Park, 2012, Preece, 2016). For instance, in Motha's (2006) study, the racial identity dilemma of Katie, a Korean-born woman participating in the study, showcased how her authority was called into question and that this was due to a sense of shame she felt about her race. Preece's (2016) case study discussed how social class may be perceived as an identity ascribed to individuals based on their positioning within their respective social class system and inhibited by these individuals whose beliefs and linguistic practices are shaped by it.

*Identity and its emphasis on the role of power relationships*

The use of language is always related to issues of identity and power. When we speak, we position ourselves in relation to others, and we are also positioned by these others. Post-structuralist approaches highlight how we use language to legitimise particular identities and devalue others. People use language varieties not solely because of who they are, but they perform/index who they are by using different language varieties (Pennycook, 2007). Based on Bourdieu's (1991) concept of different capitals (economic, cultural, social) which can facilitate and/or constrain one's interactions with others, linguistic practices are seen as sites of social struggle, characterised by unequal power relations. Individuals might attempt to present a combination of the right linguistic, social and cultural capital/resources (e.g. accents, dresses, behaviours) to be accepted as a member of a community of practice but cannot always control their positioning due to some aspects over which they have little or no control (e.g. racial phenotypes, physical appearance that conforms to local notions of beauty). For instance, a highly proficient English and Chinese bilingual teachers of English with an Asian-looking appearance may not enjoy the same privileges as teachers of English as a white, American expatriate in the context of foreign language education in China. Users of 'non-standard' varieties of language may struggle with a sense of illegitimacy inflicted upon them by the socially ascribed, non-native speaker status.

*Identity as shaped and negotiated at the crossroads of the past, present and future (Block, 2007)*

L2 learner and teacher identities in the language classroom are not always situated by 'here-and-now', but also in the future aspect of who they aspire or think they ought to be. Identities are equally shaped by past experiences. For example, to make sense of L2 teachers' pedagogical actions, all aspects of their life that have impacted on a language teachers' identity need to be accounted for.

## Motivational perspectives on L2 identities

The fluid and multiple nature of identity has also had an impact of motivational studies in second language learning. This is somewhat due to a sociolinguistic shift of English as a global language, whereby English has come to be seen as everyone's rightful property, and therefore part of their linguistic identity. Such views have invalidated the concept of historical integrative motivational constructs, which sees native speakers as the targeted learning model (Gardner, 1985). This has seen motivational perspectives shift closer to self/identity perspectives, to explore how learners view their position in an imagined (or immediate) global community of English speakers. Conceptualised from a 'self' perspective, motivation is now viewed to form part of one's identity (Dörnyei & Ushioda, 2009;

Lamb, 2017). This also hints at the possibility that important facets of L2 learner identities may lie in their hopes and desires to become a certain kind of person, locating an imagined self in relation to particular imagined communities of practice (Kanno & Norton, 2003; Pavlenko & Norton, 2007).

Based on their empirical findings (Dörnyei *et al.*, 2006) and drawing on the theories of 'possible selves' (Higgins, 1987) in mainstream psychology, Dörnyei's (2009) L2 Motivational Self Systems suggests that concept of ideal L2 self would be better able to explain complex and dynamic nature of L2 learning and identity formation than the previous mainstream concept of integrative motivation. The model consists of three main parts:

(1) Ideal L2 Self denotes the person we would like to become and acts as a powerful motivator.
(2) Ought-to L2 Self refers to the attributes we believe we ought to possess to avoid negative outcomes.
(3) L2 Learning Experience concerns executive motives related to the immediate learning environment and experience.

The underlying hypothesis is that learners are motivated to study an L2 if they develop strong and plausible visions of themselves as future users of the L2. In other words, if the image of oneself as an EIL user in a global context is deeply rooted in learners' ideal or ought-to self, this will be a powerful motivating factor to acquire the competence necessary for achieving that imagined ideal. Research has found that the ideal L2 self, while dependent on the context, is the most significant component of the tripartite model when it comes to predicting L2 motivation among L2 learners (e.g. Csizér & Lukács, 2010; Taguchi *et al.*, 2009).

The concept of identities and motivations have also been discussed in relation to L2 teachers (e.g. Hiver, 2013; Kubanyiova, 2007, 2009, 2012). In line with the L2 motivational self system, Kubanyiova (2009) proposed the Possible Language Teacher Self framework, which explores that the personal meanings that teachers attach to their own identity development. In terms of teacher engagement in a teacher development programme, this can be best understood through 'an overarching metaphor of their socially constructed, personally meaningful and vivid images of who they would like to become, felt they ought to become, or feared they might become' (Kubanyiova, 2017: 102). As with the case of L2 learners, the ideal language teacher self was found to be prevalent in teachers' mental lives and has an impact on their classroom practices. Insights into the content of the participants' possible selves not only enhance our understanding of what motivates language teachers to act the way they do but can also offer a fuller picture of who they are.

The L2-self, which posits at its core the notion of 'ideal self' or a kind of someone with attributes that one would like to have, may be challenged by the multiplicity of identities. Within the context of English as a global language, L2 English learners may have to decide whether their ideal self belongs to the global EIL community or if it is gravitated towards mastering the prestigious standard varieties of English (e.g. British or American English). Uncertainties about the desired goal can indeed affect learners' motivation, suggesting that identities are continually negotiated in social interactions and that learners' imagined identities and communities can play a key role in language learning and teaching. L2 learners may imagine themselves as members of an imagined L2 community and the teacher can help in sustaining a positive, motivating relationship with that setting. However, teachers need to bear in mind that learners' sense of self may not always accurately represent their actual abilities. Some learners may have developed unrealistic or impractical self-concepts and identity goals. They might, for instance, aim for a native speaker ideal self in their learning English, which can potentially lead to frustration and also misjudgement of their competence and eventually debilitation of their self-confidence. Teachers can encourage learners to have faith in their vision, yet need to be aware that 'personal growth cannot be achieved by destroying that dream and imposing on them someone else's convictions' (Kramsch & Zhang, 2017: 218). Instead, a better strategy is to offer personalised language practices that are grounded in realities in a supportive learning context where the students' personal biographies are taken into account. This could be achieved through projects that involve imaginative tasks that allow learners to make their vision explicit through communication such as role-playing various imagined persona in specific situations in diverse imagined contexts (see Hadfield & Dörnyei, 2013 for ideas). Only when teachers understand how their learners see themselves (be it their current or imagined future selves) can they work with each learner to help them set customised meaningful goals, find suitable learning strategies and do away with perceived problems that could occur.

## Summing them all up: L2 English learner and teacher identities

When we talk about English language learner or language teacher identity, we are interested in their sense of who they are in relation to settings (contexts) and the multiple roles enacted in English language learning and teaching. We are also interested in their language learning histories, and other relevant social dimensions deemed as important to their identity construction. Language teacher identity, in particular, evolves from an interaction among three sets of factors:

(1) teachers' personal biography, which includes related social identity categories (e.g. race, ethnicity, gender, age, sexuality, nationality, etc.), language expertise (e.g. language proficiency) and experience (language learning histories, professional teaching experiences);

(2) immediate, locally situated socio-educational contexts (e.g. institutional policies, curriculum) (Varghese *et al.*, 2005);
(3) prevalent ideologies surrounding English language education and English teachers' identities and roles (i.e. what constitutes good or preferred English language teachers, pedagogical practices and qualifications).

Each of these is not in themselves sufficient to shape one's sense of professional identities as an English teacher. It is rather the extent to which the teachers themselves identify with these dimensions and the ways in which their self-concepts are interpreted or ascribed by others (Clarke, 2008; Duff & Uchida, 1997). As a consequence, there may be a contradiction between how people view themselves and how they are seen by others (Blommaert, 2006). Teacher identity is therefore an ongoing process of individuals' interpretation of themselves and is part of being recognised as teachers in the profession of teaching (Gee, 2001).

Combining the multiple insights gained from major approaches (e.g. social psychology, post-structural theories), identity work of a language teacher involves cognition, agency and individual interpretations of the experiences in particular contexts and cultures in which they are embedded. In this way, L2 teacher identity is inherently socially situated but not 'passively' subject to contextual influences. L2 teachers are regarded as individuals who agentively construct their sense of self and make sense of the world through the filters of their own unique cognitions and social contexts, both of which are dynamic across time and place. Although the precise definitions of self-concept and identity in the context of second language learning and teaching are elusive at best, they do not need to be viewed in competition with each other as each of the terms has something to tell us about the self. As made clear by Mercer and Williams (2014), the most comprehensive picture of the self can only be obtained through a combination of insights from a vast array of theoretical stances. Bringing together all magnitudes of how we see our 'self' reveals just how vast and complex an individual's sense of self is, and how it spans across time to incorporate experiences in our past, our hopes for the future and the present moment we are living.

## NES-NNES Dichotomy, Globalisation and EIL Identity

### Native vs non-native English speakers' identities

In the era of globalisation, English has given L2 users opportunities to not only develop their identity in interaction with other people but also express such identity in their perceptions of who they are and who they want to become as a result of such interaction. An increase in use of English as an international lingua franca in global language contact zones and multicultural spaces has called into question a dualistic view of native and non-native English speakers, which was introduced in Chapter 1, and elaborated further in subsequent chapters. An emerging interest in L2 teacher identity is motivated by a number of concerns relevant to language teaching. Among these is the issues of power, status and legitimacy experienced by L2 teachers who have been positioned as non-native teachers of English (Varghese *et al.*, 2005). Non-native English speaker identities, especially experiences of non-native English-speaking teachers in the TESOL profession, have over the past two decades been the focus of examination by a number of scholars (see Braine, 2010). Consistent among the findings of this body of work is how native-speakerism has played an important role in the identity construction and development of the non-native language teachers.

In language classrooms, due to the deeply rooted notion that the most ideal language teacher is the native speaker, the native speakership of the teacher has brought forth extant power relationships in the field of language education. Many language teacher education programmes rely on a traditional native speaker model and do not adequately attend to non-native English speaker learners, overlooking opportunities to address relevant sociocultural and psychological issues (e.g. Kamhi-Stein, 2009; Llurda, 2014; Mahboob, 2010; Matsuda, 2012). In constructing our L2 identity, we rely on our perception of the sociolinguistic relationship we have with our interlocutors. As our perception is often framed by our language ideology, it can be argued that our sense of self is formed and shaped through the lens of a deeply held language ideology. Should the underlying ideology that guides the ways we think and behave be that of native-speakerism, we then resort to this pre-packaged set of beliefs to position our self with respect to other people, resulting in the native/non-native dichotomy that separates and claims superiority of one group over the other. For many L2 English users, their sense of self becomes negatively affected by linguistic insecurity and unfairness.

Today's globalised community is incredibly complex due to increasing mobility of people and information, multilingualism, multiculturalism and the various interpretations of contexts unique to each individual brought about by globalisation. It has become ever more challenging to conceptualise contexts or cultures in any unified monolithic manner. Thus, the relationship between the language learner and social world has become equally complex. English is no longer exclusively tied to its original national and cultural base, functioning instead as an international lingua franca. Learning a second language for the purpose of communicating in a global sphere now means learning new strategies as well as new ways of looking at oneself. Using English in EIL contexts therefore enables L2 learners to explore and reappraise their identities. This is evident in English as a Medium of Instruction (EMI) contexts, where participating in the EMI programme can contribute to students' and teachers' identity formation, providing them a learning space where the native speaker ideals are excluded from their ideal selves. It is also where their sense of multilingual and international identities is developed (Doiz & Lasagabaster, 2018; Henry, 2017).

As previously mentioned, recent conceptualisations of identity construction highlight it as complex, fluid and dynamic. Identity is always in the process of changing and shifting during one's lifetime (Darvin & Norton, 2015; De Costa & Norton, 2017). We may be born into a certain language community but then feel more attached to and become proficient in a particular form of communication associated with another language community later in life. This process of identity formation occurs via an act of learning in which the sense of who we are and what we can do gets transformed. As with any change, L2 learners and how they learn are unlikely to stay the same. This implies that teachers of English, especially those who were once learners themselves, cannot simply recycle the same English lessons (previously given to them as learners of the language some time ago) with their own students. While the subject of teaching is still English, it is not the same English taught decades ago. As learners and teachers move along different language learning journeys across settings and time frames, they are constructing new ways of relating their sense of self to the new worlds and new ways of expressing their identities through a new medium (Ushioda, 2013), bringing with them manifold identities reflecting the multiple roles, social groups and settings with which they are connected.

The potential impact of globalisation on ELF identity construction has been examined from both the perspectives of learners (e.g. Sung, 2014a, 2017) and teachers (e.g. Jenkins, 2007; Kumaravadivelu, 2012b; Pedrazzini & Nava, 2011). When using English in lingua franca contexts, L2 learners may be motivated by different reasons. Common findings suggest that while some L2 users wish for a global, cosmopolitan identity which affords them with a sense of connectedness and belonging to a global community, some may want to display their L1 identity by tailoring their English to pursue their local needs and interests (e.g. Canagarajah, 2005; Sung, 2017; Ushioda, 2013). Research has also found that some L2 speakers intentionally maintain their L1 accent to convey their local linguistic-cultural identity instead of conforming to the nativist ideals (Jenkins, 2014). It is also possible that some L2 speakers of English may identify with and thus become a member of both the global and local communities of practice, thereby forming hybrid identities when engaging in ELF communication (Pennycook, 2007). According to Phan (2008), these hybrid identities are obtained on the basis of one's core identities. Phan observed that, despite their exposure to the Western influence (e.g. modes of thinking, values, pedagogical practices, etc.) via TESOL courses, the Western-trained Vietnamese teachers often displayed a strong sense of belonging to their own culture's value systems, constantly referring to their national identity which functioned as a stronghold on which they negotiated their other identities. By holding on to the core Vietnamese values, these teachers were able to manage dynamic changes while maintaining the sense of continuity in their identity formation.

The explosive growth of contexts where English along with other major languages are used as a lingua franca points to the needs to replace the native/non-native dichotomy with an approach in which linguistic practices enable language learners and teachers to assert their agency and feel empowered. Greater focus should be on preparing current and future practitioners for their profession with special attention to the teachers' diverse skills, linguistic resources and transnational identities. While the teaching of English as a Second Language (ESL) or English as a Foreign Language (EFL) have been wrought by the native speaker ideology, which positions English language learners as different from (and in most cases) deficient compared to speakers of standardised varieties of English, the EIL paradigm sees the English used by English language learners as a flexible linguistic resource. Teachers who embrace EIL philosophies will ensure that L2 learners are granted sufficient opportunities to use English in developing new forms of identities which are not necessarily confined within traditionally defined national or cultural frames but bear more resemblance to the concept of 'international posture' (Yashima, 2002), which entails an interest in international affairs and an open-minded attitude towards cultural diversity. In addition, digital advances have transformed our perception of space and time in this world. Social media allow L2 learners to engage in a kind of learning and communication that is not fixed in physical settings but available both online and offline. The digital world made possible by globalisation has opened the door for learners and teachers to explore options in constructing their identity.

## Why Study L2 Learner and Teacher Identity?

The magic of self-knowledge was best captured by Lao Tzu: 'He who knows others is wise; he who knows himself is enlightened'. This widely known Daoist proverb says something about human nature: our perpetual desire to 'know' who we are. We are now living in a world where ambiguity has become part of everyday life, where it becomes increasingly problematic to phrase an answer to seemingly straightforward questions such as 'where are you from?' and 'what is your mother tongue/first language?'. As Blommaert and Backus (2011) rightly capture: 'Societies now face fundamental challenges of knowledge: knowing who is who, what we are and what it is we do' (2011: 4). Language learners and teachers engaging in cross-cultural interactions on global stages could benefit from a heightened awareness of language, identity and sociocultural factors that impact on their development of multilingual competence. Such awareness can be cultivated, as hinted in the saying above, through our ability to self-introspect, to reflect on and to be in awareness of who we are as an English teacher and what we carry with us to the language classroom – personal histories, aspirations, trepidation – the entire constellation of attributes and characters. Self-reflection encourages us to embrace our personal history and all the events that make us who we are today. The sheer force of self-introspective practices can fundamentally alter teachers' viewpoints. When teachers infuse reflection time in their pedagogical toolkit, their professional life becomes a continual drip of therapy as they are continuously seeing things differently. By making self-reflection a habit, teachers are given multiple readings of the self of their learners and their own, which in turn grants them greater clarity on what they could do to improve the learning and teaching experience (see Farrell, 2018 for more reflective practices).

In the world where everything is constantly in a state of flux, the unique ability as humans to self-introspect and to use this knowledge to guide our future goals and actions will remain important. Whether as a learner or a teacher, our perception of who believe or feel we are (self-concept) helps us monitor and evaluate our behaviour and select appropriate strategies that facilitate our language use while navigating our daily life encounters to make sense of the world around us. This awareness about ourselves is also closely linked to our sense of agency, which involves our willingness as well as ability to take control of, and to be responsible for, our actions. Many teachers may initially find the idea of teaching EIL unfamiliar, something beyond their limits where they might not immediately succeed. They may feel like they are in the dark, not knowing even where to begin. The mere act of creating opportunities for oneself to cultivate the sense of self-awareness is a first essential step to open up a whole realm of possibilities. Such initiative indicates that we care enough to exert effort and exercise our agency to see an advantage in gaining the experience in a pedagogical approach we do know not so much about.

Indeed, this form of self-introspection also extends its application and benefits to our learners. Given that the ultimate goal of any language classroom is the utmost service brought to the learners, it is advisable, if not obligatory, for language teachers to be informed of who their students are. This appreciation of each individual learner's self along with the learning experiences they bring to the classroom not only allows us to empathise and create a meaningful social connection with them but also equips us with a valuable pedagogical toolkit that helps us achieve different tasks – from anticipating their concerns to interpreting behaviours and giving well-considered feedback.

So what happens when we do not know ourselves or our learners well enough? In the same vein with beliefs and attitudes (discussed in the previous chapter), teachers' sense of self can affect their practices and students' learning. Unaware of their deeply internalised native speaker ideology, teachers may inadvertently categorise students with a 'non-native English learner' label upon whom the native-like ideals are imposed. To prevent this, teachers can engage in a critical self-reflection by interrogating established ways of thinking about issues surrounding English and the teaching of the language through telling their own stories on which constructive feedback from those who share similar or different experiences can be obtained (Norris, 2017). This is exemplified in Rose and Montakantiwong (2018), in which Anya, one of the authors, in narrating her initial attempt to implement her EIL vision she had constructed during her studies in a TESOL programme in an English course she was teaching, came to an upsetting awareness that her desired language teacher self as someone who embraces linguistic diversity with multilingual repertoires had failed to materialise when put to the test in an actual classroom. Through a critical reflection, Anya became aware that her practice was still chained to native speaker ideals and that the repercussions of her pedagogical actions were in stark contrast to the vision to which she had initially aspired. While the experience can be unsettling and disappointing, the approach can prompt teachers to engage in creative conflicts (Dörnyei & Kubanyiova, 2014). This is evident in Anya's reflective comment: 'The dismay I felt led me to contemplate what I could have otherwise offered to the students, and to my own professional teacher self' (Rose & Montakantiwong, 2018: 94). Such a story suggests that the fog of what is unknown about ourselves can blind our vision. The aspect of our self we are ignorant of (or deliberately ignore) can harm not only to our students' learning but also to our sense of self-worth. Although a conscious examination of our beliefs and teaching practices can stir up disconcerting emotions, as illustrated in Anya's autoethnographic narrative, the practice can trigger an awakening realisation of our original vision and help us to remain true to it. In this sense, our attempt to learn more about our not-so-visible self may possibly be the most fundamental step in making the students' learning, and thus our teaching experience the best it can potentially be.

## What Does the Research Tell Us?

The following table outlines studies on the topic of teacher and learner identity.

Sung (2014) investigated the perceptions of local and/or global identities among nine L2 learners of English when communicating in ELF contexts. While some L2 learners would like to present themselves as global citizens in ELF communication, others wished to assert their local identity by maintaining their local accent during ELF interactions.

Jenkins (2007) examined in Chapter 7 of the book how English teachers' attitudes may affect the teachers' identities. Teachers expressed ambivalent attitudes in that while they would like to attain an imagined native speaker of Inner Circle English varieties they also hold high regard for their L1 and nationality which they signal in their localised accent.

**Table 8.1** Example studies on teacher and learner identity

| Researchers | Topic | Participants | Research design | Data collection method |
| --- | --- | --- | --- | --- |
| Sung, 2014a | EIL learner identity | Cantonese-speaking undergraduate students in an EMI university in Hong Kong (N = 9) | Qualitative approach | Two rounds of in-depth semi-structured interviews |
| Jenkins, 2007 | ELF teacher identity | Non-native speaker English teachers (N = 17) | Qualitative approach | In-depth, semi-structured interviews |
| Park, 2012 | Identity constructions and negotiations of non-native English-speaking teachers | East Asian women teachers of English in MATESOL programmes (N = 1) | Narrative approach | Electronic autobiographical narratives, electronic journal entries, individual interviews |
| Higgins and Ponte, 2017 | Teacher identity formation through multilingual pedagogy | In-service elementary teachers who participated in a one-year professional development (PD) project on multilingual language learners (N = 7) | Collaborative action research | Interviews, teacher assignments, classroom observations and teacher conferences with field supporters |
| Zheng, 2017 | L2 teachers' enactment of translingual teacher identities | English department International teaching assistants learning how to teach College Composition classes at a public university in the United States (N = 2) | Ethnographic multiple case study approach | Participant observation, semi-structured interviews, survey, course-related documents |
| Xu, 2013 | Imagined identities and professional identity change | Novice Chinese EFL teachers in a B.A. EFL teacher education programme at a university in China (N = 4) | Qualitative approach (longitudinal) | Individual interviews, journal protocols and classroom observations |
| Kubanyiova, 2012 | L2 teachers' Conceptual Change | Teachers of English as a foreign language (EFL) participating in a teacher development programme (N = 8) | Grounded theory ethnography | Observation, in-depth interviews, questionnaires to students, focus group interviews with students |
| Doiz and Lasagabaster, 2018 | EMI language teacher selves | EMI student teachers attending the Multilingualism Program (MP) in a public university in northern Spain (N = 13 for teachers and 15 for students) | Qualitative approach | Focus group discussions |

Park's (2012) narrative inquiry examined experiences of two non-native English-speaking teachers who managed to assert agency over their L2 teacher identities by working with an inspiring and supportive non-native English-speaking teacher educator. The study foregrounds the positive impact of pre-service teacher education on teachers' development of critical attitudes toward native-speakerism, which results in an increase in professional self-esteem and confidence.

Based on Gee's (2001) and McGriff's (2015) discourse-oriented framework, Higgins and Ponte (2017) report how teachers form their professional identities while incorporating multilingual pedagogies into the realities of contemporary classroom. The study highlights the influence the teachers' ethonolinguistic histories has on their views about multilingualism in their teaching contexts and the role multilingual pedagogies play in enabling the teachers' critical reflection on issues surrounding languages, identities and classroom practices.

Zheng (2017), by drawing on Canagarajah's (2013) translingualism and the notion of identity-as-pedagogy (Morgan, 2004), explores what it means for international teaching assistants to be an effective translingual teacher. The study demonstrates how a teacher's translingual identity enacted via adoption of a translingual approach in pedagogical practices can be used beneficially and strategically in ways that not only legitimise language teacher identities but also enhance their learning outcomes.

Kubanyiova's (2012) study focused on the development of self-concepts in eight L2 teachers in Slovakia. Using grounded theory ethnography, she investigated how different language teacher selves influenced their pedagogical strategies and the overall development as English teachers. This longitudinal study offers pedagogical insights into the vital roles of values and teaching philosophies underpinning a language teacher's vision of his/her desired identity in facilitating one's identity transformation.

Xu (2013) employed the constructs of 'imagined vs practiced identity' in her longitudinal study of four Chinese novice EFL teachers. The study explores the individual transformation from the imagined to practiced identity that underlined the novice teachers' professional experience teaching in K-12 schools in China. Although the scope and span of possible images created is limitless, the study suggests that it is only through engaging in real practices can we turn these imagined states to practiced identities.

In Doiz and Lasagabaster's (2018) study, three focus group discussions were arranged to explore the interaction between the L2 motivational self system (Dörnyei, 2005, 2009) and the learning/teaching experiences of university students and teachers in EMI settings from three different faculties. Findings indicated that the *Ideal L2 teacher-self* played a more prominent role than their ought-to selves among EMI teachers.

## Implications for Teachers in Global Contexts

As discussed throughout the chapter, the concept of identity is a complex, multi-layered phenomenon. One may attempt the impossible task of deriving a single definition or an exhaustive list of perspectives, but such a list will not hold up for very long. Like languages, none of which exists in a homogeneously unchanging form, language learners and teachers are continually inhabiting (and ascribed by others) new and emergent positions. Globalisation speeds up the process, and many millennial learners and teachers may already realise that their self-concept is inevitably undergoing constant change and negotiation due to our rapidly changing world.

Given our ultimate interest in helping L2 learners to develop a healthy sense of their L2 self, we first need to consider how teachers themselves in everyday TESOL classroom construct and negotiate their L2 teacher selves over time. A greater emphasis must be placed on language teacher identities. In order to understand teachers, we must understand 'the professional, cultural, political, and individual identities which they claim or which are assigned to them' (Varghese *et al.*, 2005: 22). What must be done is to expand the scope of inquiry to encompass not only language learners' perceptions but also those of the teachers. This knowledge will allow us to better understand ways in which language teacher cognitions of English language and its pedagogy can transform their classroom instructions and create language learning opportunities for their students in classrooms, which, in turn, illuminates how the learners' learning experience can be improved (Kubanyiova, 2017).

So what does it mean to be an L2 teacher of English in the 21st century? Contemporary debates have called attention to the ways in which L2 teacher identities have evolved in the wake of globalisation and neoliberal movement. As evident in two journal special issues of on language teacher identity in *TESOL Quarterly* (Varghese *et al.*, 2016) and *Modern Language Journal* (De Costa & Norton, 2017), language teacher identity is deeply embedded in the teaching practices and policy making of TESOL professionals. Throughout the chapter we have combined various perspectives about the L2 identities of both learners and teachers, and we now know that the eternally changing, positioned and fluid nature of language teacher identity problematises the essentialist and monolingual descriptions that permeate the profession. The exponential rise in global encounters between users of different lingua-cultural repertoires has additionally rendered the native/non-native distinction less relevant for the teaching of an international lingua franca. This is especially salient as the major objective of teaching EIL is to prepare learners to become agents of transculturation (Dogancay-Aktuna & Hardman, 2012), global citizens (Byram & Parmenter, 2015), translingual cosmopolitans (Canagarajah, 2013), or multilingual subjects (Kramsch, 2009).

It has become clear that L2 teachers, irrespective of their ascribed native or non-native status, can capitalise on their agency to make change, redefining their role from a passive victim of outdated beliefs rekindled by the societal force to a more empowering one. For language teachers, the matter has therefore become less about who can teach standard varieties of English (e.g. American or British English) but who can teach pragmatic, intercultural skills that enable its learners to attain a global identity unbounded by the limited identity categories based on race, ethnicity, social class, or gender. In removing a monolingual lens in TESOL, and instead highlighting the translingual mindset of L2 practitioners, Kramsch and Zhang (2017) encourage L2 teachers to see themselves as 'multilingual instructors' whose multilingual mindset allows them to obtain a sense of liberation and empowerment. By viewing ourselves as multilingual instructors, we consider how the multiple dimensions of identity (e.g. national, linguistic, ethnic, gender, class, educational, etc.) of both our learners and ourselves affect how we carry out our practices and thus make better-informed pedagogical decisions. Ignorance or lack awareness compromises not only our healthy sense of self as a teacher but also that of our students.

L2 teachers with a multilingual mindset also seek to redefine the ways they perceive social reality. While it may be difficult to eradicate ideologies (e.g. native-speakerism) deeply rooted in our past language learning experiences, we can change how we think about them and therefore the kind of association we choose to form with them when moving forward. Instead of holding on to the now-obsolete deficit view of English learners, L2 teachers can embrace an EIL-oriented view where their past experiences as learners of the language are reconceived in terms of knowledge or resources. The perk of being an English teacher who shares with their students the linguistic and cultural knowledge of learning the language is the competitive edge afforded to them via their prior experience as learners themselves. They know where the students are most likely to struggle because they have walked that path before. L2 English teachers are also in a position where they can look retrospectively at their own journey, combining insights from that history with the know-how gained in professional training. The role of power and struggle in L2 learning suggests that teachers are in the best position to make sure that a language classroom will provide a safe supportive learning space where all learners feel competent and welcome to participate and express their multiple identities.

With intercultural communication opening up new spaces and resources for identity construction, teachers should actively familiarise themselves with various issues associated with identity in the classroom in order to better facilitate students in their 'shuttling' between different varieties of English and different speech communities (Canagarajah, 2013). This can be achieved through the teachers' meta-understanding of

EIL as heterogeneous in multilingual classrooms that have increasingly become a norm rather than an exception. EIL-oriented teacher education can facilitate this process. For example, acknowledged of the impossibility to attain the *Ideal EMI teacher self* (the L2 speaker who speaks the L2 like a native), most teachers in Doiz and Lasagabaster's (2016) study aimed for the more realistic local ideal EMI teacher self for whom English functioned as a lingua franca. Here, ELF acted as a motivating factor that allowed these teachers to 'leave their complexes aside' (2016: 141) and position themselves as confident communicators of English. The authors also noted that achieving these aspired selves could also be a cumbersome mission for many due to restrictive binary categorical identity options such as the dominant native/non-native speaker discourse. This suggests a clear implication for pre- and in-service teacher education to consider the varying experiences of teachers with respect to privilege and marginalisation in the local and international contexts of English language teaching. Teacher education programmes should offer TESOL practitioners a discursive space where they can exercise agency in forming an empowering their own L2 teacher self-concept.

In the English language classroom context, L2 teachers may design classroom practices that promote students' sense of ownership of the English language, enhance the range of identity options available to language learners, and foster students' critically reflective, and multilingual, identities. Teachers can, for example, have learners describe their perception of themselves as learners of English as a global language. This can be materialised in any form, in writing or speaking, online or offline. These self-portraits will provide teachers with some insights into their learners' world, which the teachers can use to help the students in their learning about the language and, indeed, about themselves.

## Post-reading Activities

### Reflect

This chapter has emphasised throughout how L2 learners and teachers may significantly benefit from the power of self-knowledge. Given the much-touted advocacy for a learner-centred approach in our pedagogical practices, think of a language class you used to teach (or will likely teach) and then consider steps that need to be taken in order to understand how your students see themselves. To what extent are you aware of how your learners view themselves with regard to learning English as a global language? How do you imagine your students would describe themselves as L2 English learners (strengths, weaknesses, characteristics, learning styles, aspirations, etc.)? How might you elicit this information from the learners?

### Discuss

(1) This chapter has noted the overlapping and interdependent nature of social categories such as race, ethnicity, gender, class and religion. Which of these identity categories do you think impact the perceived legitimacy of English language teachers the most? In what ways can attending to identity-related issues in TESOL facilitate our understanding of the connection between a sense of privilege experienced by one group and marginalisation faced by the other?

(2) Based on Bourdieu's notion of social, economic and cultural capital (1991), to what extent are the L2 imagined selves of each learner determined by the degrees of capital/resources available to them? In what way do you think the ideologies held by each individual L2 learners can affect their formation of their future identity as a global English-speaking citizen in the face of globalisation?

(3) Complete the following sentence: I believe that an ideal/good L2 English teacher should… because …

### Apply

Research has shown that language and identity are inextricably interwoven. Design an EIL task for your future English language classroom where learners' linguistic resources and issues of identities are brought together. Keep in mind that the goal is to create safe spaces where students can feel comfortable to communicate struggles and conflicts that may emerge from EIL learning.

## Resources for Further Reading

Barkhuizen, G. (ed.). (2017) *Reflections on Language Teacher Identity Research*. New York: Routledge.

An edited collection of papers, this book by Gary Barkhuizen provides a comprehensive sketch of developments in teacher identity research and offers a working definition of language teacher identity by combining perspectives from a diverse range of theoretical frameworks and dimensions (cognitive, emotional, ideological and historical). Inclusive and accessible, the collection includes a recommended reading list for those interested in learning more about language teacher identity and open to multiple theoretical, methodological and empirical stances.

Kramsch, C. and Zhang, L. (2017) *The Multilingual Instructor: What Foreign Language Teachers Say about their Experience and Why it Matters*. Oxford: Oxford University Press.

Drawing on an ecological approach and a complexity thought model, the book narrates the life stories of foreign language teachers, native and non-native, of the particular language they were teaching in an American instructional context. It explores how these multilingual instructors construct their perception of their teaching selves, give meaning to their professional lives and deal with multilingual experience in the classroom. Based on ethnographic studies carried out at the Berkeley Language Centre, the authors revisit the age-old debate around nativeness/non-nativeness and the many challenges, from institutional to ethical, encountered by these multilingual instructors. Although the book does not specifically target English language teachers, observations and theoretically based and data-driven lines of argument prove to be highly relevant and insightful for all L2 teachers.

Dörnyei, Z. and Kubanyiova, M. (2014) *Motivating Learners, Motivating Teachers: Building Vision in the Language Classroom.* Cambridge: Cambridge University Press.

The book expands on theoretical issues associated with the motivational perspective of the learners and teachers' future selves, discussed in this chapter. Its greatest value lies in its pedagogical applications, arguing that teacher motivation needs to be tackled before we can move on to consider how teachers can foster the motivation of their learners. As the authors write: 'in order to be able to have something worthwhile to give to our students, we need to look after ourselves and nurture our own motivational basis' (p. 123). Not only do the authors give a detailed explanation on how the L2 Self Motivational Framework can be employed with language teachers, but they also offer a range of practical classroom activities in various language-learning contexts.

Cheung, Y.L., Said, S.B. and Park, E. (eds) (2015) *Advances and Current Trends in Language Teacher Identity research.* New York: Routledge/Taylor & Francis.

The volume investigates how the discourses associated with native speaker superiority can disempower and perpetuate a sense of inadequacy and illegitimacy among teachers who have been labelled as non-native.

**In addition to the above books, there are a number of special journal issues that deal with language teacher identity:**

Varghese, M.M., Motha, S., Trent, J., Park, G. and Reeves, J. (eds) (2016) Language teacher identity in multilingual settings. *TESOL Quarterly* 50 (3), 541–783.

De Costa, P.I. and Norton, B. (eds) (2017) Transdisciplinarity and language teacher identity (special issue). *Modern Language Journal* 101 (S1), 1–105.

Yazan, B. and Lindhal, K. (eds) (2019) An identity-oriented lens to TESOL teachers' lives: from teacher education to classroom contexts. *TESOL Journal.*

# Part 4

# Initiating Change in TESOL

# 9 Initiating Change: An Invitation to Teachers and Teacher Educators

## Pre-reading Activities

### *Think*

Based on Morgan's (1986) work on organisational metaphors, Cameron and Green (2004) suggest that we can view organisations in four different ways: organisations as machines; organisations as political systems; organisations as organisms; and organisations as flux and transformation. These different metaphors also imply different views about the role a change leader should play in the change process. The *machine* metaphor suggests that the change leader be the chief designer and implementer of the changes; the *political* metaphor says that the role of change leader is that of a powerful speaker and behind-the-scene negotiators; the *organism* metaphor implies that the leader of change act as a coach or a counsellor; and the *flux and transformation* metaphor frames the leader as a facilitator of emergent change. Think about which of these metaphors might apply to leading EIL curricular change.

### *Discuss*

Now imagine yourself as someone who would like to introduce EIL practices within your own teaching/learning English context. Discuss the following:

(1) Which view of change leader's role do you feel most drawn to personally?
(2) What are the implications for you as a leader of change in terms of understanding the dynamics of your teaching context (current and future)?
(3) What might or might not work when it comes to curricular innovation?

## Introduction

Throughout the book we have highlighted how the fast-changing sociolinguistic landscape of the world is pointing to a macro-level change in TESOL. For this to happen, we need to recognise that EIL curricular innovation and its execution are contingent upon meticulous planning in which a number of factors are taken into consideration. This chapter echoes Rose and Galloway's (2019) view, in which calls for change should be driven not only by theoretical assumptions, but also on-the-ground research into actual practices. This chapter first discusses an agentive role that individual teachers could take on to bring about monitored change at different levels within their working contexts. EIL teaching must foreground *teacher* and *learner agency* in bringing about the kind of change they wish to see in the classroom. In other words, we need to listen to and learn from *early adopters* of EIL practice. Teachers are the *main actor* (or *change agent*) to be able to visualise what good EIL pedagogy might look like in a real-life classroom.

The chapter then looks at what change might look like for teacher educators, who are working with pre-service and in-service teachers in TESOL accreditation programmes. It examines the powerful role that teacher educators can play in building pedagogical knowledge around EIL for future teachers. As this is one area within which there has been substantial research, this chapter outlines a number of studies that have reported on the impact of EIL course-content within TESOL programmes on teachers' attitudes and practice.

## Individual Teachers as Change Agents

The world we live in continues to change at an intense rate, and the educational institutions that teachers work in are also changing dramatically in terms of their strategies, structures and systems. These changes, of course, impact on the expectations that institutions place on staff, whether these be programme directors, experienced teachers, or newly recruited teachers. Many readers of this book have (or will have) experience within the language teaching profession when they have had to grapple with some form of change. Regardless of the level or degree of change, successful and sustainable organisational transformation cannot be effectively managed unless several factors are taken into account. This section outlines some guided suggestions for teachers aspiring to introduce and implement EIL change within their own teaching environments.

### Starting point: Teachers as a changemaker

Wherever change is to be introduced and implemented, it must first begin with teachers. EIL-oriented teachers must realise that they need to first and foremost acquire a solid theoretical foundation of concepts and issues surrounding EIL as a paradigm. As Dogancay-Aktuna and Hardman (2018) argued, EIL pedagogy can become a classroom reality without teachers having to despairingly seek and pin all their hopes on prescribed EIL 'how-to' teaching tips. Given well-founded understandings of EIL, teachers will (and should) be able to decide whether or not (and how) their own sense-making of EIL can be most appropriately operationalised within their own educational contexts.

## Understand the teaching and learning context through ethnographic analysis

Regardless of the type of change, or the extent to which change is to be introduced, we must bear in mind that those people on the receiving end are human beings. The success or failure of change is ultimately dependent on these individuals. To devise well-designed change implementation plans, which meet the needs and interests of those within it, we need to first understand the 'culture' on its own terms. In other words, we need to unravel cognitions, perceptions and meanings of EIL held by those inhabiting the system – the supposed receivers and doers of the innovation. Such processes cannot be taken for granted as we have no rights to assume that EIL or any pedagogical innovation will always be positively received.

As Nativespeakerism is deeply rooted, an 'epistemic break' (Kumaravadivelu, 2012a) away from the status quo may prove a challenging endeavour unless we understand how teachers select and interpret information from their teaching environment (e.g. policy texts on English language education) and act on those interpretations. As Chapter 2 has outlined, any curriculum development is started from, and informed by, good needs analysis. Needs analysis considers not only a learner's *necessities* and *lacks* in the language in terms of their future use, but also their *wants*. Thus, by treating learners as individuals, teachers can help educate them about their likely future needs of English use, which will in turn influence their personal orientation as future global language users.

## Using metaphors to identify how we approach organisational change

Each teacher has their own assumptions about how organisations work in general, developed through a combination of experience and education. The use of metaphor is one of the several ways in which these assumptions can be expressed. Different metaphors of change lead to different assumptions about what teachers do. By looking at the type of leadership that follows from a specific approach to organisational change, teachers wishing to be successful leaders of change can make use of the four key metaphors (Morgan, 1986). These metaphors can help teachers understand the different beliefs and assumptions about change that exist and accordingly make a thoroughly considered plan. These different frameworks and ways of approaching change can be utilised at an individual, team and organisational level, although the easiest and most sensible way is to begin with one's own perception. Table 9.1 displays both benefits as well as downsides of each metaphor and how using each (or all) of the four metaphors can offer insights for those wishing to be successful leaders of change.

Table 9.1 displays how each metaphor brings about different conceptions of organisational innovation initiatives. It also outlines the ensuing roles enacted by those wishing to be successful leaders of change.

If teachers see their teaching context as in need of clear goals and structure, they may be using a *machine metaphor* as a perception filter. The machine metaphor also implies that setting goals and driving them through to completion are responsibilities of the change leader who should be at the top of the organisational structure. Over-orientation toward this metaphor results in micromanagement of outcomes and too little risk taking.

If a teacher talks about their organisation as if it was *a political system*, they may see change as truly possible only if it was led by influential people functioning as the figurehead exercising paramount authority whose main duty involves garnering followers by means of communication of an attractive future vision and negotiation. Hidden agendas and political scheming are also a possibility, so manipulation needs to be kept in check.

If a teacher describes their teaching organisation as *an organism*, they see people's involvement during the change process as mandatory. Supported by the leader whose primary role is that of coach, counsellor and consultant, these people must also organically feel the need for change. Overuse of the metaphor may run the risk of moving too slowly and too late.

If a teacher sees change as something that emerges and thus cannot be managed, they may have adopted *a flux and transformation metaphor* in which each and every one is part of the system, whatever position they hold. Here, leaders act as a facilitator of emergent change, encouraging open discussions about conflicts and tensions that need to be dealt with while avoiding being vague and directionless.

These four of Morgan's organisational metaphors allow us to explore the range of existing assumptions that with regard to how organisational change works. While it is useful to be able to identify to which metaphor you feel most drawn, we believe that change may be optimally brought about when we selectively combine these different perspectives, capitalising the utmost benefits offered by each while taking necessary precautions to avoid the tunnel-vision pitfall. Implementing EIL practices in a context-sensitive manner requires flexibility and openness. It is also multi-dimensional in terms of styles and approaches. Teachers can steer clear of getting wrapped up in one way of doing things and attain more complete insights into the change process if they can bring themselves to embrace various views about how change can be approached.

**Table 9.1** Metaphors of change (adapted from Cameron & Green, 2009: 139–140)

| Metaphor | Nature of change | Changemaker's roles | Types of leadership required | Typical pitfalls for changemakers |
|---|---|---|---|---|
| Machine | Change must be goal-driven whereby desired outcomes set at the beginning pave the direction. Careful planning is a must. Resistance can be managed. | Chief designer and implementer of the changes. | Project management, Goal setting, Monitoring and Controlling | Micro-management allows little experimenting or taking risks. |
| Political system | Change requires a powerful coalition behind it and must be supported by a powerful person capable of negotiations. | Powerful speaker and behind-the-scene negotiators | Visionary, Building a powerful coalition, Connecting agendas | Change leaders put their own agenda first, resulting in dwindling trust among people. Manipulation also means compliance instead of commitment. |
| Organism | Change is adaptive. Individuals and groups need to be aware of the 'felt need' for change and supported through the process. End state can be collaboratively designed and worked towards. | Coach and counsellor | Coaching and supporting | Change may never happen, or does happen, but too little too late. Emphasis is on reacting rather than initiating. |
| Flux and transformation | Change cannot be managed; it emerges out of conflict and tension. Managers are part of the process. Their job is to highlight gaps and contradictions. | Facilitator of emergent change | Enabling fruitful connections among team members, Amplifying issues. | When change effort becomes vague and directionless, change leaders and others involved are likely to become confused and frustrated as a sense of progress to motivate future effort is lacking. |

## Forming a changemaker squad

In addition to familiarising themselves with current EIL issues to maintain up-to-date understandings of the field, aspiring EIL-oriented teachers wishing to make a difference in their students' lives may need to take on different roles. These roles vary from promoting EIL principles among students to facilitating other teachers in carrying out EIL-oriented activities.

But how do teachers as leaders of a change process ensure that all the necessary roles are carried out? A wise approach perhaps is to not go at it alone. Bringing about change and transformation is a complex endeavour, and it is not possible for one teacher, no matter how active, enthusiastic and committed they may be, to undertake this considerable task without some sort of collaboration. Ascendancy of a team has become one of the most prominent themes of organisational life in the 21st century. Much of today's work is organised through team collaboration to ensure success. While very little has been investigated about the role of teams in implementing EIL-oriented change at an organisational level (see Mora & Golovátina-Mora, 2017; and Kang, 2017), we would like to suggest that for change to be long-lasting and achieve wider and greater impact, a team of change agents sharing common goals needs to be in place.

Instead of attempting to perform all these roles individually, teachers are encouraged to team up with other teachers, setting a stage where one can voluntarily participate and decide for themselves which role they could play in carrying out such change. After all, it is better for our students to have more than just one teacher able and willing to act as a role model of effective EIL learning situations while simultaneously providing constant support. Drawing on O'Neill's (2000) four specific leadership roles necessary for successful and sustained change efforts in organisations, teachers may want to observe how these different roles are configured within their teaching/learning context. These four key roles for successful change include: Sponsor; Implementer; Change agent; and Advocate. Each of these are outlined in turn below.

### Sponsor (head of department/programme, policymakers, board of committee)

Sponsors have the authority to make change happen. Entitled with the capacity to legitimises and sanction the change, sponsors may exercise direct command over individuals who will implement the change and control resources such as time and money. For a successful implementation of EIL practices, sponsors must demonstrate a clear vision for the change in which goals and measurable outcomes for the initiative are identified.

### Implementer (teacher practitioners – all)

Implementers are a key player in charge of carrying out the change. They have direct line responsibilities to the sponsor. Their responsibilities include providing the team with on-the-ground feedback from the field. Being closest to the change allows implementers to notice issues that may be overlooked by other team members, thereby saving the team from neglecting obstacles that require immediate solutions. One of the largest saboteurs of successful innovation stems from false compliance at the beginning of the initiative, which effects later adoption in the innovation cycle. Implementers can circumvent such issues and can better commit to a change effort by listening, inquiring and clarifying other team members' questions and concerns.

### Change agent (e.g. course coordinator, researcher-practitioner)

A facilitator of the change, change agents help sponsors and implementers stay aligned with one another. Whether the change initiative turns out to be effective, balanced and long-lasting depends on how well change agents manage resources (time and people) and avoid taking on too much. While having no direct line of authority over implementers, change agents may act as data gatherers, educators, advisors, meeting facilitators and coordinators among team members.

### Advocate (e.g. researcher)

Advocates are often passionate and highly motivated to make the change happen. However, without sponsors to help lobby for change, realising such change is difficult. It is important that advocates be competent in promoting EIL ideas by showing their compatibility with issues that are most relevant to the teaching organisation's missions and goals.

A simple yet flexible way of defining who does what in any process of change is often necessary in today's globalised scenarios where existing hierarchy becomes blurred and roles and duties overlap. EIL teachers may find this framework useful for kicking off and sustaining EIL-oriented change, and for judging how other teachers/stakeholders in their community can be part of the change process and realise their capacity to effect meaningful change. These steps should provide teachers as a changemaker with a clear foundation on how EIL can be implemented as an organisational change, illustrating a range of different well-thought-out roles which can be taken up by committed individuals who are 'in' for the entire duration of change. While the change may be slow, it is of utmost significance that we as a changemaker can help pave a life-changing path for our students.

## Diffusion of Innovation by Educational Managers

In educational innovation, many scholars draw on Rogers' (2003) theory of innovation diffusion to describe large-scale, planned innovation. For example, this might be relevant if an entire school or university programme wishes to make large changes to its curriculum. In such cases, the diffusion of innovation needs to be planned and executed. Rogers (2003) defines diffusion as 'the process by which an innovation is communicated through certain channels over time among the members of a social system' (2003: 5). For EIL innovation in education, therefore, diffusion could be defined as the process by which an EIL innovation is communicated through channels over time among the members of an educational institution. This theory of innovation diffusion has been used previously to describe ways to put World Englishes into pedagogical practice (Brown,

1993), and more recently Global Englishes into practice (Rose & Galloway, 2019; Galloway & Numajiri, 2019).

Important in diffusion is who adopts the innovation, and when. If a school were to implement a large-scale EIL innovation to the curriculum, it is essential that all teachers feel comfortable taking on the innovation, so this can affect the timing of diffusion. Rogers (2003) groups adopters of an innovation into five categories: innovators, early adopters, the early majority, the late majority and laggards (Rogers, 2003). Porter and Graham (2016) drew on various definitions of these adopters (Humbert, 2007; Moore, 2002; Rogers, 2003; Thackray *et al.*, 2010) to consolidate their characteristics and inform their own knowledge of technological innovation in the language classroom. Their efforts are summarised in Table 9.2, with adaptations made to shift focus to EIL innovation.

When a management team wants to instigate a wide-spread innovation, it is advisable to deal with one segment of adopters at a time (Moore, 2002). This way, feedback from each group can help with improving the innovation for the subsequent group. In the case of an innovation failing to achieve its goals, it can also be discontinued before impacting other teachers and learners. While it seems as though the 'innovators' would be the most influential group in a diffusion process, it is actually the early adopters whose work is most influential. While the innovators may be deemed as 'trail-blazers' by some, they could be viewed with scepticism

**Table 9.2** Characteristics of Rogers' five categories of innovation adopters (adapted from Porter & Graham, 2016: 751)

| Category | Characteristics |
|---|---|
| Innovators | • First to adopt a new innovation.<br>• Represent approximately 2.5% of adopters.<br>• Aggressively pursue new EIL innovation.<br>• Substantial EIL knowledge and connections to sources of innovation. |
| Early adopters | • Next to adopt new innovations.<br>• Represent approximately 13.5% of adopters.<br>• Substantial EIL knowledge, however innovations are enacted with greater discretion than innovators.<br>• Serve as examples and opinion leaders for others contemplating adoption. |
| Early majority | • Adopt at varying times after the early adopters but before the average adopters.<br>• Represent approximately 34% of adopters.<br>• Fairly comfortable with EIL ideas, but only adopt when they have compelling evidence or recommendations of its value. |
| Late majority | • Adopt innovations after the early majority.<br>• Represents approximately 34% of adopters.<br>• Typically, less comfortable with EIL ideas.<br>• Adopt an innovation due to peer pressure and necessity. |
| Laggards | • Last to adopt an innovation.<br>• Represent approximately 16% of adopters.<br>• Express aversion to EIL and resist new innovations even after necessity prompts adoption. |

by others. In particular, the Late Majority and Laggards may view the Innovators as 'rushing into' adopting new approaches and ideas, which have not been fully tested. In terms of EIL innovation, the Innovators may be more likely to be newly trained teachers, having acquired their EIL knowledge as part of their recent training. Furthermore, the Innovators are just a small percentage of the population, and thus may not hold so much influence among teachers as a whole. As a result, it is the 'early adopters' that management needs to work more closely with, as this population's discretion may be valued more by both the early and late majority as well as the innovators. Their success and support in communicating this success is vital to ensure the recruitment of the *early majority*. The professional knowledge of the early adopters is also vital is diffusing the important work of the innovators in applying their successes a wider educational context. Thus, it is the early adopters who have the greater potential to become champions of the innovation for subsequent groups, and tip the balance in favour of EIL adoption overall.

## Incorporating EIL Pedagogy into Teacher Education

An effort has been made to fill a noted 'conceptual gap' (Seidlhofer, 2004) between theory and practice. Innovations have also been incorporated to TESOL programmes on a more practical level. Some innovations have been implemented in courses and programmes, as described in Chapter 3. Other studies have emerged that incorporate EIL-oriented activities into classroom practices, as addressed in Chapter 6. Similarly, innovations have also been incorporated into TESOL teacher education, since it is one of the crucial components that facilitates the innovation cycle (Matsuda, 2006, 2017b). One area where research has also been conducted is teacher education in in pre-service programmes, seeing as Global Englishes content in relevant to preparation programmes (Chowdhury & Phan, 2014; Phan, 2007).

Teacher education can shape and influence the strong opinions that teachers hold about their roles in the English language classroom. These varying cognitions (discussed in Chapter 8) do not always reflect an understanding of the way English is used in reality, nor do they always capture the need for learners to acquire skills to communicate successfully with L1 and L2 English speakers. For example, teachers tend to consider themselves as custodians of Standard English (Bayyurt, 2006, 2012; Bayyurt & Sifakis, 2017; Sifakis, 2009; Sifakis & Sougari, 2005). A call has been made for the need for teachers to re-evaluate these perceptions (Bayyurt & Sifakis, 2017; Sifakis, 2007, 2014). Most studies that implemented EIL innovations claimed that teachers still strongly believed that their students should learn standard native-English varieties – a view that has attributed to the gap between the ideals of EIL and current TESOL practices (Galloway, 2017; Hino, 2017; Kang, 2017; Zacharias, 2017). Some teachers felt frustrated by EIL-oriented pedagogy because they felt unable to obtain definitive answers for their EIL-related questions, which were mostly context dependent (Galloway, 2017; Manara, 2014; Rose, 2017). Furthermore, many in-service teachers felt unable to implement the innovations, due to limitations of the assigned curriculum, a lack of teaching materials, or a fixed schedule (Galloway, 2017; İnal & Özdemir, 2015). Additionally, some teacher educators who got involved in teacher preparation programmes, courses and units, lacked awareness or were not fully convinced by EIL principles (Selvi, 2017).

Thus, as mentioned in Vettorel and Lopriore (2017), all changes appear to take time due to a lack of awareness, disagreement, rejection, resistance and reluctance from programme administrators, teacher educators, pre- and in-service teachers and students. Additionally, school authorities and stakeholders, such as parents or investors, are still inclined to conform to teaching environments which favour native speaker norms and Standard English (Manara, 2014; Giri & Foo, 2014). In order to move change forward, more action research incorporating EIL-oriented pedagogic actions into TESOL and TESOL teacher education is essential (Galloway, 2017; Rose & Galloway, 2019). In more recent years, we have seen a growing number of action research and classroom research projects on implementing EIL innovations, many of which have been discussed in Chapter 2, Chapter 3 and Chapter 6. In this chapter, we add to these with an exploration of action research style projects which have explored innovation in teacher education courses.

## What the Research Tells Us

Some of the projects that have reported on change in teacher education are summarised in Table 9.3. In these studies, the change desired was often measured in terms of a raised awareness or change in attitudes of teachers towards EIL.

The ELF-TEd project was conducted by Sifakis and Bayyurt (2015), which was part of a larger project reported in Chapter 8 (see Bayyurt & Sifakis, 2015a, 2015b). The EFL-aware teacher education consisted of three phases: theoretical, application and evaluation. These phases included learning about ELF, implementing a mini action research project and evaluating the project. Focus group interviews revealed that the participants became fully aware of the role of English globally and changed their attitudes toward the way they teach. They also gained confidence as teachers and L2 speakers of English. Nevertheless, they also indicated that it would take time to make change happen in their teaching practices. The study also highlighted the issues affecting teaching related to the local school context and pressures from parents and other stakeholders. The study emphasised that it was essential to help teachers understand the concept of ELF and its instruction and the extent to which they could integrate the instruction in real life.

**Table 9.3** Examples of EIL-oriented teacher education projects and influences on pre- and in-service teachers' and teacher educators' attitudes

| Researchers | Participants | Projects | Main attitudinal data |
|---|---|---|---|
| Sifakis and Bayyurt (2015) | Primary, secondary and university teachers (N = 12, 11 from Turkey and 1 from Greece) | The online EFL-aware teacher education consisted of three phases that included study about ELF and implementing a mini action research project. | Focus group interviews |
| Hall et al. (2013) | Pre- and in-service teachers and teacher trainers from multiple countries (N = 17) | The online course introduced new concepts relevant to Global Englishes and provided reflective activities. | Participants' feedback |
| Lopriore (2016) | Pre- and in-service teachers in Italy (A total of N = 250) | The blended and online courses involved ELF components, which included research about ELF uses and ELF-informed lesson planning. | Questionnaires, focus group interviews and written reflections |
| Luciana (2015) | Trainees attending one-year postgraduate course in TESOL. (N = 8) | ELF-informed data-based tasks. | Trainees' interactions during the sessions |
| Vettorel (2015, 2016) and Vettorel and Corrizzato (2016) | In-service teachers in Italy. (N = 139) | Teacher education courses included awareness raising of Would Englishes and ELF, reflections on them in ELT, coursebook evaluations and WE- and ELF-oriented lesson planning in their local context. | Questionnaires, online discussion forums, classroom discussions, groups work, final reports and lesson plans |
| Rose and Galloway (2019) | Pre- and in-service teachers mainly from China. (N = 57) | GELT-informed option course included topics like World Englishes, EIL, ELF and translanguaging research, the role of English in different contexts and GELT. | Questionnaires, interviews and focus groups interviews. |

Another online project was conducted by Hall *et al.* (2013). The course introduced new concepts relevant to Global Englishes and provided reflective activities that allowed participants to reflect and think about the pedagogical implications, often for their own local context. Based on the participants' feedback, the majority of participants became fully aware of Global Englishes and showed a possibility of changing their beliefs and practices. There were a few participants who still were not convinced by the notion of Global Englishes, due to its complexity and ambiguity. The responses of many participants suggested that the course had the potential to trigger change in their own beliefs and practices and in some cases also encouraged them to promote the change in others. The study also indicated that it was unclear whether the teachers actually implemented the innovations in their classrooms; and it was premature to expect any substantial change within the timeframe of the study.

Similarly, Lopriore (2016) also conducted blended and online courses that partly involved ELF components. The participants were asked to research current examples of English use and then to write ELF-aware lesson plans. In terms of the effect on changes in their teaching practices, the study pointed out how difficulties did not lie in teachers' resistance to changes or in their attitudes towards new ways of using and teaching English. Rather the difficulty was created by the limited time available to them for practising new forms of teaching, selecting and adjusting materials and implementing new activities/lessons in their local contexts.

Luciana (2015) implemented some ELF-informed, data-based research tasks into teacher training courses. Findings from teachers' interactions during the sessions were positive, indicating the effectiveness of the ELF-informed activities, which similar in findings to the other studies. The study especially highlighted that the participants showed a greater sensitivity toward the variation of English as language users. Nevertheless, many teachers were uncertain whether they would include the ELF-informed activities in their teaching.

Vettorel (2015, 2016) and Vettorel and Corrizzato (2016) implemented teacher education courses in Italy that included World Englishes- and ELF-informed approaches with 139 in-service teachers. The findings of the study indicated that teachers were very open to the course content. Nevertheless, potential problems that could conceived as 'barriers' for inclusion of WE- and ELF-oriented approaches in the participants' teaching practices were revealed. Those included the difficult, complex and ambiguous nature of the notions of WE and ELF, lack of materials and time, difficulties in assessment and a lack of suitable role models.

Rose and Galloway (2019) reported on their GELT-informed course with pre- and in-service teachers, who were mainly from China. The study confirmed the positive influence of the course on their attitudes towards English and TESOL, with the teachers becoming more aware of Global Englishes, which allowed them to reflect critically on English and TESOL practice. Numerous barriers to change were also revealed, especially the pressures from parents and policymakers to adhere to traditional practices. This same population of teachers is used in Galloway and Numajiri's (2019) investigation of attitudes towards Global Englishes ideas in an MA TESOL program in the United Kingdom.

## Implications for Teachers and Teacher Educators in Global Contexts

Overall, as summarised in Rose and Galloway (2019), World Englishes-, ELF-, EIL- and Global Englishes-informed teacher education courses have been shown to affect attitudes positively. However, although many trainee teachers are open to EIL innovations at a theoretical level, they are unsure of the actions required to put them into practice. This may be because there are a number of barriers for teachers to overcome in order to fully instigate change. The barriers outlined by Rose and Galloway (2019) include: attachment to standards; a lack of awareness of EIL; assessment; parental attitudes; a lack of materials; and teacher training.

Some of these barriers may be better dealt with by applying more organic and transformative styles of innovation management. In terms of attachment to standards, some teachers may be resistant to change and believe in the current standards they themselves have worked tirelessly to teach, and in many cases master themselves. This may be particularly problematic in the 'machine' and 'political system' metaphors of change, where resistance could occur against top-down innovations. In such cases, other dynamic forms of innovation might be more appropriate. A lack of awareness of EIL might also be a barrier, and this is where the slow introduction of innovation via the types of adopters can be effective – starting with one group at a time. The early adopters are especially important, as they are able to report on their experiences of the innovation to inform later adopters. Here, the 'flux and transformation' metaphors may become useful when teacher changemakers take initiatives by amplifying gaps and tensions between new realities and the teaching organisation's current practices to speed up the change process.

Other barriers require a more machinic or political style of innovation to dismantle. For example, parents are a further barrier to innovation, especially for younger-aged learners in school contexts where 'helicopter' or 'tiger' parents are present, who play an active role in their child's education. In such cases, a more systematic approach such as the machine metaphor or political system would be more appropriate for innovation. In this way, the innovation will have the clout of powerful and respected people leading the innovation, who are in a position to authoritatively inform the parents of the importance of the EIL curricular innovation. Similarly, a lack of EIL materials as barriers to innovation is better dealt with from a top down approach, as this may require policy changes, including the freeing up teacher time for materials development. As discussed in Chapter 5, assessment can also be a powerful barrier to EIL innovation, especially if the curriculum is connected to high-stakes standardised tests. For much EIL scholarship, assessment is the 'elephant in the room'. If changes to these tests are not possible, accommodations will need to be made to the innovations to meet students' dual needs for passing these tests, while also preparing them for future EIL use.

A final barrier to innovation is teacher education. In order to prepare teachers to teach EIL in the future, more EIL content needs to be included in teacher training programmes, of the kind outlined in this chapter. In order to fill this gap, a call has been made for action research,

accompanied by more contextualised reflection of teacher education programmes (Lopriore, 2016; Rose & Galloway, 2019; Vettorel, 2016). Some
pedagogical ideas such as lessons, activities and tasks that incorporated
EIL perspectives into teacher preparation courses were presented in
Matsuda (2017), and thus may be useful to counter this barrier.

The type of action research we are seeing in teacher education also
needs to extend into English language classrooms once EIL-informed
teachers leave education and enter into their classes. We especially need
action research or teacher research about how the teachers who took the
EIL-informed teacher education courses then implemented the innovations into their practices. Such research will help to contribute to our
understanding of the impact of innovation on attitudes of learner, practitioners, policymakers and parents. Although classroom practices essentially are always a matter of local decision (Seidlhofer, 2011), successes in
one context can be used to inform potential change in another. Innovations
can be adopted and adapted to better inform us on how to best engage
learners and teachers with EIL practices. This will ultimately encourage
practitioners and stakeholders to change their norm-bound attitudes.

## Post-reading Activities

### Reflect

This chapter suggests that adopters can be categorised into five types
according to their characteristics. If your school were to adopt a new
EIL-oriented curriculum, think about which type of adopter you
might be.

### Discuss

(1) A large section of this chapter has focused on innovation in teacher
education, yet many experienced teachers never return to education after completing their initial teacher accreditation. How can
we ensure EIL knowledge is transferred to such teachers?
(2) If a major barrier to wide-scale EIL innovation is ideological (i.e.
teachers, parents and learners are attached to native English and
native English-speaking teachers), how should management and
innovators overcome these barriers, which are deeply ingrained in
one's belief system?
(3) In many teaching contexts, small-scale EIL innovation is part of
an 'organism' or 'flux' metaphorical approach, in that teachers
often have the freedom to deviate from a set curriculum in small
ways. Looking at the pitfalls of these types of innovation in
Table 9.1, discuss ways in which these can be overcome.

> **Apply**
>
> Read one of the studies in Table 9.3 to gather more information on the teacher education innovation and its reported effect. Drawing on the concepts covered in this book thus far, what improvements or changes could be recommended to the programme? Outline specific examples and discuss ways in which you could measure the effectiveness of such changes.

## Resources for Further Reading

### For teachers

Kiczkowiak, M. and Lowe, R.J. (2019) *Teaching English as a Lingua Franca: The Journey from EFL to ELF*. London: Delta Publishing.

One of the widely stated barriers to innovation is a lack of suitable materials for teachers to draw upon, as many teachers are busy people and need to rely on existing commercial textbooks to inform their teaching. Luckily, we are seeing a lot of new books emerge on the market that offer alternative resources for teachers. In this book, the authors reformulate traditional views of TESOL within an EIL ideology (that they conceptualise as an EFL to ELF transition), to prepare students for future use of the language in global contexts. The authors hope to affect a shift in current pedagogy and practice in TESOL by providing this teacher-targeted resource. The book begins with a 25-page long overview of key concepts such as nativespeakerism and ELF. This is then followed by a bank of around 70 downloadable classroom activities organised around key concepts, such as: communication strategies, intercultural competence, creating an EIL mindset through awareness raising, and business English as a lingua franca.

### For teacher educators

Matsuda, A. (2017) *Preparing Teachers to Teach English as an International Language*. Bristol: Multilingual Matters.

This volume compiles a series of how teachers in various parts of the world put into practice the perspectives and insights gained from research into the international use of English. Frameworks for the development of EIL-aware/EIL-informed teacher education programmes are outlined in Part 1, while the rest of the publication gives a detailed overview of the programmes, courses and units within courses that have been developed and implemented in countries representative of all three of Kachru's circles. Included in each chapter is a section where the authors provide honest accounts of the challenges encountered while implementing EIL ideas in their own classrooms, which can be beneficial for teacher educators and teacher practitioners alike. Those looking for some inspiration on how to apply EIL theories in their teacher education practices should find tips and ideas for EIL-oriented lessons, activities and tasks in the final chapter useful.

# 10 Initiating Change: An Invitation to Researcher-Practitioners

## Pre-reading Activities

### *Reflect*

This chapter suggests that more research activity is needed that links teaching with research. Think about the topics that need to be researched, and the methods that could be used to report on EIL classroom activities. What type of data could be collected from these activities to show their effect on learners and learning?

### *Discuss*

(1) Is there a difference between research-informed teaching, and teaching-informed research? If so, how are they different?

(2) Often teachers are busy people who do not have the time for research, nor is it important to their professional careers for promotion and performance evaluation. In what ways, then, can we encourage more research on classroom-based practices?

(3) How do you respond to the following criticism: 'Research on single classrooms is not useful, as each classroom and the individuals within them are different. Thus, the findings of one classroom that EIL activities were successful, cannot be used to draw conclusions that these activities would work in other classrooms'.

## Introduction

The previous chapter explored innovation in language teaching and language teacher education. In this chapter, we make a call for the reporting of such innovation by practitioner-researchers. We begin by exploring the divide between practitioners and researchers in language education in order to highlight the urgent need for more research to fill this gap. To understand how new EIL ideas can be best incorporated into existing language classrooms we need more research within the nexus of teaching and research. Teachers, rather than researchers, are in the optimal place to lead such research. This will ensure research is teaching informed. We also explore the possibilities of better collaboration between researchers with methodological knowledge, and teachers with pedagogical knowledge and research site access. This chapter then moves on to discuss areas of needed future research in terms of the areas and topics which are in desperate need of investigation.

To equip teachers with the research tools needed to conduct such research, we then provide an overview of the various methodologies that would be most suited to the research topics and for researcher-practitioner practice-based research. These include a call for action research where we can observe EIL theories in 'live' action. This is useful as the teachers' experiences can be fed back to a larger network of scholarship (Global Englishes, World Englishes, ELF, EIL), leading to our improved understanding of how to best put EIL into practice in a variety of contexts so that our students' learning experience will be optimized, and our professional growth will be enhanced. We also introduce a number of other traditional and alternative approaches to researching EIL in practice, and provide an overview some example studies which showcase a range of methodologies.

## The Researcher Practitioner and the Teaching-Research Nexus

McKinley (2019) has recently problematized a lack of research activity at what he calls the 'teaching-research nexus'. He argues that, 'TESOL research was traditionally led by researcher-practitioners, who acknowledged real-world English language teaching problems (in alignment with developments in establishing applied linguistics as a field of study) as the basis for research enquiries' (2019: 1). However, as the TESOL professional has intellectualized, we have seen a separation of researchers and teachers: researchers research; teachers teach; and fewer published studies are being conducted by researchers who are also teachers in language classrooms. As a result of this divide, some scholars (e.g. Marsden & Kasprowicz, 2017) have noted that language teachers no longer engage a lot with the research literature. Much of this research seems out of touch with the issues that teachers are interested in.

In response to this divide, Rose (2019) has recently called for more teaching-informed research. He argues that at the moment, the flow between teaching and research is largely unidirectional – researchers often discuss the future 'pedagogical implications of their research' but rarely look to teachers to inform future direction of their research. To re-activate research within the nexus, collaboration between teachers and researchers is key. Action research (discussed later in this chapter) is one methodology which embraces the unique role of the researcher-practitioner. The reality, however, is that many teachers are too busy to conduct research. Moreover, research activity is often not required (and sometimes discouraged by school management) as the role of the teacher is seen to be measured by student outcomes, rather than research output (Rose, 2019).

To solve this issue, more collaboration between researchers and teachers is needed. In such collaboration the teacher must be positioned to be able to offer projects the wealth of their pedagogical knowledge and context-specific knowledge, rather than being positioned as a gatekeeper for access to the research site. Projects should be co-constructed so that the research is seen to help investigate relevant issues for the teaching context. The role of the teacher is paramount to the success of such collaborative research. McKinley (2019) explains:

> In such collaborative TESOL research, the one who teaches, rather than the teacher, would be a researcher-practitioner, or perhaps for lack of a better expression, a *holistic TESOL professional*, who is part of the evolution of the nexus of teaching and research in higher education. (2019: 5)

A holistic TESOL professional is a teacher who has the necessary pedagogic and research knowledge to engage in the activities which are much needed in the teaching-research nexus. This chapter therefore aims to explore the topics and methodologies that such holistic TESOL professionals can draw upon in future investigations of EIL in practice.

## Research Topics in Teaching EIL

This section provides sample topics pertaining to teaching EIL that can be empirically investigated in the future. While not exhaustive in coverage, we posit **six** areas in need of urgent review.

### Learner and teacher attitudes towards EIL

Regarding learners' attitudes, a strong preference towards the native speaker English varieties from the Inner Circle was revealed. The native speaker varieties also were seen as benchmarks against which other varieties can be measured. There appear to be limitations about research instruments, such as a verbal-guise technique, questionnaire and interviews that still include using geographic boundaries to describe English varieties and do not capture attitudes toward English today. We should go beyond those traditional boundaries in research (Galloway & Rose, 2015; Rose & Galloway, 2019). Rose and Galloway (2019) also address this issue:

> Global Englishes sees measures that encourage hard boundaries around 'varieties' as problematic for researching attitudes in the twenty-first

century, where populations are mobile, and geographic boundaries no longer accurately dictate the way English is used within and across historical speech communities. (Rose & Galloway, 2019: 116)

Regarding teachers' attitudes, although some teachers embraced the idea of EIL (Blair, 2015), others had strong orientations that their learners should learn native speaker varieties as a model (Dewey, 2015a; Sougari & Faltzi, 2015). İnal and Özdemir (2015) found that pre-service teachers were open to ELF considerably more than academia and in-service teachers. Ali (2014) and Doan (2014) pointed out that teacher educators' dependency on native speaker norms due to lack of their awareness of the notion of EIL, leading to scepticism and concerns over the feasibility of EIL pedagogy. As Marlina (2014) mentioned, some teachers still stick to the ideas that not only it is impractical but also a waste of their time to teach diverse varieties of English; and it is better to keep teaching contents simple, learning Standard native English. However, their familiarity with ELF appeared to influence positively teachers' attitudes towards ELF, showing the importance of including ELF in the teaching programmes (İnal & Özdemir, 2015; Sougari & Faltzi, 2015). Most research studies were qualitatively oriented using questionnaires and interviews with a small number of teachers. More careful development of research instruments, such as a questionnaire that can be used in multiple contexts, would be helpful to contribute toward developing contextualized interventions adaptable to different situations for filling in the gap between theories and practices.

## Research on implementing EIL innovations

A growing number of studies involve action research or classroom-based research on implementing EIL innovations for learners, as mentioned in previous chapters such as Chapter 2 and Chapter 6. The studies implemented EIL-oriented pedagogic actions and revealed conflicting attitudes. The students acknowledged the importance of English as a global language and accepted the existence of diverse varieties of English. Yet they expressed preferences toward native English and a desire to use English like native speakers. Thus, further investigations should take a closer look at this ambiguity in attitudes (Baker, 2012; Galloway, 2013, 2017b; Jenkins, 2007; Sung, 2015).

These studies included classroom activities such as classroom discussions, native speaker and accent identification task using the textbook 'World Englishes' (Kirkpatrick, 2007), a presentation task, a debate and telecollaboration exchanges and outside the classroom activities, such as listening journals, English communication with students of different backgrounds, online discussions and telecollaboration exchanges from home. Various research instruments, such as written reflections, online surveys, interviews, observations and participants' comments, were used in order to investigate attitudes toward English after the implementation of EIL-oriented activities. Particularly, written reflections seemed to play an important role not only as a research tool but also as a pedagogical tool to give students opportunities to reflect critically on their current perceptions about English. Allowing students to reflect constantly on their existing perceptions during and after the activities were crucial in order to prepare them for engaging in successful ELF interactions and going beyond the existing norms.

In addition to the activities proposed by the pedagogy-focused research, there are more suggestions for practical examples of EIL-oriented activities, such as Galloway (2017), Matsuda and Duran (2012) and Vettorel and Lopriore (2015). Recently textbooks for English as a global language have been published; included are textbooks, such as Kirkpatrick's (2007) '*World Englishes: Implications for international communication and English language teaching,*' Jenkins' (2015) '*Global Englishes: A resource book for students*' and Galloway and Rose's (2015) '*Introducing Global Englishes*'. These textbooks include audio CD or useful online exercises that can be used in the EIL classroom.

Most language attitude research has been limited to a single activity. A single activity may not result in a change in attitudes toward EIL, and there is a need to incorporate EIL elements in a series of English language classes and courses. Further work is needed to explore the possibility of implementing various EIL-oriented activities in a systematic manner during a series of English language classes and courses over a longer period (Rose & Galloway, 2019; Sung, 2015). One of few longitudinal studies is Galloway's (2011, 2013, 2017b) study investigating Japanese university students' language attitudes and the impact of her Global Englishes courses on her students using pre-test and post-test surveys, interviews and focus groups.

## Teaching materials research

Studies into ELT materials have focused on a variety of textbooks and EIL-oriented elements and most have found an over emphasis on the native speaker model as mentioned in Chapter 4. Many of these studies have focused on analyzing materials and textbooks used for a particular context, most commonly secondary school textbooks in the Expanding Circle (see Caleffi, 2016; Matsuda, 2002; Rose & Syrbe, 2018; Vettorel, 2018; Yuen, 2011). Studies such as Caleffi (2016), Vettorel (2018), Yuen (2011) examined rather specific elements of EIL, namely ELF, Communication strategies, foreign cultures, respectively. Caleffi (2016) found little incorporation of non-native speaker accents and ELF communication, Vettorel's (2018) study, however, found opportunity to practice communication strategies in more recent textbooks published after 2000. Regarding cultures, Yuen's (2011) study corroborates the native speaker model, as most textbooks favoured English-speaking cultures over foreign ones. Matsuda (2003b) as well as Syrbe and Rose (2018) took a broader look examining a variety of EIL-related factors. Though the studies are from different learning context (Japan and Germany, respectively) they both found similar results and an over-reliance on the native speaker and standard English. Further studies such as Naji Meidani and Pishghadam (2012) and Rose and Galloway (2019) examined globally used textbook according to various EIL-related factors. While both found a tendency towards the native speaker model, both studies also show a difference among the textbooks towards some very positive trends, especially in Rose and Galloway (2019).

Though there are increasingly more research projects into textbook and materials with regards to EIL, the geographic and research focus is still too narrow. Many more studies into Outer Circle contexts are needed to better understand the extent to which local standards are applied in teaching. Another shortcoming of current research is their almost exclusive focus on materials as they are with little insight into how these materials are used by teachers. Future research should look into how materials are utilized critically and how and where teachers substitute. Further, a look at substitute materials is necessary to better be able to understand how and in what ways different resources can be used.

## Assessment

The existing research relating EIL to assessment and testing practice can be described as meagre at best. The area that has received the most attention is the use of different accents in assessing listening comprehension, as was done by Abeywickrama (2013) and Ockey et al. (2016). Both studies examined the effect accents have on test-takers listening comprehension but yielded rather inconclusive results. While Abeywickrama' (2013) study suggest that non-native accents do not affect listening comprehension, Ockey et al.'s (2016) study suggests that strength and familiarity with native English speaker's accents do have an effect on listening comprehension. Clearly, more research is needed here. Uysal's (2009) study is the only one we reviewed to examine IELTS, and even though the analysis is thorough, the focus on EIL is rather superficial. Khan's (2009) study does offer more detailed in-sight but is focused on a very specific context and the results are thus not easily applicable to other contexts. It becomes obvious that there is great need for research into assessment and EIL in a variety of contexts focusing on a variety of issues. For one, research needs to explore the extent to which standardized tests such as TOEFL and IELTS are used across the globe as gatekeepers to education and employment, and more specifically the extent to which they are accurate and valid in predicting success in education. Specific emphasis should be put on EMI in Inner, Outer and Expanding

Circle context to closely examine students' linguistic needs, in order to evaluate the usefulness of specific tests and assessments. Secondly, researchers should look into locally produced and used language assessment, in order to determine the use of local norms. As argued in Chapter 5, there is a strong need to move towards usage-based approaches in assessment, which measures how students can strategically use the language. However, this requires substantial research into the usefulness of specific activities as well as how constructs and norms could be and should be defined for such tests.

## Students' specific needs in a global world

A practical overview of the importance of needs analysis for curriculum development was outlined in Chapter 2. However, there is also a need to conduct needs analysis from a research perspective, which is vital to ensure targeted EIL provision. Overall, we need more robust research that can help to inform us of how students will use English in a variety of global contexts. Research in this area usually is in the form of: surveys with learners' post-graduation; workplace fieldwork; and corpus-based investigations. Starfield (2016) argues that in terms of workplace research, researcher-practitioners could collect data in the domains where their students will work post-graduation, in order to investigate their needs. For example, one needs analysis study at a Hong Kong workplace, analyzed audio-recordings and ethnographic observations in the workplace (Handford & Matous, 2011). Such methods have been adopted by ELF researchers exploring domains such as business (e.g. Kankaanranta & Louhiala-Salminen, 2007, 2010; Kankaanranta & Planken, 2010; Louhiala-Salminen et al., 2005). Corpus-based methods aim to gather a diverse and wide-ranging bank of publicly available discourse for analysis. Research emerging from the VOICE (Vienna-Oxford International Corpus of English) is an example of such research; however, more diverse corpora are needed to better understand the way L2 English speakers use English in the 21st century in a variety of contexts.

## EIL in teacher education

While Chapters 8 and 9 explored the importance of EIL in teacher education, more research in this context is needed to better comprehend the impact of a raised awareness of EIL on actual practice. Few studies have explored the long-term effects of EIL content within teacher education programmes, and even fewer still have investigated impact on future practices. Of the five studies in teacher education outlined in the previous chapter, most reported on the actual innovations within teacher education courses, and their impact on reflective practice or short-term attitudes. What is needed is longitudinal research to track teachers when they go into the workplace after teacher training to see whether their EIL education transforms into actual classroom innovative practices. Such research can inform us of the areas where impact on practice is the greatest; it can also inform us of the barriers to innovation in situations where EIL ideals are not adopted by the teachers.

## Research Methodologies for Investigating EIL Innovation

This section provides suggested methodologies to research EIL in pedagogical practice. Many of these suggestions are adapted from Rose and Galloway (2019), with some additions of our own.

### Action research

Action research is a form of inquiry that can help teachers investigate and evaluate their teaching practices toward a deeper understanding in and improvement in their own situations (Burns, 2005b, 2009b). Action research could contribute to development of generalisable theoretical knowledge and policymaking although it is less well illustrated (Borg, 2013). Teachers are part of the practices they are investigating and are active and 'critical participants in the action and researchers of the action' (Burns, 2015: 189) as opposed to traditional research where professional researchers conduct research that includes practitioners. It involves a systematic and rigorous process involving a number of cycles of planning, action, observation and reflection. The iterative process is not straight forward and subject to change.

In the past, action research has been criticized due to its lack of methodological rigour (Ellis, 2010). In order to demonstrate the quality of research, action research should include cross checking, testing through practical application, checking compatibility with educational aims and democratic values, and checking compatibility with teaching demands (Burns, 2015). Additionally, collaboration between academics and teachers would be valuable (Borg, 2013). A few EIL-informed studies have incorporated action research. Bayyurt and Sifakis (2015a, 2015b) and Sifakis and Bayyurt (2015) incorporated a mini action research project into their teacher education project. Researchers collaborated with local teachers in Vettorel's (2010, 2013, 2014, 2017) study. Galloway (2011, 2013, 2017) investigated her own classes to improve her teaching practices, which was underpinned by other research-informed methodologies surrounding, such as focus groups and interviews.

Since the purpose of action research is to solve the local concerns and problems and to change and improve their practice, it is common for action researchers mainly to use qualitative methods (Burns, 2005a, 2005b, 2015). Regarding the data collection, researchers observe and record what people do and/or ask people for their views and opinions. Observation involves techniques such as an ethnographic approach with fieldnotes and researcher journal, diary and logs. Those are written for various purposes from something more personal to something more objective and factual reflections on or simple observations of events or people. For the investigation of people's views and opinions, commonly used techniques collecting documents (policies, curricula, lesson plans, student work, test results) providing evidence that reflects people's activities, interviews and questionnaires.

## Survey research and questionnaires

Survey research is typified by the use of questionnaires, but can include other methods that aim to generalize the beliefs and behaviours of a population. Questionnaires are among the commonly used research tools eliciting written data through closed and/or open-ended questions. Closed questions involve selecting one or more responses and lead to tabulation and quantification (percentages, averages, frequency), while respondents formulate their own answers for open-ended questions and offer qualitative data from which the researcher derives themes, patterns and trends. Question content may include behaviour, beliefs, knowledge, attitudes and attributes. Considerable attention should be given to wordings of questions to avoid unclear, ambiguous and useless questions. Decisions also need to be made about instructions, order of questions, questionnaire length and the language and proficiency levels required to complete the questionnaire. Pilot testing is essential to evaluate questionnaire items for variation, meaning, redundancy, scalability and non-response, and the questionnaire as a whole for flow, timings and respondent interest and attention. De Vaus (2013) gives a checklist for questionnaire design.

Regarding an example of questionnaire development for action research, Galloway (2011, 2013, 2017a) conducted classroom-based research to investigate 116 Japanese students' attitudes towards English and impacts of a Global Englishes courses on their attitudes. The term, classroom-based research, was used instead of action research because, unlike action research, the study not only investigated to solve issues in her own teaching practices but also aimed to contribute to theory development. In this way, the study had many features typical of an intervention study, such as a quasi-experimental design, with use of a comparison group. The questionnaire was used as one of the research instruments for investigating attitudes, factors influencing attitudes and attitude change. The questionnaire included demographic and background information including language learning history, experience abroad, proficiency and familiarity with varieties of English. Closed and open attitudinal questions were included to investigate students' attitudes and measure changes in them, such as asking students to choose from varieties of English to which they may not have had exposure and to answer four-point Likert scale items for measuring the intensity of attitudes and asking how much the students' English education had prepared them to use English with people from around the world. Regarding the results, positive orientations to native English were found and familiarity, motivations, pedagogical beliefs and learning experience appeared to affect those attitudes. Changes in students' attitude were confirmed in a post-course questionnaire. Also, the findings from the open-ended questions yielded three themes: native ownership of English, English as a global language and the influence of the Global Englishes class.

As mentioned in the study (Galloway, 2011, Galloway, 2017b), the influence of the researcher's position as a teacher and native speaker on the students' questionnaire responses should not be underestimated. Also, the tendency of survey respondents to answer questions in a manner that are viewed favourably by others in general should be taken into account. Thus, in addition to making comparisons across different types of data, using more than one data-collection method is recommended (Burns, 2015). Not only comparing quantitative data with qualitative data in the questionnaire but also conducting interviews and focus groups increases confidence that the findings of the study are not simply the result of using a particular method (Burns, 2015).

## Ethnographic field research

Ethnography refers to research methods that position individuals as the main object of study – interested in their real-life, lived experiences. To allow for an in-depth picture of teachers as change agents as well as other contextual variables to emerge, *ethnography* is deemed as highly suitable for an inquiry to such complex issues as L2 English teachers and their cognition. In situating EIL in the English language teaching context within the Language Teacher Cognition framework (Borg, 2015), it is evident that researching such concept as complex and unobservable as teachers' beliefs calls for a research design that combines multiple sources of data (e.g. interviews, observation, documents) so as to gain trustworthy results. Ethnography is often accompanied with *field research*, where a researcher aims to explore these complexities in real-life settings – in the field. Ethnographic field research, therefore, aims to explore real-life people in real-life settings in order to look at their research constructs in action.

While field research often indicates that the researcher is external to the field research site, there are many ways to conceptualise researcher positionality. For example, it is possible for a researcher-practitioner to conduct ethnographic field research with their own learners by adopting a *complete participant* researcher role. That is, the teacher becomes a participant in their own research. Of course, this role is accompanied by difficulties regarding data collection, but can be overcome through the keeping of good researcher notes after (and sometimes during) classroom activities, as well as audio or video recording, and collection of field documents such as students' writing, for later analysis.

## Narrative inquiry

Global Englishes can also reap benefits from reflexive methods such as narrative inquiry, autoethnography, joint ethnography and community dialogue method. As a form of sense-making, ***narrative inquiry*** helps us shape our comprehension of various, complex happenings in the world. Stories typically move chronologically from the past to the present and often open up future possibilities. Hearing a story thus may change how we view our present options, make sense of what has already happened and evaluate our directions going forward. Teachers as change agent may use storytelling to work with their teams to make sense of their own past, present and future, or to convey to their teams how they are making sense of it all. Because narratives also come with a plot, characters and emotional and sensory detail, we can render our story more engaging and real through a realistic account of how a proposed change is going to look or feel like.

## Autoethnography, duoethnography and S-STEP

Teachers can also resort to *autoethnography* to explore how their ideologies about language inform their present classroom practices. This can be carried out as a joint effort (*duoethnography*) among teachers where meanings are collectively made, deeper questions explored, key issues reframed and refreshing new insights reached. Such collaborative inquiry, instead of being used to convince others of a particular course of action, has the potential to resuscitate dormant wisdom and bring about powerful actions. Another useful method is *World Café*,[1] a reflective practice that encourages participants to reflect upon their personal values and knowledge and share them with others in a less formal environment. As a community engagement strategy, it encourages participants to raise their views about a particular topic within a relaxed and comfortable setting (Brown & Isaacs, 2005). It can thus be used in practice to stimulate discussion on reflection on the meaning of Global Englishes and how it impacts upon the overall teaching and learning experience of students and teachers. This method has been used in a variety of contexts, including health care (Macfarlane *et al.*, 2017), social work (Fouché & Light, 2011), consumer services (Ritch & Brennan, 2010), organizational management (Lagrosen, 2017) and recently in higher education (Estacio & Karic, 2016) and special education (Parker-Katz *et al.*, 2018).

Another reflective-practice oriented methodology, which has been making inroads into teacher education, is S-STEP (Self-Study of Teacher Education Practices). S-STEP offers a way to engage in research that has pedagogical practice at its core:

S-STEP is a methodology that draws upon a variety of research frameworks and methods, including narrative, case study, (auto)ethnography, and action research. It employs 'traditional' qualitative data sources (including journaling, videotapes of teaching, interviews, teaching artefacts), as well as less common data sources... to explore questions about one's practice. (Peercy & Sharkey, 2018: 2)

S-STEP is directly aimed at a different type of practitioner researcher: language teacher educators. Language teacher educators work directly with teachers as part of their role, but often within a research domain, such as in professional courses in universities or colleges as part of teacher accreditation. Language teacher educators (LTE), therefore, 'are in a position to link their in-depth research knowledge with pedagogical practices, and to work with those entrenched in (or about to enter) the teaching profession' (Rose, 2019: 900). Peercy and Sharkey (2018) suggest 'that a deeper understanding of the teacher educator as scholar, as practitioner, as researcher, is critical to the LTE knowledge base' (2018: 2). While the application of S-STEP methodology in educational research is becoming more mainstream in the broader field of teacher education (e.g. Loughran, 2004), it is still relatively new to the field of TESOL education practices, and thus has innovative potential to exert a larger influence within language teaching research, by TESOL educators.

## What Does the Research Tell Us?

In each chapter in this book, we explicitly explore the methodologies used for EIL research to report on classroom practices. Next, we present

**Table 10.1** Example research methodologies related to EIL in practice

| Study | Topic | Methodology |
|-------|-------|-------------|
| Manara (2013) | The struggle of moving towards EIL in Indonesia | Narrative Inquiry on competing and conflicting narratives of professionalism |
| Sung (2016) | Student's attitudes to ELF and World Englishes exposure | Survey research into student attitudes, consisting of questionnaire and interviews |
| Galloway (2017a) | Attitudinal change via EIL classroom activities | Action research that followed quasi-experimental design |
| Sung (2014) | Case study of learners' EIL experiences | Multiple case study, drawing on in-depth qualitative interviews |
| Lowe and Kiczkowiak (2016) | Nativespeakerism and teacher identity | Duo-ethnography (joint autoethnography) to explore the researcher-practitioners' lived experiences |
| Baker (2009) | ELF and intercultural communication | Ethnographic field research to explore ELF-oriented communication |

some studies which have used a range of these methodologies to provide real-life examples in action. These papers are outlined in Table 10.1.

In Manara (2013), the author reports on a study that follows four teachers' narratives of teaching (and learning) English. Through narrative inquiry, the study uncovers the struggles that the teachers face in reconciling their professional identities, which include a high awareness of EIL, with other competing ideologies in the Indonesian TESOL professional community, which is dominated by Western and Anglophone perspectives.

Lowe and Kiczkowiak (2016) explore the ways in which power, privilege and prejudice surrounding the native speaker interact in the field of English language teaching. This paper utilizes a duoethnography (joint autoethnography) to explore the complexities of personal experience to disrupt the power of nativespeakerism in language teaching. This paper acted as a methodological blueprint for Rose and Montakantiwong's (2018) later article, where the practitioner-researchers engaged in a duoethnography of their own experiences integrating EIL ideas within their classrooms in Japan and Thailand. Through the sharing of these experiences, the authors are able to reflect on these experiences to inform future practice.

In a study by Sung (2016) he reports on the results of a survey research of 326 English language learners within the EAP courses of the university at which he teaches. This is accompanied by 28 in-depth qualitative interviews with the students. This survey research examined the students' perception towards EIL activities that aimed to expose them to different varieties of English.

Baker (2009) reports on ethnographic qualitative field research, which investigated seven users of English in a Thai university, who were engaged in intercultural communication. Data collection took place 6-months covering one academic term. The researcher can be positioned as a practitioner-researcher in this research, because the research site was his former place of employment, and thus he drew on a teacher-researcher identity due to his professional connections to the teachers, students and curriculum.

Galloway (2017a) is presented here as a type of action research, where a researcher-practitioner reports on innovations in her own classroom – an issue the researcher discusses further in Galloway (2017c). This study might be more appropriately described as a quasi-experiment in terms of its rigid methods and pre-test post-test design (as opposed to action research cycles), but nonetheless is a solid example of a teacher reporting on their own practices and navigating the pitfalls of practitioner-led research.

## Implications for TESOL Researcher-Practitioners

In this chapter, we have looked ahead to future research directions within the area of EIL and language teaching from which research-practitioners involved in the TESOL industry may find some suggestions for topics, relevant methodological tools and useful techniques. Our intention is to facilitate necessary future changes towards implementing EIL-oriented practices, and to bridge the gap between the theories and the more practical aspects of such theories underlying EIL-related paradigms. To facilitate a smooth transition between theories and practices, we specifically encourage researcher-practitioners to engage in the work that documents the existing modus operandi of the teaching institution and gauges the feasibility of EIL principles being taken up in actual language classrooms. Unless on-the-ground evidence of how change can be operationalised is provided, theories and all the recommendations for pedagogical initiatives will be left to wither on the vine. Theoretical concepts only become and stay powerful when they are alive in practice. This is also true for EIL, a concept whose power and long-lasting relevance lies in the extent to which practitioners use and explore it.

## Post-reading Activities

### Reflect

This chapter has introduced various topics for future research as well as methodologies. Reflect on both the topics and the methods in this chapter and think about which appeal the most to you as a future practitioner-researcher.

### Discuss

(1) What are the potential barriers to conducting research within the nexus of teaching and research? How can these be overcome?

(2) Are reflective methodologies such as autoethnographies, World Café and narrative inquiry rigorous methods for researching EIL? How can a researcher-practitioner ensure the results of these types of individualized study are taken seriously within the research community?

(3) Most of the time, research into EIL is led by applied or sociolinguists approaching their projects from a rather academic or abstract point of view thus creating a gap between academia and practice. However, changes in practice are only possible as grass roots movements led by teachers. What do you think can be done by linguists and teachers alike to overcome this gap, and to move closer towards teaching EIL?

> ### Apply
>
> Read one of the studies presented in Table 10.1 for further detail on what the researchers did. Based on this work, design a follow-up study to this research in a teaching context with which you are familiar. Think about who your sample learners will be, what aspect of EIL you will research, and how you will collect the data. Write up, or present, your hypothetical study.

## Note

(1) See overview of procedure at http://www.theworldcafe.com/key-concepts-resources/world-cafe-method/; http://designresearchtechniques.com/casestudies/world-cafe/

## Resources for Further Reading

Rose, H. (2019) Researching English as an International Language. In G. Barkhuizen (ed.) *Qualitative Research Topics in Language Teacher Education* (p. 331–136). New York: Routledge.

This chapter outlines key considerations for choosing a topic of research associated with EIL innovation. It is squarely focused on qualitative research topics and research questions surrounding practical and classroom-based issues. These include: Evaluation of the curriculum for EIL content; research into the approaches for teaching EIL; exploring attitudes of learners towards variation in English; challenges associated with English medium instruction; and multilingualism in TESOL classrooms.

Burns, A. (2010) *Doing Action Research in English Language Teaching: A Guide for Practitioners*. Abingdon: Routledge.

This reader-friendly book introduces action research for practitioners in language teaching across the world and aims to help them get started in action research. Based on one of the models of action research, it describes vital phases of action research such as plan, action, observe and reflect along with ideas and excerpts from the action research all over the world. Chapter 2 looks at planning action research that include identifying research questions. Chapter 3 includes data collection methods such as how to ask questions and discuss the research issues and how to observe and describe the situation and participants. How to analyse the collected qualitative and quantitative data is explained in Chapter 4. The last chapter focuses on the reflection phase that include how to reflect on the research as a whole and how to move on to next steps. In the postscript, it provides two concrete examples of the approaches teacher action researchers can take in order to present their research.

# References

Abeywickrama, P. (2013) Why not non-native varieties of English as listening comprehension test input? *RELC Journal* 44 (1), 59–74.

Ali, F. (2014) Implementing EIL paradigm in ELT classrooms: Voices of experienced and pre-service English language educators in Malaysia. In R. Marlina and R.A. Giri (eds) *The Pedagogy of English as an International Language: Perspectives from Scholars, Teachers, and Students* (pp. 95–100 ). New York, NY: Springer.

Alsagoff, L., McKay, S.L., Hu, G. and Renandya, W.A. (eds) (2012) *Principles and Practices of Teaching English as an International Language*. Abingdon: Routledge.

Alsup, J. (2006) *Teacher Identity Discourses: Negotiating Personal and Professional Spaces*. Mahwah, NJ: Lawrence Erlbaum.

Atay, D. (2008) The beliefs and dilemmas of Turkish prospective teachers of English. In S. Dogancay-Aktuna and J. Hardman (eds) *Global English Teaching and Teacher Education: Praxis and Possibility* (pp. 83–99) Alexandria, VA: TESOL.

Atkinson, D. (ed.) (2011) *Alternative Approaches to Second Language Acquisition*. Routledge.

Bachman, L.F. and Palmer, A. (2010) *Language Assessment in Practice: Developing Language Assessments and Justifying their Use in the Real World*. Oxford University Press.

Baker, C. (1992) *Attitudes and Language*. Clevedon: Multilingual Matters.

Baker, C. (2001) *Foundations of Bilingual Education and Bilingualism* (3rd edn). Clevedon: Multilingual Matters.

Baker, W. (2009) The cultures of English as a lingua franca. *TESOL Quarterly* 43 (4), 567–592.

Baker, W. (2011) Intercultural awareness: Modelling an understanding of cultures in intercultural communication through English as a lingua franca. *Language and Intercultural Communication* 11 (3), 197–214.

Baker, W. (2012) Using e-learning to develop intercultural awareness in ELT: A critical evaluation in a Thai higher education setting. *ELT Research Papers* 12 (3), 1–43.

Baker, W. and Jarunthawatchai, W. (2017) English language policy in Thailand. *European Journal of Language Policy* 9 (1), 27–44.

Bao, D. (2015) Flexibility in second language materials. *The European Journal of Applied Linguistics and TEFL* 4 (2), 37–52.

Barkhuizen, G. (ed.) (2017) *Reflections on Language Teacher Identity Research*. London: Routledge.

Barnawi, O.Z. (2018) *Neoliberalism and English Language Education Policies in the Arabian Gulf*. London: Routledge.

Barnawi, O.Z. and Phan, L.H. (2015) From Western TESOL classrooms to home practice: A case study with two 'privileged' Saudi teachers. *Critical Studies in Education* 56 (2), 259–76.

Bauman, Z. (2001) *Identity*. Cambridge: Polity.

Baxter, J. (2016) Positioning language and identity: Poststructuralist perspectives. In S. Preece (ed.) *The Routledge Handbook of Language and Identity* (pp. 34–49) London: Routledge.

Bayyurt, Y. and Akcan, S. (eds) (2015) *Current Perspectives on Pedagogy for English as a Lingua Franca: Developments in English as a Lingua Franca*. Berlin: De Gruyter Mouton.

Bayyurt, Y. (2006) Non-native English language teachers' perspective on culture in English as a Foreign Language classrooms. *Teacher Development* 10 (2), 233–47.

Bayyurt, Y. (2012) Proposing a model for English language education in the Turkish sociocultural context. In Y. Bayyurt and Y. Bektaş- Çetinkaya (eds) *Research Perspectives on Teaching and Learning English in Turkey: Policies and Practices* (pp. 301–312). Frankfurt: Peter Lang.

Bayyurt, Y. and Altinmakas, D. (2012) A WE-based English communication skills course at a Turkish university. In A. Matsuda (ed.) *Principles and Practices of Teaching English as an International Language* (pp. 169–182). Bristol: Multilingual Matters.

Bayyurt, Y. and Sifakis, N. (2017) Foundations of an EIL-aware teacher education. In A. Matsuda (ed.) *Preparing Teachers to Teach English as an International Language*. Bristol: Multilingual Matters, pp. 3–18.

Bayyurt, Y. and Sifakis, N.C. (2015a) Developing an ELF-aware pedagogy: Insights from a self-education programme. In P. Vettorel (ed.) *New Frontiers in Teaching and Learning English* (pp. 55–76). Newcastle-upon-Tyne: Cambridge Scholars.

Bayyurt, Y. and Sifakis, N.C. (2015b) ELF-aware in-service teacher education: A transformative perspective. In H. Bowles and A. Cogo (eds) *International Perspectives on English as a Lingua Franca. Pedagogical Insights* (pp. 117–135). Basingtoke: Palgrave Macmillan.

Bhatt, R.M. (2001) World Englishes. *Annual Review of Anthropology* 30, 527–550.

Bhatt, R.M. (2005) Expert discourses, local practices, and hybridity: The case of Indian Englishes. In S. Canagarajah (ed.) *Reclaiming the Local in Language Policy and Practice* (pp. 25–54). Mahwah, NJ: Lawrence Erlbaum Associates.

Björkman, B. (2014) An analysis of polyadic English as a lingua franca (ELF) speech: A communicative strategies framework. *Journal of Pragmatics* 66, 122–138.

Blair, A. (2015) Evolving a post-native, multilingual model for ELF-aware teacher education. In Y. Bayyurt and S. Akcan (eds) *Current Perspectives on Pedagogy for English as a Lingua Franca* (pp. 89–102). Berlin: De Gruyter Mouton.

Block, D. (2007) *Second Language Identities*. London: Continuum.

Block, D. and Corona, V. (2014) Exploring class-based intersectionality. *Language, Culture and Curriculum* 27 (1), 27–42.

Blommaert, J. (2006) Language policy and national identity. In T. Ricento (ed.) *An Introduction to Language Policy: Theory and Method* (pp. 120–139). London: Blackwell.

Blommaert, J. and Backus, A. (2011) Repertoires revisited: 'Knowing language' in superdiversity. *Working Papers in Urban Language and Literacies*, 67. London: King's College.

Borg, S. (2013) *Teacher Research in Language Teaching: A Critical Analysis*. Cambridge: Cambridge University Press.

Borg, S. (2015) *Teacher Cognition and Language Education: Research and Practice*. London: Bloomsbury.

Bourdieu, P. (1991) *Language and Symbolic Power*. Cambridge: Polity Press.

Bowles, H. and Cogo, A. (2015) *International Perspectives on English as a Lingua Franca: Pedagogical Insights*. Houndmills: Palgrave Macmillan.

Braine, G. and Selvi, A.F. (2018) NNEST Movement. *The TESOL Encyclopedia of English Language Teaching*, 1–6.

Braine, G. (2010) *Nonnative Speaker English Teachers: Research, Pedagogy, and Professional Growth*. New York, NY: Routledge.

Braine, G. (2013) The nonnative speakers (NNS) movement and its implications for ELT in Asia. In N.T. Zacharias and C. Manara (eds) *Contextualizing the Pedagogy of*

*English as an International Language: Issues and Tensions* (pp. 12–39). Newcastle upon Tyne: Cambridge Scholars Publishing.

Brown, K. (1993) World Englishes in TESOL programs: An infusion model of curricular innovation. *World Englishes* 12 (1), 59–73.

Brown, H. and Barrett, J. (2017) Duoethnography as a pedagogical tool that encourages deep reflection. In J. Norris and R.O. Sawyer (eds) *Theorizing Curriculum Studies, Teacher Education, and Research through Duoethnographic Pedagogy* (pp. 85–110). New York: Palgrave Macmillan.

Brown, J. and Isaacs, D. (2005) *The World Café: Shaping our Futures Through Conversations that Matter.* San Francisco, CA: Berrett-Koehler.

Bruthiaux, P. (2003) Squaring the circles: Issues in modeling English worldwide. *International Journal of Applied Linguistics* 13 (2), 159–178.

Brutt-Griffler, J. (2002) *World English: A Study of its Development.* Clevedon: Multilingual Matters.

Burns, A. (2005) Action research: An evolving paradigm? *Language Teaching* 38 (2), 57–74.

Burns, A. (2005b) Action research. In E. Hinkel (ed.) *Handbook of Research in Second Language Teaching and Learning* (pp. 241–256). Mahwah, NJ: Lawrence Erlbaum.

Burns, A. (2009) *Doing Action Research in English Language Teaching: A Guide for Practitioners.* Abingdon: Routledge.

Burns, A. (2009b) Action research in second language teacher education. In A. Burns and J.C. Richards (eds) *The Cambridge Guide to Second Language Teacher Education* (pp. 289–297). Cambridge: Cambridge University Press.

Burns, A. (2015) Action research. In J.D. Brown and C. Coombe (eds) *The Cambridge Guide to Research in Language Teaching and Learning* (pp. 99–104). Cambridge: Cambridge University Press.

Burns, A., Freeman, D. and Edwards, E. (2015) Theorizing and studying the language-teaching mind: Mapping research on language teacher cognition. *Modern Language Journal* 99 (3), 585–601.

Byram, M. and Parmenter, L. (2015) Global citizenship. In J.M. Bennett (ed.) *SAGE Reference Publication: The SAGE Encyclopedia of Intercultural Competence.* Thousand Oaks, CA: SAGE.

Caleffi, P. (2016) ELF in the speaking and listening activities of recently published English-language coursebooks. Intercultural Communication. New Perspectives from ELF.

Cameron, E. and Green, M. (2009) *Making Sense of Change Management: A Complete Guide to the Models, Tools and Techniques of Organizational Change* (2nd edn). London: Kogan Page.

Canagarajah, A.S. (2007) Lingua franca English, multilingual communities, and language acquisition. *The Modern Language Journal* 91, 923–939.

Canagarajah, A.S. (2012) Teacher development in a global profession: An autoethnography. *TESOL Quarterly* 46, 258–279.

Canagarajah, S. (1999) *Resisting Linguistic Imperialism in English Teaching.* Oxford: Oxford University Press.

Canagarajah, S. (2005) *Reclaiming the Local in Language Policy and Practice.* Mahwah, NJ: Lawrence Erlbaum.

Canagarajah, S. (2006) Changing communicative needs, revised assessment objectives: Testing English as an international language. *Language Assessment Quarterly: An International Journal* 3 (3), 229–242.

Canagarajah, S. (2013) *Translingual Practice: Global English and COSMOPOLITAN relations.* London: Routledge.

Canagarajah, S. (2014) Theorizing a competence for translingual practice at the contact zone. In S. May (ed.) *The Multilingual Turn: Implications for SLA, TESOL and Bilingual Education* (pp. 78–102). New York, NJ: Routledge.

Canagarajah, S. (2016) Translingual writing and teacher development in composition. *College English* 78 (3), 265–273.

Cargile, A.C. and Bradac, J.J. (2001) Attitudes toward language: A review of speakere-valuation research and a general process model. In W.B. Gudykunst (ed.) *Communication Year 25* (pp. 347–382). Mahwah, NJ: Erlbaum Associates.

Cargile, A.C, Giles, H., Ryan, E.B. and Bradac, J.J. (1994) Language attitudes as a social process: Conceptual model and new directions. *Language and Communication* 14 (3), 211–236.

Cargile, A.C., Takai, J. and Rodríguez, J.I. (2006) Attitudes toward African-American vernacular English: A US export to Japan? *Journal of Multilingual and Multicultural Development* 27 (6), 443–456.

Chalhoub-Deville, M. and Wigglesworth, G. (2005) Rater judgment and English language speaking proficiency. *World Englishes* 24 (3), 383–391.

Chiba, R., Matsuura, H. and Yamamoto, A. (1995) Japanese attitudes toward English accents. *World Englishes* 14, 77–86.

Chowdhury, R. and Phan, L.H. (2014) *Desiring TESOL and International Education: Market Abuse and Exploitation*. Bristol: Multilingual Matters.

Clarke, M. (2008) *Language Teacher Identities: Co-constructing Discourse and Community*. Clevedon: Multilingual Matters.

Cogo, A. and Dewey, M. (2012) *Analysing English as a Lingua Franca: A Corpus-driven Investigation*. London: Continuum.

Commissie, E. (2012) Special Eurobarometer 386, Europeans and their languages. Retrieved from http://ec.europa.eu/public_opinion/archives/ebs/ebs_386_en. pdf

Cook, V.J. (1999) Going beyond the native speaker in language teaching. *TESOL Quarterly* 33 (2), 185–209.

Cook, V.J. (2008) *Second Language Learning and Language Teaching*. London: Routledge.

Cook, V.J. (2012) Multi-competence. In C. Chapelle (ed.) *The Encyclopaedia of Applied Linguistics* (pp. 3768–3774). Chichester: Wiley-Blackwell.

Cook, V.J. (2016) Premises of multicompetence. In V. Cook and L. Wei (eds) *The Cambridge Handbook of Linguistic Multicompetence*. Cambridge: Cambridge University Press.

Coombe, C. (2018) Introduction to assessment and evaluation. *The TESOL Encyclopedia of English Language Teaching*. doi: 10.1002/9781118784235

Creese, A. and Blackledge, A. (2010) Translanguaging in the bilingual classroom: A pedagogy for learning and teaching? *The Modern Language Journal* 94 (1), 103–115.

Crystal, D. (2003) *English as a Global Language*. Cambridge: Cambridge University Press.

Crystal, D. (2018) *The Cambridge Encyclopaedia of the English Language*. Cambridge: Cambridge University Press.

Csizér, K. and Lukács, G. (2010) The comparative analysis of motivation, attitudes and selves: The case of English and German in Hungary. *System* 38, 1–13.

Dalton-Puffer, C., Kaltenboeck, G. and Smit, U. (1997) Learner attitudes and L2 pronunciation in Austria. *World Englishes* 16 (1), 115–123.

D'Angelo, J. (2012) WE-informed EIL curriculum at Chukyo: Towards a functional, educated, multilingual outcome. In A. Matsuda (ed.) *Principles and Practices of Teaching English as an International Language* (pp. 121–139). Bristol: Multilingual Matters.

D'Angelo, J. (2014) The WEs/EIL paradigm and Japan's NS propensity: Going beyond the 'friendly face' of west-based TESOL. In R. Marlina and A.R. Giri (eds) *The Pedagogy of English as an International Language: Perspectives from Scholars, Teachers, and Students* (pp. 221–238). Cham, Switzerland: Springer International Publishing.

Darvin, R. and Norton, B. (2015) Identity and a model of investment in applied linguistics. *Annual Review of Applied Linguistics* 35, 36–56. doi:10.1017/s0267190514000191

Davies, A. (1991) *The Native Speaker in Applied Linguistics*. Edinburgh: Edinburgh University Press.

Davies, A. (1996) Proficiency or the native speaker: What are we trying to achieve in ELT? In G. Cook and B. Seidlhofer (eds) *Principle and Practice in Applied Linguistics* (pp. 145–157). Oxford: Oxford University Press.

Davies, A. (2003) *The Native Speaker: Myth and Reality*. Clevedon: Multilingual Matters.

Davies, A. (2013) *Native Speakers and Native Users: Loss and Gain*. Cambridge: Cambridge University Press.

Davies, A., Hamp-Lyons, L. and Kemp, C. (2003) Whose norms? International proficiency tests in English. *World Englishes* 22 (4), 571–584.

De Costa, P.I. and Norton, B. (2017) Introduction: Identity, transdisciplinarity, and the good language teacher. *The Modern Language Journal* 101(S1), 3–14. doi:10.1111/modl.12368

De Vaus, D. (2013) *Surveys in Social Research*. Abingdon: Routledge.

Decke-Cornill, H. (2003) 'We would have to invent the language we are supposed to teach': The issue of English as lingua franca in language education in Germany. *Language, Culture and Curriculum* 15 (3), 251–263.

Dewey, M. (2012) Towards a post-normative approach: Learning the pedagogy of ELF. *Journal of English as a Lingua Franca* 1 (1), 141–70.

Dewey, M. (2014) Pedagogic criticality and English as a lingua franca. *Atlantis Journal of the Spanish Association of Anglo-American Studies* 36 (2), 11–30.

Dewey, M. (2015a) ELF teacher knowledge and professional development. In H. Bowles and A. Cogo (eds) *International Perspectives on English as a Lingua Franca. Pedagogical Insights* (pp. 176–93). Basingstoke: Palgrave Macmillan.

Dewey, M. (2015b) Time to wake up some dogs! Shifting the culture of language in ELT. In Y. Bayyurt and S. Akcan (eds) *Current Perspectives on Pedagogy for English as a Lingua Franca* (pp. 121–134). Berlin: De Gruyter Mouton.

Dewey, M. and Patsko, L. (2018) ELF and teacher education. In J. Jenkins, W. Baker and M. Dewey (eds) *The Routledge Handbook of English as a Lingua Franca*. Abingdon: Routledge.

Doan, N.B. (2014) Teaching the target culture in English teacher education programs: Issues of EIL in Vietnam. In R. Marlina and R.A. Giri (eds) *The Pedagogy of English as an International Language: Perspectives from Scholars, Teachers, and Students* (pp. 79–93). New York, NY: Springer.

Dogancay-Aktuna, S. and Hardman, J. (2012) Teacher education for EIL: Working toward a situated meta-praxis. In A. Matsuda (ed.) *Principles and Practices of Teaching English as an International* Language (pp. 103–118). Bristol: Multilingual Matters.

Dogancay-Aktuna, S. and Hardman, J. (2018). Teaching of English as an International Language in various contexts: Nothing is as practical as good theory. *RELC Journal* 49 (1), 74–87.

Doiz, A. and Lasagabaster, D. (2016) The motivational self system in English-medium instruction at university. In A. Doiz and D. Lasagabaster (eds) *CLIL Experiences in Secondary and Tertiary Education: In Search of Good Practices*. Bern: Peter Lang.

Doiz, A. and Lasagabaster, D. (2018) Teachers' and students' second language motivational self system in English – medium instruction: A qualitative approach. *TESOL Quarterly* 52 (3), 657–679.

Dörnyei, Z. (2005) *The Psychology of the Language Learner: Individual Differences in Second Language Acquisition*. Mahwah, NJ: L. Erlbaum.

Dörnyei, Z. (2009) The L2 motivational self system. In Z. Dörnyei and E. Ushioda (eds) *Motivation, Language Identity and the L2 Self* (pp. 9–42). Bristol: Multilingual Matters.

Dörnyei, Z. and Ushioda, E. (eds) (2009) *Motivation, Language Identity and the L2 Self*. Bristol: Multilingual Matters.

Dörnyei, Z. and Ryan, S. (2015) *The Psychology of the Language Learner Revisited.* Abingdon: Routledge.

Dörnyei, Z. and Taguchi, T. (2009) *Questionnaires in Second Language Research: Construction, Administration, and Processing.* London: Routledge.

Dörnyei, Z., Csizér, K. and Németh, N. (2006) *Motivation, Language Attitudes and Globalisation: A Hungarian Perspective.* Clevedon: Multilingual Matters.

Douglas Fir Group (2016) A transdisciplinary framework for SLA in a multilingual world. *The Modern Language Journal* 100 (S1), 19–47.

Duff, P. and Uchida, Y. (1997) The negotiation of teachers' sociocultural identities and practices in postsecondary EFL classrooms. *TESOL Quarterly* 31, 451–486. doi:10.2307/3587834

Educational Testing Service. (2013) TOEFL® and TOEIC® Programs Set Global Standard for English-Language Assessment. Retrieved from http://www.etsglobal.org/Global/Eng/About-us/News/TOEFL-R-and-TOEIC-R-Programs-Set-Global-Standard-for-English-Language-Assessment

Edwards, J. (1982) Language attitudes and their implications among English speakers. In E.B. Ryan and H. Giles (eds) *Attitudes Toward Language Variation: Social and Applied Contexts* (pp. 1–19). London: Edward Arnold.

Elder, C. and Davies, A. (2006) Assessing English as a lingua franca. *Annual Review of Applied Linguistics* 26, 282–301.

Ellis, R. (2010) Second language acquisition, teacher education and language pedagogy. *Language Teaching* 43 (2), 182–201.

Estacio, E.V and Karic, T. (2016) The World Café: An innovative method to facilitate reflections on internationalisation in higher education. *Journal of Further and Higher Education* 40 (6), 731–745.

Evans, B.E. and Imai, T. (2011) 'If we say English, that means America': Japanese students' perceptions of varieties of English. *Language Awareness* 20 (4), 315–326.

Farrell, T. (2018) *Reflective Language Teaching: Practical Applications for TESOL Teachers* (2nd edn). London: Bloomsbury Academic.

Farrell, T.S.C. and Ng, J. (2003) 'Do Teachers' Beliefs of Grammar Teaching Match Their Classroom Practices? A Singapore Case Study'. In A.V. Brown and E.L. Low (eds) *English in Singapore: Research on Grammar* (pp. 128–137). Singapore: McGraw Hill.

Farrell, T.S.C. and Yang, D. (2017) Exploring an EAP teacher's beliefs and practices in teaching L2 speaking: A case study. *RELC Journal.*

Field, J. (2003) The fuzzy notion of 'intelligibility': A headache for pronunciation teachers and oral testers. *IATEFL Special Interest Groups Newsletter,* 34–38.

Firth, A. (1996) The discursive accomplishment of normality: On 'lingua franca' English and conversation analysis. *Journal of Pragmatics* 26, 237–259.

Firth, A. and Wagner, J. (1997) On discourse, communication, and (some) fundamental concepts in SLA research. *The Modern Language Journal* 81 (3), 285–300.

Fouché, C. and Light, G. (2011) An invitation to dialogue: 'The World Café' in social work research. *Qualitative Social Work* 10 (1), 28–48.

Fraser, S. (2006) Perceptions of varieties of spoken English: Implications for EIL. In R. Kiely, P. Rea-Dickins, H. Woodfield and G. Clibbon (eds) *Language, Culture, and Identity in Applied Linguistics* (pp. 79–97). London: British Association for Applied Linguistics in association with Equinox.

Friedrich, P. (2000) English in Brazil: Functions and attitudes. *World Englishes* 19 (2), 215–223.

Friedrich, P. (2012) ELF, Intercultural communication and the strategic aspect of communicative competence. In A. Matsuda (ed.) *Principles and Practices of Teaching English as an International Language.* Bristol: Multilingual Matters.

Fullan, M. (1993) *Change Forces: Probing the Depths of Educational Reform.* New York: The Falmer Press.

Gaitas, S. and Alves Martins, M. (2015) Relationships between primary teachers' beliefs and their practices in relation to writing instruction. *Research Papers in Education* 30 (4), 492–505.

Galloway, N., Kriukow, J. and Numajiri, T. (2017) Internationalisation, higher Education and the growing demand for English: An investigation into the English medium of instruction (EMI) movement in China and Japan. *ELT Research Papers*. London: British Council.

Galloway, N. (2011) An Investigation of Japanese Students' Attitudes Towards English. Unpublished doctoral dissertation. University of Southampton.

Galloway, N. (2013) Global Englishes and English language teaching (ELT): Bridging the gap between theory and practice in a Japanese context. *System* 41 (3), 786–803.

Galloway, N. (2014) 'I get paid for my American accent': The story of one multilingual English teacher (MET) in Japan. *Englishes in Practice* 1 (1), 1–30.

Galloway, N. (2017a) *Global Englishes and Change in English Language Teaching.* Abingdon: Routledge.

Galloway, N. (2017b) Global Englishes for language teaching: Preparing MSc TESOL students to teach in a globalized world. In A. Matsuda (ed.) *Preparing Teachers to Teach English as an International Language* (pp. 69–86). Bristol: Multilingual Matters.

Galloway, N. (2017c) Researching your own students: Negotiating the dual teacher-researcher role. In J. McKinley and H. Rose (eds) *Doing Research in Applied Linguistics Realities, Dilemmas, and Solutions* (pp. 146–156). London: Routledge.

Galloway, N. and Numajiri, T. (2019) Global Englishes Language Teaching: Bottom-up Curriculum Implementation. *TESOL Quarterly*. Advanced online version, https://doi.org/10.1002/tesq.547

Galloway, N. and Rose, H. (2013) "They envision going to New York, not Jakarta": The differing attitudes toward ELF of students, teaching assistants, and instructors in an English-medium business program in Japan. *Journal of English as a Lingua Franca* 2 (2), 229-253.

Galloway, N. and Rose, H. (2014) Using listening journals to raise awareness of Global Englishes in ELT. *ELT Journal* 68 (4), 386–396.

Galloway, N. and Rose, H. (2015) *Introducing Global Englishes*. Abingdon: Routledge.

Galloway, N. and Rose, H. (2018) Incorporating Global Englishes into the ELT classroom. *ELT Journal* 72 (1), 3–14.

Gao, X. (2019) The Douglas Fir group framework as a resource map for language teacher education. *The Modern Language Journal* 103, 161–166.

García, O. and Li, W. (2018) Translanguaging. *The Encyclopedia of Applied Linguistics*, 1–7. DOI: 10.1002/9781405198431.wbeal1488

Gardner, R.C. (1985) *Social Psychology and Second Language Learning: The Role of Attitude and Motivation*. London: Edward Arnold.

Gardner, R.C. (2010) *Motivation and Second Language Acquisition: The Socio-Educational Model*. New York, NY: Peter Lang Publishing.

Gardner, R.C. and Lambert, W.E. (1959) Motivational variables in second language acquisition. *Canadian Journal of Psychology* 13 (4), 266–272.

Gardner, R.C. and Lambert, W.E. (1972) *Attitudes and Motivation in Second Language Learning*. Rowley, MA: Newbury House.

Garrett, P. (2007) Language attitudes. In C. Llamas, L. Mullany and P. Stockwell (eds) *The Routledge Companion to Sociolinguistics* (pp. 116–121). New York, NY: Routledge.

Garrett, P. (2010) *Attitudes to Language: Key Topics in Sociolinguistics*. Cambridge: Cambridge University Press.

Gee, J.P. (2001) Identity as an analytic lens for research in education. *Review of Research in Education* 25, 99–125.

Gilmore, A. (2007) Authentic materials and authenticity in foreign language learning. *Language Teaching* 40 (2), 97–118.

Giri, R.A. and Foo, J.M.S. (2014) On teaching EIL in a Japanese context: The power within and power without. In R. Marlina and R.A. Giri (eds) *The Pedagogy of English as an International Language: Perspectives from Scholars, Teachers, and Students* (pp. 239–256). New York: Springer.

Giroux, H.A. (1988) Literacy and the pedagogy of voice and political empowerment. *Educational Theory* 38 (1), 61–75.

Graddol, D. (1999) The decline of the native speaker. *AILA Review* 13, 11–30.

Graddol, D. (2006) *English Next: Why Global English may Mean the End of 'English as a Foreign Language.'* London: British Council.

Gramley, S. (2012) *The History of English: An Introduction.* London, New York: Routledge.

Grau, M. (2005) English as a global language: What do future teachers have to say? In C. Gnutzmann and F. Intemann (eds) *The Globalisation of English and the English Language Classroom* (pp. 261–274). Tübingen: Gunter Narr Verlag.

Grazzi, E. (2015) ELF and the development of intercultural communicative competence: An Italian-American telecollaboration project. In P. Vettorel (ed.) *New Frontiers in Teaching and Learning* (pp. 179–204). Newcastle-upon-Tyne: Cambridge Scholars Publishing.

Grazzi, E. and Maranzana, S. (2016) ELF in intercultural telecollaboration. A case study. Intercultural communication. In L. Lopriore and E. Grazzi (eds) *Intercultural Communication: New Perspectives from ELF* (pp. 109–128). Roma: TrE-Press.

Griffee, D.T. (2012) *An Introduction to Second Language Research Methods: Design and Data.* Berkeley, CA: TESL-EJ Publications.

Haarmann, H. (1986) *Language in Ethnicity: A View of Basic Ecological Relations.* New York, NY: Mouton de Gruyter.

Hadfield, J. and Dörnyei, Z. (2013) *Motivating Learning.* Harlow: Longman.

Hall, C.J. (2014) Moving beyond accuracy: From tests of English to tests of 'Englishing'. *ELT Journal* 68 (4), 376–385. doi:10.1093/elt/ccu016

Hall, C., Wicaksono, R., Liu, S., Qian, Y. and Xiaoqing, X. (2013) *English Reconceived: Raising Teachers' Awareness of English as a 'Plurilithic' Resource through an Online Course. ELT Research Papers 13–05.* London: British Council.

Hall, G. (2009) International English language testing: A critical response. *ELT Journal* 64 (3), 321–328.

Hammad, E.A. and Ghali, E.M.A. (2015) Speaking anxiety level of Gaza EFL pre-service teachers: Reasons and sources. *World Journal of English Language* 5 (3), 53–64.

Hammond, L. (2015) Early childhood educators' perceived and actual metalinguistic knowledge, beliefs and enacted practice about teaching early reading. *Australian Journal of Learning Difficulties* 20 (2), 1–16.

Hamp-Lyons, L.I.Z. and Davies, A. (2008) The Englishes of English tests: Bias revisited. *World Englishes* 27 (1), 26–39.

Handford, M. and Matous, P. (2011) Lexicogrammar in the international construction industry: A corpus-based case study of Japanese–Hong-Kongese on-site interactions in English. *English for Specific Purposes* 30 (2), 87–100.

Hazel, S. (2016) Why native English speakers fail to be understood in English–and lose out in global business. The Conversation. Retrieved Jan 1, 2020 from http://theconversation.com/why-native-english-speakers-fail-to-be-understood-in-english-and-lose-out-in-global-business-54436

He, D. and Li, D.C.S. (2009) Language attitudes and linguistic features in the "China English" debate. *World Englishes* 28 (1), 70–89.

He, D. and Zhang, Q. (2010) Native speaker norms and China English: From the perspective of learners and teachers in China. *TESOL Quarterly* 44 (4), 769–789.

Hebbani, A. and Hendrix, K.G. (2014) Capturing the experiences of international teaching assistants in the U.S. American classroom. *New Directions for Teaching and Learning* 138, 61–72.

Henry, A. (2017) L2 motivation and multilingual identities. *Modern Language Journal* 101, 548–565.

Higgins, C. and Ponte, E. (2017) Legitimating multilingual teacher identities in the mainstream classroom. *Modern Language Journal* 101 (S1), 15–28.

Higgins, E. (1987) Self-discrepancy: A theory relating self and affect. *Psychological Review* 94 (3), 319–340.

Hilgendorf, S.K. (2018) Beyond center and periphery: Plurality with inclusivity. *World Englishes* 37 (3), 472–483.

Hino, N. (2012) Participating in the community of EIL users through real-time news: Integrated practice in teaching English as an international language (IPTEIL). In A. Matsuda (ed.) *Principles and Practices of Teaching English as an International Language* (pp. 183–200). Bristol: Multilingual Matters.

Hino, N. (2017) Training graduate students in Japan to be EIL teachers. In A. Matsuda (ed.) *Preparing Teachers to Teach English as an International Language* (pp. 159–70). Bristol: Multilingual Matters.

Hino, N. and Oda, S. (2015) Integrated practice in teaching English as an international language (IPTEIL): A classroom ELF pedagogy in Japan. In Y. Bayyurt and S. Akcan (eds) *Current Perspectives on Pedagogy for English as a Lingua Franca* (pp. 30–50). Berlin, Germany: Mouton de Gruyter.

Hiver, P. (2013) The interplay of possible language teacher selves in professional development choices. *Language Teaching Research* 17 (2), 210–227.

Hoffstaedter, P. and Kohn, K. (2014) Task design for intercultural telecollaboration in secondary schools: Insights from the EU project TILA. Research-publishing.net.

Hoffstaedter, P. and Kohn, K. (2015) Cooperative lingua franca conversations in intercultural telecollaboration exchanges between pupils in secondary foreign language education. *Research Report on the EU Project TILA* (*"Telecollaboration for intercultural language acquisition"*). Retrieved February 19, 2019, from http://www.tilaproject.eu/

Holliday, A. (2006) Native-speakerism. *ELT Journal* 60 (4), 385–387.

Holliday, A.R. (2005) *The Struggle to Teach English as an International Language.* Oxford: Oxford University Press.

Holliday, A.R. (2015) Native-speakerism: Taking the concept forward and achieving cultural belief. In A. Swan, P.J. Aboshiha and A.R. Holliday (eds) *(En)Countering Native-speakerism* (pp. 11–25). London: Palgrave.

Holliday, A.R. and Aboshiha, P.J. (2009) The denial of ideology in perceptions of 'nonnative speaker' teachers. *TESOL Quarterly* 43 (4), 669–689.

Honna, N. and Takeshita, Y. (2014) English as an international language and three challenging issues in English language teaching in Japan. In R. Marlina and A.R. Giri (eds) *The Pedagogy of English as an International Language: Perspectives from Scholars, Teachers, and Students* (pp. 65–78). Cham: Springer International Publishing.

Hos, R. and Kekec, M. (2014) The mismatch between non-native English as a foreign language (EFL) teachers' grammar beliefs and classroom practices. *Journal of Language Teaching and Research* 5 (1), 80–87.

House, J. (2003) English as a lingua franca: A threat to multilingualism? *Journal of Sociolinguistics* 7 (4), 556–578.

Hu, G. and Lindeman, S. (2009) Stereotypes of Cantonese English, apparent native/non-native status, and their effect on non-native English speakers' perception. *Journal of Multilingual and Multicultural Development* 30 (3), 253–269.

Ilieva, R. and Waterstone, B. (2013) Curriculum discourses within a TESOL program for international students: Affording possibilities for academic and professional identities. *TCI (Transnational Curriculum Inquiry)* 10 (1), 16–37.

İnal, D. and Özdemir, E. (2015) Re/considering the English language teacher education programs in Turkey from an ELF standpoint: What do academia, pre-service and in- service teachers think? In S. Ackan and Y. Bayyurt (eds) *Current Perspectives on Pedagogy for English as a Lingua Franca* (pp. 135–152). Berlin: Mouton de Gruyter.

Inoue, N. and Stracke, E. (2013) Non-native English speaking postgraduate TESOL students in Australia: Why did they come here? *University of Sydney Papers in TESOL* 8, 29–56.

Jenkins, J. (2000) *The Phonology of English as an International Language: New Models, New Norms, New Goals*. Oxford: Oxford University Press.

Jenkins, J. (2006) Current perspectives on teaching world Englishes and English as a lingua franca. *TESOL Quarterly* 40 (1), 157–181.

Jenkins, J. (2007) *English as a Lingua Franca: Attitude and Identity*. Oxford: Oxford University Press.

Jenkins, J. (2014) *English as a Lingua Franca in the International University – the Politics of Academic English Language Policy*. New York, NY: Routledge.

Jenkins, J. (2015a) *Global Englishes: A Resource Book for Students*. Abingdon: Routledge.

Jenkins, J. (2015b) Repositioning English and multilingualism in English as a Lingua Franca. *Englishes in Practice* 2 (3), 49–85.

Johnson, K.E. (1994) The emerging beliefs and instructional practices of preservice English as a second language teachers. *Teaching and Teacher Education* 10 (4), 439–452.

Joseph, J.E. (2016) Historical perspectives on language and identity. In S. Preece (ed.) *Routledge Handbook of Language and Identity* (pp. 19–33). London and New York: Routledge.

Kachru, B.B. (1976) Models of English for the Third World: White man's linguistic burden or language pragmatics? *TESOL Quarterly*, 221–239.

Kachru, B.B. (1985) Standards, codification and sociolinguistic realism: The English language in the outer circle. In R. Quirk and H.G. Widdowson (eds) *English in the World: Teaching and Learning the Language and Literatures* (pp. 11–30). Cambridge: Cambridge University Press.

Kachru, B.B. (1986) *The Alchemy of English: The Spread, Functions, and Models of Non-native Englishes*. Oxford: Pergamon Press.

Kachru, B.B. (1991) Liberation linguistics and the Quirk concern. *English Today* 25, 3–13.

Kachru, B.B. (1992) Teaching World Englishes. In B.B. Kachru (ed.) *The Other Tongue: English Across Cultures* (2nd edn). Urbana, IL: University of Illinois Press.

Kachru, B.B. and Nelson, C. (2001) World Englishes. In A. Burns and C. Coffin (eds) *Analysing English in a Global Context: A Reader*. London: Routledge in association with Macquarie University and the Open University.

Kamhi-Stein, L. (2009) Teacher preparation and nonnative English-speaking educators. In A. Burns and J.C. Richards (eds) *The Cambridge Guide to Second Language Teacher Education* (pp. 91–101). Cambridge: Cambridge University Press.

Kang, S.Y. (2017) US-based teacher education program for 'local' EIL teachers. In A. Matsuda (ed.) *Principles and Practices of Teaching English as an International Language* (pp. 51–68). Bristol: Multilingual Matters.

Kankaanranta, A. and Louhiala-Salminen, L. (2007) Business communication in BELF (Business English as a Foreign Language). *Business Communication Quarterly* 70 (1), 55–59.

Kankaanranta, A. and Louhiala-Salminen, L. (2010) 'English? – Oh, it's just work!' A Study of BELF Users' Perceptions. *English for Specific Purposes* 29 (3), 204–9. https://doi.org/10.1016/j.esp.2009.06.004

Kankaanranta, A. and Louhiala-Salminen, L. (2018) ELF in the domain of business – BELF: What does the B stand for? In J. Jenkins, W. Baker and M. Dewey (eds) *The Routledge Handbook of English as a Lingua Franca* (pp. 309–320). Abingdon: Routledge.

Kankaanranta, A. and Planken, B. (2010) Belf competence as business knowledge of internationally operating business professionals. *Journal of Business Communication* 47 (4), 380–407.

Kanno, Y. and Norton, B. (2003) Imagined communities and educational possibilities: Introduction. *Journal of Language, Identity and Education* 2, 241–249. doi:10.1207/s15327701jlie0204_1

Khan, S.Z. (2009) Imperialism of international tests: An EIL perspective. In F. Sharifian (ed.) *English as an International Language: Perspectives and Pedagogical Issues* (pp. 190–205). Bristol: Multilingual Matters.

Kirkpatrick, A. (2006) Which model of English: Native-speaker, nativized or lingua franca? In R. Rubdy and M. Saraceni (eds) *English in the World: Global Rules, Global Roles* (pp. 71–83). London: Continuum.

Kirkpatrick, A. (2007) *World Englishes: Implications for International Communication and English Language Teaching.* Cambridge: Cambridge University Press.

Kirkpatrick, A. (2011) English as an Asian lingua franca and the multilingual model of ELT. *Language Teaching* 44 (2), 212–224.

Kirkpatrick, A. (2012) English as an Asian Lingua Franca: The 'Lingua Franca Approach' and implications for language education policy. *Journal of English as a Lingua Franca* 1 (1), 121–139.

Kirkpatrick, A. and Xu, Z. (2002) Chinese pragmatic norms and "China English". *World Englishes* 21 (2), 269–279.

Kohn, K. (2015) A pedagogical space for ELF in the English classroom. In Y. Bayyurt and S. Akcan (eds) *Current Perspectives on Pedagogy for English as a Lingua Franca* (pp. 51–68). Berlin, Germany: Mouton de Gruyter.

Kohn, K. and Hoffstaedter, P. (2015) Flipping ntercultural communication practice: Opportunities and challenges for the foreign language classroom. In J. Colpaert, A. Aerts, M. Oberhofer and M. Gutiérez-Colón Plana (eds) *Task Design & CALL. Proceedings of the Seventeenth International CALL Conference*, 6-8 July 2015 (pp. 338–345). Antwerpen: Universiteit Antwerpen.

Koskun, A. (2011) Future English teachers' attitudes toward EIL pronunciation. *Journal of English as an International Language* 6 (2), 46–68.

Kramsch, C. (2009) *The Multilingual Subject.* Oxford: Oxford University Press.

Kramsch, C. and Zhang, L. (2017) *The Multilingual Instructor: What Foreign Language Teachers Say about their Experience and Why it Matters.* Oxford: Oxford University Press.

Kubanyiova, M. (2007) Teacher development in action: An empirically-based model of promoting conceptual change in in-service language teachers in Slovakia. Unpublished PhD thesis, University of Nottingham, Nottingham, UK.

Kubanyiova, M. (2009) Possible selves in language teacher development. In Z. Dörnyei and E. Ushioda (eds) *Motivation, Language Identity and the L2 Self* (pp. 314–332). Bristol: Multilingual Matters.

Kubanyiova, M. (2012) *Teacher Development in Action: Understanding Language Teachers' Conceptual Change.* Basingstoke: Palgrave.

Kubanyiova, M. (2017) Recognizing the local in language teacher identity. In G. Barkhuizen (ed.) *Reflections on Language Teacher Identity* (pp. 100–106). New York: Routledge.

Kubota, R. (2009) Rethinking the superiority of the native speaker: Toward a relational understanding of power. In N.M. Doerr (ed.) *The Native Speaker Concept: Ethnographic Investigations of Native Speaker Effects* (pp. 233–248). Berlin: De Gruyter Mouton.

Kubota, R. (2015) Introduction: Race and language learning in multicultural Canada. *Journal of Multilingual and Multicultural Development* 36 (1), 1–2.

Kubota, R. (2019) Confronting epistemological racism, decolonizing scholarly knowledge: Race and gender in applied linguistics. *Applied Linguistics.* Advanced online: https://doi.org/10.1093/applin/amz033

Kubota, R. and Lin, A. (2006) Race and TESOL: Introduction to concepts and theories. *TESOL Quarterly* 40 (3), 471–493.

Kumaravadivelu, B. (2012a) Individual identity, cultural globalization and teaching English as an international language: The case for an epistemic break. In L. Alsagoff, S.L. McKay, G. Hu and W.A. Renandya (eds) *Teaching English as an International Language: Principles and Practices* (pp. 9–27). Abingdon: Routledge.

Kumaravadivelu, B. (2012b) *Language Teacher Education for a Global Society.* New York: Routledge.

Kumaravadivelu, B. (2016) The decolonial option in English teaching: Can the subaltern act? *TESOL Quarterly* 50 (1), 66–85.

Kuo, I.C. (2006) Addressing the issue of teaching English as a Lingua Franca. *ELT Journal* 60 (3), 213–221.

Lagrosen, Y. (2017) The Quality Café: Developing the World Café method for organisational learning by including quality management tools. *Total Quality Management and Business Excellence* 1–13.

Lamb, M. (2004) Integrative motivation in a globalizing world. *System* 32, 3–19. doi: 10.1016/j.system.2003.04.002

Lamb, M. (2017) The motivational dimension of language teaching. *Language Teaching* 50, 301–346.

Ladegaard, H.J. and Sachdev, I. (2006) 'I like the Americans... but I certainly don't aim for an American accent': Language attitudes, vitality and foreign language learning in Denmark. *Journal of Multilingual and Multicultural Development* 27 (2), 91–108.

Lee, H. (2012) World Englishes in a high school English class: A case from Japan. In A. Matsuda (ed.) *Principles and Practices of Teaching English as an International Language* (pp. 154–168). Bristol: Multilingual Matters.

Lee, J. (2018) Teacher as change agent: Attitude change toward varieties of English through teaching English as an international language. *Asian Englishes*, 1–16.

Lee, J.S. and Lee, K. (2018) Informal digital learning of English and English as an international language: The path less traveled: IDLE and EIL perception. *British Journal of Educational Technology*, 08/29/2018.

Leung, C. (2014) Communication and participatory involvement in linguistically diverse classrooms. In S. May (ed.) *The Multilingual Turn. Implications for SLA, TESOL and Bilingual Education* (pp. 123–46). New York: Routledge.

Li, D. and Edwards, V. (2013) The impact of overseas training on curriculum innovation and change in English language education in western China. *Language Teaching Research* 17 (4), 390–408.

Li, G. (2017) Preparing culturally and linguistically competent teachers for English as an international language education. *TESOL Journal* 8 (2), 250–276.

Li, L. and Walsh, S. (2011) 'Seeing is believing': Looking at EFL Teachers' beliefs through classroom interaction. *Classroom Discourse*, 2 (1), 39–57.

Lim, S. and Burns, A. (2018) 'Native-Speakerism... I Think We Need to Change Our Perception': Sociocultural perspectives on Cambodian pre-service teacher education. In *English Language Teacher Preparation in Asia* (pp. 98–114). Routledge.

Lin, A. (2013) Toward paradigmatic change in TESOL methodologies: Building plurilingual pedagogies from the ground up. *TESOL Quarterly* 47 (3), 521–545.

Lippi-Green, R. (1997) *English with An Accent: Language, Ideology, and Discrimination in the United States.* London: Routledge.

Llurda, E. (2005) Non-native TESOL students as seen by practicum supervisors. In E. Llurda (ed.) *Non-native Language Teachers: Perceptions, Challenges and Contributions to the Profession* (pp. 131–154). New York, NY: Springer.

Llurda, E. (2014) Native and non-native teachers of English. In C. Chapelle (ed.) *The Encyclopedia of Applied Linguistics* (pp. 1–5). Chichester: Wiley-Blackwell.

Lopriore, L. (2016) ELF in teacher education: A way and ways. In L. Lopriore and E. Grazzi (eds) *Intercultural Communication. New Perspectives from ELF* (pp. 167–188). Rome: Roma TrE-Press.

Lopriore, L. and Vettorel, P. (2015) Promoting awareness of Englishes and ELF in the English language classroom. In H. Bowles and A. Cogo (eds) *International Perspectives on English as a Lingua Franca. Pedagogical Insights* (pp. 13–34). Basingtoke: Palgrave Macmillan.

Lortie, D.C. (1975) *Schoolteacher: A Sociological Study.* Chicago, IL: University of Chicago Press.

Loughran, J.J. (2004) A history and context of self-study of teaching and teacher education practices. In J.J. Loughran, M.L. Hamilton, V.K. LaBoskey and T. Russell (eds) *International Handbook of Self-Study of Teaching and Teacher Education Practices* (pp. 7–39). Dordrecht: Springer.

Louhiala-Salminen, L., Charles, M. and Kankaanranta, A. (2005) English as a lingua franca in Nordic corporate mergers: Two case companies. *English for Specific Purposes* 24 (4), 401–421.

Lowe, R.J. and Kiczkowiak, M. (2016) Native-speakerism and the complexity of personal experience: A duoethnographic study. *Cogent Education* 3 (1), 1264171.

Luciana, P. (2015) Raising trainee teachers' awareness of language variation through data-based tasks. *New Frontiers in Teaching and Learning English* (pp. 76–102). Newcastle-upon-Tyne: Cambridge Scholars.

MacFarlane, A., Galvin, R., O'Sullivan, M., McInerney, C., Meagher, E., Burke, D. and LeMaster, J. (2017) Participatory methods for research prioritization in primary care: An analysis of the World Café approach in Ireland and the USA. *Family Practice* 34 (3), 278–284.

Mahboob, A. (2010) *The NNEST Lens: Non-native English Speakers in TESOL.* Newcastle: Cambridge Scholars Publishing.

Mahboob, A. and Talaat, M. (2008) English language teachers and teacher education in Pakistan. In S. Dogancay-Aktuna and J. Hardman (eds) *Global English Teaching and Teacher Education: Praxis and Possibility* (pp. 3–25). Alexandria, VA: TESOL.

Manara, C. (2013) The struggle of moving towards EIL: Competing and conflicting narratives of professionalism in an Indonesian context. In N.T. Zacharias and C. Manara (eds) *Contextualizing the Pedagogy of English as an International Language: Issues and Tensions* (pp. 150–167). Newcastle upon tyne: Cambridge Scholars Publishing

Manara, C. (2014) 'So what do you want us to do?': A critical reflection of teaching English as an international language in an Australian context. In R. Marlina and R.A. Giri (eds) *The Pedagogy of English as an International Language: Perspectives from Scholars, Teachers, and Students* (pp. 189–202). New York: Springer.

Marlina, R. (2014) The pedagogy of English as an international language (EIL): More reflections and dialogues. In R. Marlina and A.R. Giri (eds) *The Pedagogy of English as An International Language: Perspectives from Scholars, Teachers, and Students* (pp. 1–22). Cham: Springer International Publishing.

Marlina, R. and Giri, A.R. (eds) (2014) *The Pedagogy of English as an International Language: Perspectives from Scholars, Teachers, and Students.* Cham: Springer International Publishing.

Marlina, R. and Giri, R.A. (eds) (2014) *Pedagogy of English as an International Language: Perspectives from Scholars, Teachers and Students.* New York, NY: Springer.

Marsden, E. and Kasprowicz, R. (2017) Foreign language educators' exposure to research: Reported experiences, exposure via citations, and a proposal for action. *The Modern Language Journal* 101 (4), 613–642.

Marshall, S. and Moore, D. (2013) 2B or not 2B plurilingual? Navigating languages literacies, and plurilingual competence in postsecondary education in Canada. *TESOL Quarterly* 47 (3), 472–499.

Martínez Agudo, J. (2018) *Emotions in Second Language Teaching: Theory, Research and Teacher Education.* Cham: Springer.

Matsuda, A. (2003a) Incorporating World Englishes in teaching English as an international language. *TESOL Quarterly* 37 (4), 719–729.

Matsuda, A. (2003b) The ownership of English in Japanese secondary schools. *World Englishes* 22 (4), 483–496.

Matsuda, A. and Matsuda, P.K. (2018) Teaching English as an international language: A WE-informed paradigm for English language teaching. In E.L. Low and A. Pakir (eds) *World Englishes: Rethinking Paradigms*. Abingdon: Routledge.

Matsuda, A. and Friedrich, P. (2011) English as an international language: A curriculum blueprint. *World Englishes* 30 (3), 332–344.

Matsuda, A. (2009) Desirable but not necessary? The place of world Englishes and English as an international language. In F. Sharifian (ed.) *English as An International Language: Perspectives and Pedagogical Issues* (pp. 169–89). Bristol: Multilingual Matters.

Matsuda, A. (2002) International understanding through teaching world Englishes. *World Englishes* 21 (3), 436–440.

Matsuda, A. (2006) Negotiating ELT assumptions in EIL classrooms. In J. Edge (ed.) *(Re) Locating TESOL in an Age of Empire* (pp. 158–170). Basingstoke: Palgrave MacMillan.

Matsuda, A. (2012) *Principles and Practices of Teaching English as An International Language*. Bristol: Multilingual Matters.

Matsuda, A. (2017a) Introduction. In A. Matsuda (ed.) *Preparing Teachers to Teach English as an International Language* (pp. xiii–xxi). Bristol: Multilingual Matters.

Matsuda, A. (ed.) (2012) *Principles and Practices of Teaching English as an International Language*. Bristol: Multilingual Matters.

Matsuda, A. (ed.) (2017) *Preparing Teachers to Teach English as an International Language*. Bristol: Multilingual Matters.

Matsuda, A. and Duran, C.S. (2012) EIL activities and tasks for traditional EFL classrooms. In A. Matsuda (ed.) *Principles and Practices of Teaching English as an International Language* (pp. 201–238). Bristol: Multilingual Matters.

Matsuda, A. and Friedrich, P. (2012) Selecting an instructional variety for an EIL curriculum. In A. Matsuda (ed.) *Principles and Practices of Teaching English as an International Language. New Perspectives on Language and Education* (pp. 17–27) Bristol: Multilingual Matters.

Matsuura, H., Chiba, R. and Yamamoto, A. (1994) Japanese college students' attitudes towards non-native varieties of English. In D. Graddol and J. Swann (eds) *Evaluating Language* (pp. 52–61). Clevedon: Multilingual Matters.

Mauranen, A. (2003) The corpus of English as lingua franca in academic settings. *TESOL Quarterly* 37 (3), 513–527.

Mauranen, A., Hynninen, N. and Ranta, E. (2010) English as an academic lingua franca: The ELFA project. *English for Specific Purposes* 29 (3), 183–190.

May, S. (2014b) Introducing the 'Multilingual Turn'. In S. May (ed.) *The Multilingual Turn. Implications for SLA, TESOL and Bilingual Education* (pp. 1–6). New York, NJ: Routledge.

May, S. (ed.) (2014a) *The Multilingual Turn: Implications for SLA, TESOL, and Bilingual Education*. Routledge.

McArthur, T. (1987) The English languages? *English Today* 3 (3), 9–13.

McArthur, T. (2006) English world-wide in the twentieth century. In L. Mugglestone (ed.) *The Oxford History of English* (pp. xi, 485). Oxford: Oxford University Press.

McDonough, J. and Shaw, C. (2012) *Materials and Methods in ELT*. Chichester: John Wiley & Sons.

McGriff, M. (2015). Teacher identity and EL-focused professional learning in a suburban middle school. *Action in Teacher Education* 37, 82–98.

McIntyre, D. (2009) *History of English: A Resource Book for Students*. London: Routledge.

McKay, S.L. (2002) *Teaching English as an International Language: Rethinking Goals and Approaches*. Oxford: Oxford University Press.

McKay, S.L. (2012) Principles of teaching English as an international language. In L. Alsagoff, S.L. McKay, G. Hu and W.A. Renandya (eds) *Teaching English as an International Language: Principles and Practices* (pp. 28–46). New York, NY: Routledge.

McKay, S.L. and Bokhorst-Heng, W.D. (2008) *International English in its Sociolinguistic Contexts: Towards a Socially Sensitive EIL Pedagogy.* Abingdon: Routledge.

McKay, S.L. and Brown, J.D. (2016) *Teaching and Assessing EIL in Local Contexts Around the World.* New York: Routledge.

McKenzie, R.M (2008a) Social factors and non-native attitudes towards varieties of spoken English: A Japanese case study. *International Journal of Applied Linguistics* 18 (1), 63–88.

McKenzie, R.M. (2008b) The role of variety recognition in Japanese university students' attitudes towards English speech varieties. *Journal of Multilingual and Multicultural Development* 29 (2), 139–153.

McKenzie, R.M. (2010) *The Social Psychology of English as a Global Language: Attitudes, Awareness and Identity in the Japanese Context.* Berlin: Springer.

McKenzie, R.M. and Gilmore, A. (2017) "The people who are out of 'right English'": Japanese university students' social evaluations of English language diversity and the internationalisation of Japanese higher education. *International Journal of Applied Linguistics* 27 (1), 152–175.

McKinley, J. (2019) Evolving the TESOL Teaching–Research Nexus. *TESOL Quarterly* 53 (3), 875–884.

McKinley, J. and Thompson, G. (2018) Washback effect in teaching English as an international language. *The TESOL Encyclopedia of English Language Teaching*, 1–12.

McNamara, T.F. (2000) *Language Testing.* Oxford: Oxford University Press.

McNeill, B. and Kirk, C. (2014) Theoretical beliefs and instructional practices used for teaching spelling in elementary classrooms. *Reading and Writing* 27 (3), 535–554.

Medgyes, P. (1992) Native or non-native: Who's worth more? *ELT Journal* 46 (4), 340–349.

Meier, G.S. (2017) The multilingual turn as a critical movement in education: Assumptions, challenges and a need for reflection. *Applied Linguistics Review* 8 (1), 131–161.

Meierkord, C. (2000) Interpreting successful lingua franca interaction. An analysis of non-native/non-native small talk conversations in English. In A. Fetzer and K. Pittner (eds) *Conversation Analysis: New Developments.* Linguistik Online 5 Special issue. Retrieved 19 February 2019, from https://bop.unibe.ch/linguistik-online/article/view/1013/1673

Menken, K. and García, O. (eds) (2010) *Negotiating Language Policies in Schools: Educators as Policymakers.* London: Routledge.

Mercer, S. and Williams, M. (eds) (2014) *Multiple Perspectives on the Self in SLA.* Bristol: Multilingual Matters.

Mickan, P. (2012) *Language Curriculum Design and Socialisation.* Bristol: Multilingual Matters.

Mills, N. (2014) Self-efficacy in second language acquisition. In S. Mercer and M. Williams (eds) *Multiple Perspectives on the Self in SLA* (pp. 6–19). Bristol: Multilingual Matters.

Milroy, J. (2001) Language ideologies and the consequences of standardization. *Journal of Sociolinguistics* 5 (4), 530–555.

Milroy, J. and Milroy. L. (1999) *Authority in Language: Investigating Standard English* (3rd edn). London: Routledge.

Milroy, L. (1999) Standard English and language ideology in Britain and the United States. In T. Bex and R.J. Watts (eds) *Standard English: The Widening Debate.* London: Routledge.

Miniwatts Marketing Group (2018) *Internet World Stats: Usage and Population Statistics.* Retrieved 19 February 2019, from https://www.internetworldstats

Modiano, M. (2001) Linguistic imperialism, cultural integrity, and EIL. *ELT Journal* 55 (4), 339–347.

Modiano, M. (2003) Euro-English: A Swedish perspective. *English Today* 19 (2), 35–41.

Modiano, M. (2009) EIL, native-speakersim and the failure of European ELT. In F. Sharifian (ed.) *English as an International Language: Perspectives and Pedagogical Issues* (pp. 58–77). Bristol: Multilingual Matters.

Monfared, A. and Khatib, M. (2018) English or Englishes? Outer and expanding circle teachers' awareness of and attitudes towards their own variants of English in ESL/EFL teaching contexts. *Australian Journal of Teacher Education* 43 (2), 56–75.

Moore, G.A. (2002) *Crossing the Chasm: Marketing and Selling Disruptive Products to Mainstream Customers.* New York, NY: HarperCollins.

Mora, R.A. and Golovátina-Mora, P. (2017) A new model for reflexivity and advocacy for master's-level EIL in-service programs in Colombia: The notion of 'learning and teaching processes in second languages'. In A. Matsuda (ed.) *Preparing Teachers to Teach English as An International Language* (pp. 35–50). Bristol: Multilingual Matters.

Morgan, B. (2004) Teacher identity as pedagogy: Towards a field-internal conceptualisation in bilingual and second language education. *International Journal of Bilingual Education and Bilingualism* 7 (2–3), 172–188. doi:10.1080/13670050408667807

Morgan, G. (1986) *Images of Organization.* Beverly Hills: Sage.

Morrison, L. (2016) Native English speakers are the world's worst communicators. *BBC.* Retrieved Jan 1, 2020 from https://www.bbc.com/worklife/article/20161028-native-english-speakers-are-the-worlds-worst-communicators

Motha, S. (2006) Racializing ESOL teacher identities in U.S. K-12 public schools. *TESOL Quarterly* 40, 495–518. doi:10.2307/40264541

Mufwene, S.S. (2001) *The Ecology of Language Evolution.* Cambridge: Cambridge University Press.

Naji Meidani, E. and Pishghadam, R. (2012) Analysis of English language textbooks in the light of English as an International Language (EIL): A comparative study. *International Journal of Research Studies in Language Learning* 2 (2).

Nation, I.S.P. and Macalister, J. (2010) *Language Curriculum Design.* New York: Routledge.

Nguyen, H.T.M. and Hudson, P. (2010) Preservice EFL teachers' attitudes, needs, and experiences about teaching writing and learning to teach writing before their practicum: A case study in Vietnam. *The Asian EFL Journal Quarterly* 12 (2), 43–67.

Niedzielski, N. and Preston, D. (2000) *Folk Linguistics.* New York, NY: Mouton de Gruyter.

Nishimuro, M. and Borg, S. (2013) Teacher cognition and grammar teaching in a Japanese high school. *JALT Journal* 35 (1), 29–50.

Norris, J. (2017) Duoethnography. In L.M. Given (ed.) *The SAGE Encyclopedia of Qualitative Research Methods* (pp. 233–236). Thousand Oaks, CA: SAGE Publications.

Norton, B. (1997) Language, identity, and the ownership of English. *TESOL Quarterly* 31, 409–429. doi:10.2307/3587831

Norton, B. (2000) *Identity and Language Learning: Gender, Ethnicity and Educational Change* (1st edn). Harlow: Longman.

Norton, B. (2014) Identity and poststructuralist theory in SLA. In S. Mercer and M. Williams (eds) *Multiple Perspectives on the Self in SLA* (pp. 59–74). Bristol: Multilingual Matters.

Numrich, C. (1996) On becoming a language teacher: Insights from diary studies. *TESOL Quarterly* 30 (1), 131–153.

O'Neill, M. (2000) *Executive Coaching with Backbone and Heart: A Systems Approach to Engaging Leaders with their Challenges* (Jossey-Bass business and management series). San Francisco: Jossey-Bass.

Ockey, G.J., Papageorgiou, S. and French, R. (2016) Effects of strength of accent on an L2 interactive lecture listening comprehension test. *International Journal of Listening* 30 (1–2), 84–98.

Ortega, L. (2013) SLA for the 21st century: Disciplinary progress, transdisciplinary relevance, and the bi/multilingual turn. *Language Learning* 63 (suppl. 1), 1–24.

Ortega, L. (2014) Ways forward for a bi/multilingual turn in SLA. In S. May (ed.) *The Multilingual Turn. Implications for SLA, TESOL and Bilingual Education* (pp. 32–53). New York, NJ: Routledge.

Öztürk, G. and Gürbüz, N. (2017) Re-defining language teacher cognition through a data-driven model: The case of three EFL teachers. *Cogent Education* 4 (1), 1290333.

Paikeday, T.M. (1985) *The Native Speaker is Dead!* Toronto, Canada/New York, NY: Paikeday Publishing.

Paradowski, M.B. (2008) Winds of change in the English language: Air of peril for native speakers? *Novitas-Royal* 2 (1), 92–119.

Park, G. (2012) 'I am never afraid of being recognized as a NNES': One teacher's journey in claiming and embracing her nonnative-speaker identity. *TESOL Quarterly* 46, 127–151.

Park, G. (2015) Situating the discourses of privilege and marginalization in the lives of two East Asian women teachers of English. *Race, Ethnicity and Education* 18 (1), 108–133. doi:10.1080/13613324.2012.759924

Parker-Katz, M., Cushing, L., Athamanah, L., Carter, E. and Bumble, J. (2018) Fostering collaboration as transition specialists through community conversations. *Journal of Disability Policy Studies* 28 (4), 244–254.

Pavlenko, A. and Norton, B. (2007) Imagined communities, identity, and English language teaching. In J. Cummins and C. Davison (eds) *International Handbook of English Language Teaching* (pp. 669–680). New York, NY: Springer.

Pedrazzini, L. (2015) Raising trainee teachers' awareness of language variation through data-based tasks. In P. Vettorel (ed.) *New Frontiers in Teaching and Learning English* (pp. 77–101). Newcastle-upon-Tyne: Cambridge Scholars.

Pedrazzini, L. and Nava, A. (2011) Researching ELF identity: A study with non-native English teachers. In A. Archibald, A. Cogo and J. Jenkins (eds) *Latest Trends in ELF Research* (pp. 269–284). Newcastle: Cambridge Scholars.

Peercy, M.M. and Sharkey, J. (2018) Missing a S-STEP? How self-study of teacher education practice can support the language teacher education knowledge base. *Language Teaching Research*. DOI: 10.1177/1362168818777526 (pre-print).

Pennycook, A. (1994) *The Cultural Politics of English as an International Language.* London: Longman.

Pennycook, A. (1998) *English and the Discourses of Colonialism.* London: Routledge.

Pennycook, A. (2003) Global Englishes, rip slyme, and performativity. *Journal of Sociolinguistics* 7 (4), 513–533.

Pennycook, A. (2007) *Global Englishes and Transcultural Flows.* London: Routledge.

Pennycook, A. (2010) The future of Englishes: One, many or none? In *The Routledge Handbook of World Englishes* (pp. 695–710). London: Routledge.

Phan, L. H. (2007) Questioning the validity and appropriacy of presenting communicative language teaching as 'the best' teaching method in TESOL teacher training courses. In J. Mukundan, S. Menon and A. Hussin (eds) *ELT Matters 3: Developments in English Language Learning and Teaching* (pp. 232–240). Selangor, Malaysia: Universiti Putra Malaysia Press.

Phan, L.H. (2008) *Teaching English as an International Language: Identity, Resistance and Negotiation.* Clevedon: Multilingual Matters.

Phillipson, R. (1992) *Linguistic Imperialism.* Oxford: Oxford University Press.

Porter, W.W. and Graham, C.R. (2016) Institutional drivers and barriers to faculty adoption of blended learning in higher education. *British Journal of Educational Technology* 47 (4), 748–762.

Preece, S. (2016) An identity transformation? Social class, language prejudice and the erasure of multilingual capital in higher education. In S. Preece (ed.) *The Routledge Handbook of Language and Identity* (pp. 392–407). London: Routledge.

Preston, D. (1989) *Perceptual Dialectology: Non-Linguists' Views of Areal Linguistics.* Dordrecht: Foris Publication.

Quirk, R. (1985) The English language in a global context. In R. Quirk and H.G. Widdowson (eds) *English in the World: Teaching and Learning the Language and Literatures* (pp. 1–6). Cambridge: Cambridge University Press.

Quirk, R. (1990) Language varieties and standard language. *English Today* 21, 3–10.

Rampton, B.H. (1990) Displacing the 'native speaker': Expertise, affiliation and inheritance. *ELT Journal* 44 (2), 97–101.

Rashidi, N. and Meihami, H. (2016) Hidden curriculum: An analysis of cultural content of the ELT textbooks in inner, outer, and expanding circle countries. *Cogent Education* 3 (1), 1212455.

Reis, D.S. (2011) Non-native English speaking teachers (NNESTs) and professional legitimacy: A sociocultural theoretical perspective on identity transformation. *International Journal of the Sociology of Language* 208, 139–160.

Richards, J.C. (2017) *Curriculum Development in Language Teaching.* Cambridge: Cambridge University Press.

Richards, J. and Lockhart, C. (1994) *Reflective Teaching in Second Language Classrooms.* Cambridge: Cambridge University Press.

Ritch, E. and Brennan, C. (2010) Using World Café and drama to explore older people's experience of financial products and services. *International Journal of Consumer Studies* 34 (4), 405–411.

Rogers, E. (2003) *Diffusions of Innovations* (5th edn). New York: Free Press.

Rose, H. (2019) Dismantling the ivory tower in TESOL: A renewed call for teaching informed research. *TESOL Quarterly* 53 (3), 895–905. https://doi.org/10.1002/tesq.517

Rose, H. (2017) A global approach to English language teaching: integrating an international perspective into a teaching methods course. In A. Matsuda (ed.) *Preparing Teachers to Teach English as an International Language* (pp. 169–180). Bristol: Multilingual Matters.

Rose, H. (2018) Popular approaches to EAL instruction. *The TESOL Encyclopedia of English Language Teaching.* DOI: 10.1002/9781118784235.eelt0818

Rose, H. (2019) Researching English as an International Language. In G. Barkhuizen (ed.) *Qualitative Research Topics in Language Teacher Education* (pp. 331–136). New York: Routledge.

Rose, H. and Galloway, N. (2017) Debating standard language ideology in the classroom: Using the 'Speak Good English Movement' to raise awareness of Global Englishes. *RELC Journal* 48 (3), 294–301.

Rose, H. and Montakantiwong, A. (2018) A tale of two teachers: A duoethnography of the realistic and idealistic successes and failures of teaching English as an international language. *RELC Journal* 49 (1), 88–101.

Rose, H. and Syrbe, M. (2018) Assessment practices in teaching English as an international language. *The TESOL Encyclopedia Of English Language Teaching.* doi: 10.1002/9781118784235

Rose, H. and Galloway, N. (2019) *Global Englishes for Language Teaching.* Cambridge: Cambridge University Press.

Rose, H. and Montakantiwong, A. (2018) A tale of two teachers: A duoethnography of the realistic and idealistic successes and failures of teaching English as an international language. *RELC Journal* 49 (1), 88–101. https://doi.org/10.1177/003368821774620

Rosenhan, C. and Galloway, N. (2019) Creativity, self-reflection and subversion: Poetry writing for Global Englishes awareness raising. *System* 84, 1–13. https://doi.org/10.1016/j.system.2019.04.005

Ryan, S. (2006) Language learning motivation within the context of globalisation: An L2 self within an imagined global community. *Critical Inquiry in Language Studies: An International Journal* 3, 23–45. doi:10.1207/S15427595CILS0301_2

Sadeghi, K. and Ghaderi, F. (2018) Assessment norms. *The TESOL Encyclopedia of English Language Teaching.* doi: 10.1002/9781118784235

Sadeghpour, M. and Sharifian, F. (2017) English language teachers' perceptions of world Englishes: The elephants in the room. *Asian Englishes* 19 (3), 242–258.

Sampasivam, S. and Clément, R. (2014) The dynamics of second language confidence: Contact and interaction. In S. Mercer and M. Williams (eds) *Multiple Perspectives on the Self in SLA* (pp. 23–35). Bristol: Multilingual Matters.

Saraceni, M. (2009) Relocating English: Towards a new paradigm for English in the world. *Language and Intercultural Communication* 9 (3), 175–186.

Sarnoff, I. (1970) *Social Attitudes and the Resolution of Motivational Conflict.* Harmondsworth: Penguin.

Sasayama, S. (2013) Japanese college students' attitudes towards Japan English and American English. *Journal of Multilingual and Multicultural Development* 34 (3), 264–278.

Schneider, E.W. (2012) Contact-induced change in English worldwide. In T. Nevalainen and E.C. Traugott (eds) *The Oxford Handbook of The History of English.* doi: 10.1093/oxfordhb/9780199922765.013.0049

Schön, D. (1983) *The Reflective Practitioner: How Professionals Think in Action.* London: Temple Smith.

Seidlhofer, B. (2001) Closing a conceptual gap: The case for a description of English as a lingua franca. *International Journal of Applied Linguistics* 11 (2), 133–58.

Seidlhofer, B. (2004) Research perspectives on teaching English as a lingua franca. *Annual Review of Applied Linguistics* 24, 209–239.

Seidlhofer, B. (2011) *Understanding English as a Lingua Franca.* Oxford: Oxford University Press.

Seidlhofer, B. (2018) Standard English and the dynamics of ELF variation. In J. Jenkins, W, Baker and M. Dewey (eds) *The Routledge Handbook of English as a Lingua Franca* (pp. 85–100). Abingdon: Routledge.

Selvi, A.F. (2010) All teachers are equal, but some teachers are more equal than others: Trend analysis of job advertisements in English language teaching. *WATESOL NNEST Caucus Annual Review* 1, 156–181.

Selvi, A.F. (2013) Toward EIL teacher education: Exploring challenges and potentials of MATESOL programmes in the United States. In N.T. Zacharias and C. Manara (eds) *Contextualizing the Pedagogy of English as an International Language: Issues and Tensions* (pp. 43–58). Newcastle upon Tyne: Cambridge Scholars Publishing.

Selvi, A.F. (2014) Myths and misconceptions about the non-native English speakers in TESOL (NNEST) Movement. *TESOL Journal* 5 (3), 573–611.

Selvi, A.F. (2017) Preparing teachers to teach English as an international language: Reflections from Northern Cyprus. In A. Matsuda (ed.) *Preparing Teachers to Teach English as an International Language* (pp. 114–130). Bristol: Multilingual Matters.

Selvi, A.F. and Yazan, B. (2015) *Teaching English as an International Language.* TESOL Press.

Sembiante, S. (2017) Translanguaging and the multilingual turn: Epistemological reconceptualization in the fields of language and implications for reframing language in curriculum studies. *Curriculum Inquiry* 46 (1), 45–61.

Sharifian, F. and Marlina, R. (2012) English as an international language (EIL): An Innovative academic program. In A. Matsuda (ed.) *Principles and Practices of Teaching English as an International Language* (pp. 140–153). Bristol: Multilingual Matters.

Sifakis, N.C. (2007) The education of the teachers of English as a lingua franca: A transformative perspective. *International Journal of Applied Linguistics* 17 (3), 355–75.

Sifakis, N.C. (2009) Challenges in teaching ELF in the periphery: The Greek context. *ELT Journal* 63 (3), 230–237.

Sifakis, N.C. (2014) ELF awareness as an opportunity for change: A transformative perspective for ESOL teacher education. *Journal of English as a Lingua Franca* 3 (2), 317–335.

Sifakis, N.C. (2017) ELF awareness in English language teaching: Principles and processes. *Applied Linguistics* 40 (2), 288–306.

Sifakis, N.C. and Bayyurt, Y. (2015) Insights from ELF and WE in teacher training in Greece and Turkey. *World Englishes* 34 (3), 471–484.

Sifakis, N.C. and Sougari, A.M. (2005) Pronunciation issues and EIL pedagogy in the periphery: A survey of Greek state school teachers' beliefs. *TESOL Quarterly* 39 (4), 467–488.

Sifakis, N. and Sougari, A.M. (2005) Pronunciation issues and EIL pedagogy in the periphery: A survey of Greek state school teachers' beliefs. *TESOL Quarterly* 39 (3), 467–488.

Sifakis, N. and Tsantila, N. (eds) (2018) *English as a Lingua Franca for EFL Contexts*. Bristol: Multilingual Matters.

Sifakis, N., Lopriore, L., Dewey, M., Bayyurt, Y., Vettorel, P., Cavalheiro, L., Siqueira, D., Sávio, P. and Kordia, S. (2018) ELF-awareness in ELT: Bringing together theory and practice. *Journal of English as a Lingua Franca* 7 (1), 155–209.

Sougari, A.M. and Faltzi, R. (2015) Drawing upon Greek pre-service teachers' beliefs about ELF-related issues. In S. Ackan and Y. Bayyurt (eds) *Current Perspectives on Pedagogy for English as a Lingua Franca* (pp. 153–169). Berlin: Mouton de Gruyter.

Starfield, S. (2016) English for specific purposes. In G. Hall (ed.) *The Routledge Handbook of English Language Teaching* (pp. 150–163). Abingdon: Routledge.

Strang, B. (1970) *A History of English*. London: Methuan.

Strevens, P. (1980) *Teaching English as an International Language: From Practice to Principle*. Oxford: Pergamon Press.

Sung, C.C.M. (2014a) 'Accent and identity: Exploring the perceptions among bilingual speakers of English as a lingua franca in Hong Kong.' *International Journal of Bilingual Education and Bilingualism* 17, 544–557.

Sung, C.C.M. (2014b) English as a lingua franca and global identities: Perspectives from four second language learners of English in Hong Kong. *Linguistics and Education* 26, 31–39.

Sung, C.C.M. (2015) Implementing a Global Englishes component in a university English course in Hong Kong: Student perceptions and implications for course development and implementation. *English Today* 31 (4), 42–49.

Sung, C.C.M. (2016) Exposure to multiple accents of English in the English Language Teaching classroom: From second language learners' perspectives. *Innovation in Language Learning and Teaching* 10 (3), 190–205.

Sung, C.C.M. (2018) Out-of-class communication and awareness of English as a Lingua Franca. *ELT Journal* 72 (1), 15–25.

Sung, C.C.M. (2017) Exploring language identities in English as a lingua franca communication: Experiences of bilingual university students in Hong Kong. *International Journal of Bilingual Education and Bilingualism*, 1–14.

Swan, A. (2015) Redefining English language teacher identity. In A. Swan, P. Aboshiha and A. Holliday (eds) *(En)Countering Native-Speakerism* (pp. 59–74). London: Springer.

Swan, A., Aboshiha, P.J. and Holliday, A.R. (eds) (2015) *(En)countering Native-speakerism: Global Perspectives*. London: Palgrave.

Syrbe, M. and Rose, H. (2018) An evaluation of the global orientation of English textbooks in Germany. *Innovation in Language Learning and Teaching* 12 (2), 152–163.

Taguchi, T., Magid, M. and Papi, M. (2009) The L2 motivational self system among Japanese, Chinese and Iranian learners of English: A comparative study. In Z. Dörnyei and E. Ushioda (eds) *Motivation, Language Identity and the L2 Self* (pp. 66–97). Bristol: Multilingual Matters.

Takahashi, H. (2014) Non-native English-speaking teachers' self-perceived language proficiency levels, anxieties, and learning strategies. *International Journal of Christianity and English Language Teaching* 1, 24–44.

Tanghe, S. (2014) Integrating World Englishes into a university conversation class in South Korea. *English Today* 30 (2), 18–23.

Taylor, S.K. and Snoddon, K. (2013) Plurilingualism in TESOL: Promising controversies. *Tesol Quarterly* 47 (3), 439–445.

Thackray, L. Good, J. and Howland, K. (2010) Learning and teaching in virtual worlds: Boundaries, challenges and opportunities. In A. Peachey, J. Gillen, D. Livingstone and S. Smith-Robbins (eds) *Researching Learning in Virtual Worlds* (pp. 139–158). London, England: Springer.

Timmis, I. (2002) Native-speaker norms and international English: A classroom view. *ELT Journal* 56 (3), 240–249.

Tokumoto, M. and Shibata, M. (2011) Asian varieties of English: Attitudes towards pronunciation. *World Englishes* 30 (3), 392–408.

Tomlinson, B. (2012) Materials development for language learning and teaching. *Language Teaching* 45 (2), 143–179.

Tum, D.O. (2013) A study of non-native student teachers' feelings of foreign language teacher anxiety (Unpublished doctoral dissertation). Institute of Education, University of London, London, England.

Underwood, P.R. (2012) Teacher beliefs and intentions regarding the instruction of English grammar under national curriculum reforms: A theory of planned behaviour perspective. *Teaching and Teacher Education* 28 (6), 911–925.

UNESCO (2005) *Initiative Babel*. Retrieved 19 February 2019, from https://unesdoc.unesco.org/ark:/48223/pf0000139844

UNESCO (2009) *IFAP Annual World Report* 2009. Retrieved 31 December 2019, from http://www.iis.ru/docs/IS_Policies_IFAP_World_Report_2009.pdf

Ushioda, E. (eds) (2013) *International Perspectives on Motivation: Language Learning and Professional Challenges*. Basingstoke: Palgrave Macmillan.

Uysal, H.H. (2009) A response to Graham Hall. *ELT Journal* 64 (3), 329–330.

Varghese, M.M., Motha, S., Trent, J., Park, G. and Reeves, J. (guest eds) (2016) Language teacher identity in multilingual settings (special issue). *TESOL Quarterly* 50 (3), 541–783.

Varghese, M., Morgan, B., Johnston, B. and Johnson, K.A. (2005) Theorizing language teacher identity: Three perspectives and beyond. *Journal of Language, Identity, and Education* 4, 21–44.

Vettorel, P. (2010) English(es), ELF, Xmas and trees: Intercultural communicative competence and English as a lingua franca in the primary classroom. *A Journal of TESOL Italy*, XXXVII/1, 25–52.

Vettorel, P. (2013) ELF in international school exchanges: Stepping into the role of ELF users. *Journal of English as a Lingua Franca* 2 (1), 147–173.

Vettorel, P. (2014) Connecting English wor(l)ds and classroom practices. *TEXTUS* XXVII/1 (January-April), Perspectives on English as a Lingua Franca, 137–154.

Vettorel, P. (2015) World Englishes and English as a Lingua Franca: Implications for teacher education and ELT. *Iperstoria* 6, 229–244.

Vettorel, P. (2016) WE- and ELF-informed classroom practices: Proposals from a pre-service teacher education programme in Italy. *Journal of English as a Lingua Franca* 5 (1), 107–133.

Vettorel, P. (2018) ELF and communication strategies: Are they taken into account in ELT materials? *RELC Journal* 49 (1), 58–73.

Vettorel, P. (ed.) (2015) *New Frontiers in Teaching and Learning English*. Newcastle-upon-Tyne: Cambridge Scholars Publishing.

Vettorel, P. and Corrizzato, S. (2016) Fostering awareness of the pedagogical implications of World Englishes and ELF in teacher education in Italy. *Studies in Second Language Learning and Teaching* 6 (3), 487–511.

Vettorel, P. and Lopriore, L. (2015) Promoting awareness of Englishes and ELF in the English language classroom. In H. Bowles and A. Cogo (eds) *International Perspectives on English as a Lingua Franca* (pp. 13–34). Palgrave Macmillan, London.

Vettorel, P. and Lopriore, L. (2017) WE, EIL, ELF and awareness of their pedagogical implications in teacher education programs in Italy. In A. Matsuda (ed.) *Preparing Teachers to Teach English as an International Language* (pp. 195–210). Bristol: Multilingual Matters.

Wallace, M. (1991) *Training Foreign Language Teachers: A Reflective Approach.* Cambridge: Cambridge University Press.

Wang, Y. (2013) Non-conformity to ENL norms: A perspective from Chinese English users. *Journal of English as a Lingua Franca* 2 (2), 255–282.

Wang, Y. (2015) Chinese university students' ELF awareness: Impacts of language education in China. *Englishes in Practice* 2 (4), 86–106.

Wang, Y. and Jenkins, J. (2016) 'Nativeness' and intelligibility: Impacts of intercultural experience through English as a lingua franca on Chinese speakers' language attitudes. *Chinese Journal of Applied Linguistics* 39 (1), 38–58.

Ware, P., Liaw, M.-L. and Warschauer, M. (2012) The use of digital media in teaching English as an international language. In L. Alsagoff, S.L. McKay, G. Hu and W.A. Renandya (eds) *Principles and Practices for Teaching English as an International Language* (pp. 67–84). Abingdon: Routledge.

Warschauer, M. and De Florio-Hansen, I. (2003) Multilingualism, identity, and the Internet. In A. Hu and I. De Florio-Hansen (eds) *Multiple Identity and Multilingualism* (pp. 155–179). Tübingen: Stauffenberg.

Watson, A. (2015) The problem of grammar teaching: A case study of the relationship between a teacher's beliefs and pedagogical practice. *Language and Education*, 1–15.

Wenger, E. (1998) *Communities of Practice: Learning, Meaning and Identity.* Cambridge: Cambridge University Press.

Widdowson, H.G. (2012) ELF and the inconvenience of established concepts. *Journal of English as a Lingua Franca* 1 (1), 5–26.

Widdowson, H.G. (2015) Afterword. Frontiers of English and the challenge of change. In P. Vettorel (ed.) *New Frontiers in Teaching and Learning* (pp. 227–237). Newcastle-upon-Tyne: Cambridge Scholars Publishing.

Williams, C. (1996) Secondary education: teaching in the bilingual situation. In C. Williams, G. Lewis and C. Baker (eds) (pp. 193–211). *The Language Policy: Taking Stock.* Llangefni: CAI.

Williams, M., Mercer, S. and Ryan, S. (2015) *Exploring Psychology in Language Learning and Teaching.* Oxford: Oxford University Press.

Woods, D. (1996) *Teacher Cognition in Language Teaching: Beliefs, Decision-making, and Classroom Practice.* New York, NY: Cambridge University Press.

Wu, S. and VanderBroek, L. (2008) The role of English and indigenous languages in teacher education in the Ghanaian context. In S. Dogancay-Aktuna and J. Hardman (eds) *Global English Language Teacher Education: Praxis and Possibility* (pp. 41–57). Alexandria, VA: TESOL.

Xu, H. (2013) From the imagined to the practiced: A case study on novice EFL teachers' professional identity change in China. *Teaching and Teacher Education: An International Journal of Research and Studies* 31, 79–86.

Yano, Y. (2001) World Englishes in 2000 and beyond. *World Englishes* 20 (2), 119–132.

Yashima, T. (2002) Willingness to communicate in a second language: The Japanese EFL context. *The Modern Language Journal* 86, 54–66. doi: 10.1111/1540-4781.00136

Yook, C. and Lindemann, S. (2013) The role of speaker identification in Korean university students' attitudes towards five varieties of English. *Journal of Multilingual and Multicultural Development* 34 (3), 279–296.

Young, T.J. and Walsh, S. (2010) Which English? Whose English? An investigation of 'non-native' teachers' beliefs about target varieties. *Language, Culture and Curriculum* 23, 123–137.

Young, T.J., Walsh, S. and Schartner, A. (2016) Which English? Whose English? Teachers' beliefs, attitudes and practices. *ELT Research Papers*, 16.04, London: British Council.

Yuen, K.M. (2011) The representation of foreign cultures in English textbooks. *ELT Journal* 65 (4), 458–466. doi:10.1093/elt/ccq089

Zacharias, N.T. (2014) Integrating EIL pedagogy in a pre-service teacher program. *TEFLIN Journal* 25 (2), 217–231.

Zacharias, N.T. (2017) Practicing EIL pedagogy in a microteaching class. In A. Matsuda (ed.) *Principles and Practices of Teaching English as an International Language* (pp. 159–170). Bristol: Multilingual Matters.

Zacharias, N.T. and Manara, C. (eds) (2013) *Contextualising the Pedagogy of English as an International Language: Issues and Tensions*. Newcastle upon Tyne: Cambridge Scholars Publishing.

Zheng, X. (2017) Translingual identity as pedagogy: International teaching assistants of English in college composition classrooms. *Modern Language Journal* 101 (S1), 29–44.

# Index